About the authors

Nikesh Shukla is the author of the critically acclaimed novel *Meatspace*, the Costa shortlisted novel *Coconut Unlimited* and the award-winning novella *The Time Machine*. He wrote the short film *Two Dosas* and the Channel 4 sitcom *Kabadasses*. @nikeshshukla

Varaidzo is an undergraduate student and essayist working in film and the arts. She is currently an editor at gal-dem.com. @veedzo

Himesh Patel is an English actor best known for his role as Tamwar Masood in the BBC soap opera *EastEnders*. He also starred in the award-winning short film *Two Dosas*. @himeshjpatel

Chimene Suleyman is a writer. Her debut poetry collection, *Outside Looking On*, was in the *Guardian*'s Best Books of 2014. She has performed at the Royal Festival Hall, Book Slam, Literary Death Match, the Bush Theatre, Latitude and more. She has written on race and gender for the *Independent*, Media Diversified, and *The Quietus*. @chimenesuleyman

Vera Chok is an actress, writer and performance maker. She's also founder and director of theatre company saltpeter and The Brautigan Book Club. Her writing has been published by *Rising*, *Brautigan Free Press*, *Toast*, *Yauatcha Life* and *Ether* and performed at the inaugural BareLit Festival. In 2015, Vera acted for the National Theatre and The Kenneth Branagh Company as well as created the performance piece *These 12 Things Are True*. @vera_chok

Salena Godden is one of Britain's foremost spoken word artists. She is a regular performer at international and national literary festivals in a career that is now entering its third decade. Her short stories and poetry have been anthologised by Penguin, Canongate, Serpent's Tail, Influx Press, Polygon Books and many more. She has written for BBC Radio programmes including *The Verb*, *Saturday Live*, *Loose Ends* and *From Fact to Fiction* and has authored and presented several arts documentaries for BBC Radio and Channel 4. Burning Eye Books published her debut collection *Fishing in the Aftermath* in 2014 to mark twenty years of poetry and performance. Her literary childhood memoir *Springfield Road* was successfully crowdfunded and published with Unbound. @salenagodden

Bim Adewunmi is a writer. She writes about culture for BuzzFeed, and is a columnist at the *Guardian*. @bimadew

Daniel York Loh has worked as an actor at the RSC, National Theatre and Royal Court. As a writer he has written the stage play *The Fu Manchu Complex* and, along with composer Craig Adams, was the winner of the 2016 Perfect Pitch award to create an original musical, *Sinking Water*, based on events surrounding the 2004 Morecambe Bay Chinese cockle pickers disaster, which is now in development at Theatre Royal Stratford East. @danielfyork

Miss L is an actress and the creator of 'Casting Call Woe', a site where she highlights the very worst casting calls. She regularly writes about the trials of being an actress and her work has been featured on BuzzFeed and in the *Guardian* and *Grazia* magazine. @proresting

Nish Kumar is a British stand-up comedian, actor and radio presenter. He hosts *Newsjack* on BBC Radio 4 Extra. He has appeared on *Have I Got News for You*, Russell Howard's *Stand Up Central*, *Sweat the Small Stuff*, and *The Alternative Comedy Experience*. @mrnishkumar

Reni Eddo-Lodge is a journalist and writer. Her first book, *Why I'm No Longer Talking to White People About Race*, will be released in 2017. @renireni

Darren Chetty is currently completing his PhD at UCL Institute of Education, where he teaches on the BA Education Studies course. He taught in primary schools for almost 20 years. He is the author of the award-winning paper 'The Elephant in the Room: Picturebooks, Philosophy for Children and Racism'. @rapclassroom

Kieran Yates is a freelance writer on music and politics for *NME*, *Metro* and *Dazed & Confused*. She is the co-author of *Generation Vexed* and the creator of the magazine *British Values*. @kieranyates

Coco Khan is senior editor at Complex UK and editor of arts magazine, *Kensington and Chelsea Review*. She writes about class, culture and anything to do with hot boys. @cocobyname

Inua Ellams is an award-winning poet, playwright, and performer. Across his work, identity, displacement and destiny are recurring themes, in which he tries to mix the old with the new: traditional African storytelling with contemporary poetry. @inuaellams

Sabrina Mahfouz writes plays, poems, librettos and TV. She was recently a Sky Arts Academy Scholar for Poetry and an Associate Playwright at the Bush Theatre. Her play *Chef* won a 2014 Fringe First Award. @sabrinamahfouz

Riz Ahmed is a British actor and rapper. He has starred in *The Road to Guantanamo*, *Shifty*, *Britz*, *Four Lions*, *Ill Manors*, *The Reluctant Fundamentalist* and *Nightcrawler*. He records as Riz MC, with Heems as Swet Shop Boys, and with DJ Distance as Halflife. @rizmc

Sarah Sahim is a writer of Afghan and Indian descent from the West Midlands, UK. She co-hosts the intersectional feminist podcast *Not All Women*. She has edited for *Racked* and *Broadly* and written for *Rolling Stone, Paper, Playboy* and *Pitchfork* on race, feminism, pop culture and lifestyle. @sarahsahim

Wei Ming Kam is a writer and blogger. She works for Oberon Books and is the co-founder of BAME in Publishing, a network for black, Asian and minority ethnic people who work in publishing. She has written for Fantasy Faction and Media Diversified. @weimingkam

Vinay Patel is a writer for screen and stage. His work includes *True Brits*, which premiered at the 2014 Edinburgh Fringe before transferring to the Bush Theatre, where he is currently under commission. Most recently, he wrote BBC3's *Murdered by My Father*. @vinaypatel

Musa Okwonga is a poet, author, sportswriter, broadcaster, musician, public relations consultant and commentator on current affairs – including culture, politics, sport, race, gender and sexuality. He is the author of two books on football, and he has written for *Al Jazeera America*, *New Statesman*, the *Independent*, BBC Radio 4's *Today Programme*, Channel 4 News, Sky News, the *Guardian*, *New Humanist* and the *Financial Times*. @okwonga

THE GOOD IMMIGRANT

Edited by Nikesh Shukla

unbound

This edition first published by Unbound in 2016
This paperback edition published by Unbound in 2017

Unbound
6th Floor Mutual House, 70 Conduit Street, London W1S 2GF

www.unbound.com

Text design by PDQ

Art direction by Mark Ecob
Cover design by James Jones

A CIP record for this book is available from the British Library

ISBN 978-1-78352-295-8 (trade hbk)
ISBN 978-1-78352-296-5 (ebook)
ISBN 978-1-78352-294-1 (limited edition)
ISBN 978-1-78352-395-5 (paperback)

Printed in Great Britain by Clays Ltd, St Ives Plc

8 9

For Sunnie
and
Timothy Patrick York (1967–2000)

Dear Reader,

The book you are holding came about in a rather different way to most others. It was funded directly by readers through a new website: Unbound. Unbound is the creation of three writers. We started the company because we believed there had to be a better deal for both writers and readers. On the Unbound website, authors share the ideas for the books they want to write directly with readers. If enough of you support the book by pledging for it in advance, we produce a beautifully bound special subscribers' edition and distribute a regular edition and e-book wherever books are sold, in shops and online.

This new way of publishing is actually a very old idea (Samuel Johnson funded his dictionary this way). We're just using the internet to build each writer a network of patrons. Here, at the back of this book, you'll find the names of all the people who made it happen.

Publishing in this way means readers are no longer just passive consumers of the books they buy, and authors are free to write the books they really want. They get a much fairer return too – half the profits their books generate, rather than a tiny percentage of the cover price.

If you're not yet a subscriber, we hope that you'll want to join our publishing revolution and have your name listed in one of our books in the future. To get you started, here is a £5 discount on your first pledge. Just visit unbound.com, make your pledge and type **thegood** in the promo code box when you check out.

Thank you for your support,

Dan, Justin and John
Founders, Unbound

With special thanks to Joanne Rowling

CONTENTS

NAMASTE
Nikesh Shukla   1

A GUIDE TO BEING BLACK
Varaidzo   10

MY NAME IS MY NAME
Chimene Suleyman   22

YELLOW
Vera Chok   33

KENDO NAGASAKI AND ME
Daniel York Loh   45

WINDOW OF OPPORTUNITY
Himesh Patel   57

IS NISH KUMAR A CONFUSED MUSLIM?
Nish Kumar   68

FORMING BLACKNESS THROUGH A SCREEN
Reni Eddo-Lodge   77

BEYOND 'GOOD' IMMIGRANTS
Wei Ming Kam   84

'YOU CAN'T SAY THAT!
STORIES HAVE TO BE ABOUT WHITE PEOPLE'
Darren Chetty   96

ON GOING HOME
Kieran Yates   108

FLAGS
Coco Khan   119

CUTTING THROUGH
(ON BLACK BARBERSHOPS AND MASCULINITY)
Inua Ellams   130

WEARING WHERE YOU'RE AT:
IMMIGRATION AND UK FASHION
Sabrina Mahfouz   144

AIRPORTS AND AUDITIONS
Riz Ahmed   159

PERPETUATING CASTEISM
Sarah Sahim   169

SHADE
Salena Godden   181

THE WIFE OF A TERRORIST
Miss L   198

WHAT WE TALK ABOUT
WHEN WE TALK ABOUT TOKENISM
Bim Adewunmi   208

DEATH IS A MANY-HEADED MONSTER
Vinay Patel   213

THE UNGRATEFUL COUNTRY
Musa Okwonga   224

Acknowledgements   235
Supporters   239

EDITOR'S NOTE

This book emerged out of a comment on a *Guardian* article. I know, I know, it's easy to say, don't read the comments. But I do. Because I want to know my enemy. The commenter took umbrage at an interview a journalist had done with five authors (including me) about their writing process. The journalist (Asian) had interviewed five or six people of colour. The commenter wondered why there wasn't a more prominent author interviewed for this piece. He supposed (for it is almost always a 'he') that perhaps we were all friends of the journalist, given we too were all mostly Asian. This constant anxiety we feel as people of colour to justify our space, to show that we have earned our place at the table, continues to hound us. For while I and the 20 other writers included in this book don't want to just write about race, nor do we *only* write about race, it felt imperative, in the light of that comment (and the many others like it), the backwards attitude to immigration and refugees, the systemic racism that runs through this country to this day, that we create this document: a document of what it means to be a person of colour now. Because we're done justifying our place at the table.

For people of colour, race is in everything we do. Because the universal experience is white. Another commenter (yes, yes, I know) on a short story I once wrote, was pleasantly surprised to see Indians going through the universal experience. Much as I was surprised that I was excluded from the universal experience, it hammered home the knowledge that the universal experience is white. This book collects 21 universal experiences: feelings of anger, displacement, defensiveness, curiosity, absurdity – we look at death, class, microaggression, popular culture, access, free movement, stake in society, lingual fracas, masculinity, and more.

Luckily, there are magazines and spaces emerging to give people of colour the space to write about their universal experiences, and not just write specifically on race. Check out sites like Media Diversified, gal-dem, Skin Deep, Burnt Roti, Rife Magazine.

I chose these writers for simple reasons: I know them, I rate them, I want to read more from them. I'm happy to admit that nepotism and networks played a part in my selection. And I'm happy to create a brand new old boys' network that circumvents the institutionalised ones we have to deal with on a daily basis. Because there is a secret cabal of people of colour, and contrary to the stereotypes we like to refute, we do all know each other. But that's because when we're the only ones in the room, we gravitate towards each other, and stick next to each other, because we intimately know the balance of race and universal experience particular to people of colour.

Before you enjoy these beautiful, powerful, unapologetic essays, a quick note on the title of the book: Musa Okwonga, the poet, journalist and essayist whose powerful 'The Ungrateful Country' closes the book, once said to me that the biggest burden facing people of colour in this country is that society deems us bad immigrants – job-stealers, benefit-scroungers, girlfriend-thieves, refugees – until we cross over in their consciousness, through popular culture, winning races, baking good cakes, being conscientious doctors, to become good immigrants.

And we are so tired of that burden.

NAMASTE

NIKESH SHUKLA

Namaste means hello.

Namaste means I'm bowing to you.

It's a customary greeting.

It's a respectful salutation.

It has become a bastardised metaphor for spiritualism. It's white people doing yoga, throwing up prayer hands chanting 'AUM' and saying 'namaste' like their third eyes are being opened and they can peer directly into the nucleus of spirituality.

You need to know this. Because of your skin tone, people will ask you where you're from. If you tell them Bristol, they'll ask where your parents are from. When they know you're half-Indian, one person will try to impress their knowledge of your culture on you.

I can't sleep.

It's 2am and a party is raging across the road. The flat is rented out to students on a regular basis. Your mother is, sensibly, sleeping with ear plugs in. I can hear you purring in the next room.

I know that in four hours time I have to drive you to London, to take you to see your dada and your fai and fuva. To spend time with the Indian part of your family. To say namaste to your Indian cousins, aunties and uncles.

I'm driving so I need the sleep.

It transpires that the reason the party is so loud is because someone on the top floor of the house is leaning out of his window, smoking and bellowing a conversation down to a person at street level, which, due to the peculiarities of the houses we live opposite, is about four storeys' worth of shouting. At 2am.

This is silly, I think. It's Friday night, sure, but it's a residential street. I may have been these kids once, but now I'm in my thirties. I'm a man of family now. I'm a man of red wine and Netflix. I'm a man of nights in and community cohesion. I get it. I get what life's about. It's about living like your actions affect the people you don't know, as well as the people you do.

I've done questionable shit, pissed in places I shouldn't have, left detritus for poor working souls to have to clean up the morning after, shout-screamed songs at the top of my voice running down streets where families lived, been oblivious to the rest of the world, carrying on like there's something out there in the rest of the world for me to interact with. Your mother reminds me of this the next morning when I tell her what happens next.

I tell her that I don't want to live with the thought that I'm intolerant of other people's intolerance.

I walk out of the house, just as the conversation, bellowed across four storeys, wraps up and the man on the street level leaves to the sound of his friend hoping he gets home safely. I approach the steps up to their stoop. I notice, in the shadows, a boy and a girl are sitting in the doorway of the main door, ajar, smoking.

'Excuse me,' I ask. 'Do you mind continuing your party inside?'

'Jah bless,' the girl in the doorway says. 'Namaste,' she repeats, over me.

I say it again. I change the words to become clearer. More forceful. 'Can you please continue your party inside?'

'Namaste,' she says again. I hear the boy stifle a laugh.

'Namaste,' they both say. 'Namaste, namaste, namaste, namaste, namaste,' until I'm drowned out.

I'm standing under a street lamp, wearing my white bedtime kurta and lengha pyjamas. My skin is bleached out by the fluorescence of the yellow lamp. There's probably no way they can tell I'm Indian from the lighting. It's dickery for dickery's sake.

The bellowing man leaning out of his window asks if the music's too loud. I look up to him, the voice of reason and I say again, can you please continue your party inside?

'Namaste, namaste, namaste,' the girl says.

I shout something wounded, along the lines of 'this is classy,' passive-aggressive, without a target.

I go back inside and I lie in bed staring at the ceiling, watching the arrows of passing car headlights pierce cracks in the curtains.

Eventually the party quietens. My mind doesn't. I'm rolling in a quagmire of ways to deal with this slight. Beyond writing 'Namaste, Dickheads' on a placard and placing it in my bedroom window, I don't know what to do.

The house residents go home for the summer, having moved in and warmed the house to celebrate. Any call for an apology I ask for come the autumn will be muted and months too late.

* * *

I walk past an arts space that's part bar/club, part sustainable restaurant, part hot-desking for freelance artists and part dance studio. They host morning raves and yoga classes there. Most mornings, the steps are daubed with hippies, wearing OM and Ganesha parachute pants, their hair in dreadlocks, bindis mark out the third eyes in the middle of their foreheads. They tie their dogs up to the bicycle racks using scratchy sari material and they enter the yoga studios to be natraja and ashtanga geniuses and salute the sun and greet and say goodbye to each other with a solid, heartfelt namaste.

'Namaste,' one of them says to me one morning as I walk down the road, listening to Jai Paul, swinging my two-tier tiffin up and down.

She offers me prayer hands as I pass and I see her mouthing something. I take my headphones off. Jai Paul's 'Str8 Outta Mumbai' is at its crescendo. *But you know I'll do anything for you. I'll do anything for you.*

'Namaste,' she says.

I grimace.

'Hi,' I reply.

'Namaste,' she replies and raises her prayer hands to touch to her bowing forehead.

She has faded henna on her fingers.

'It just means hello,' I say. She looks at me, confused. 'Namaste, it just means hello. That's it.'

'Namaste,' she says again, and I walk on.

I have three voices. I realise this when Nerm and his wife come to visit. You're inside your mother's stomach. Your involvement in this story comes just after your mother tells Nerm and his wife that she is pregnant, we are expecting. In his excitement, the typically expressive Nerm gestures wildly with his hands and knocks his pint of lager all over your mum's stomach. All over you.

It's funny, but it's not.

The way Nerm and I interact is an intersection of our Gujarati upbringing, our east London socialisation and acknowledgment that there's a white person in the room who needs to keep up.

Yes, bruv, we talk like goras be listening, innit. Fut-a-fut, we wipe away poi-nt spill, mite, while Katie gets fresss again. We call each other bevakoofs, cuss out each other's pronunciation, bruv. We greet with the kem cho, mite. We're cursive, glottal stopping, syllable-swapping rhythmic beasts of anarchic remixed English. Talking to him for the three hours he and his wife are in town, I feel like I'm with my peoples again. When I go home, it takes me a while to get my voice back.

It's an effort to type this way. In a way that's palatable to Westerners. In a way that's markedly different from my speaking voice, because my speaking voice holds rhythms that weren't made in the West.

My mum had three voices.

She had her white-people-phone voice, her Guj-lish talk-at-home voice and her relatives voice.

I have three voices too. I talk in Guj-lish, my normal voice and white literary party. I don't know whether my normal voice, where I feel most comfortable, most safe, even feels like me anymore. I've splintered into personas. This is the trick of living publicly online with increasing watch and scrutiny by others. When I first started out on Twitter, I had 10-odd followers, all people I knew in the real world, people I could be myself with. As my following increased, I had to become less of myself and more of the public perception of me as the writer. And it made me lose track of who I was and what voice I spoke in.

Nowadays, I ensure that whenever I tweet about literary things, I add the odd 'fam', 'bruv', 'cuz' or 'innit', just to ensure the execution of my thought or praise comes with the necessary rooting to where I'm from. I'm a hip-hop fan, and much as I agree that it's not where you're from, it's where you're at – actually, it's where you're from.

An agent who has rejected me twice tweets about an impending apocalypse because his intern referred to clothes as 'garms'. This sends me into a shame spiral. I've been using this word in two of my three voices since 1994. I reply to his tweet, saying 'slang's more important that "proper English", fam. No one talks in proper English, innit.' He doesn't reply. I delete my tweet. I know he's still smarting from when I pulled him up on a snarky tweet about diversity in publishing and his ennui towards it. His response was to say that there was a debate of merit worth having. I told him that it wasn't a debate for me, it was my life. I can't change my skin tone. White people debate it. We live it.

My conversation with Nerm makes me feel lonely.

I watch you in your mum's belly, squirming about, experimenting with spatial awareness, waking up as she and I settle down to bed after the pub. I wonder what voice you'll have? Who you'll be? What you'll sound like? And whether you'll have Gujarati reference points or if the extent of your lingual heritage will only be namaste?

I knock on my neighbour's door.

I know someone is home because a window at the top of the house is cracked open. I can just about make out the 'Keep Calm and Carry On' poster.

I wait, thinking about my opening line. I don't know whether to be angry or polite and firm, or treat it like it's a joke, like we're all friends here, like I know you guys were just dicking around and that's okay, but just know that words have impact.

Or whether to tell them how I feel.

One of the many online arguments I've had about the importance of language, how language can hurt, has been about tea. Chai means tea. Chai tea means tea tea. The number of times you see this on a menu makes you wonder why people can't be bothered to do their research. Like naan bread too. Bread bread.

A comedian, Kumail Nanjiani, an avid gamer, once expressed his delight that the *Call of Duty* series finally set a level in Karachi, the city of his childhood, now one of the top ten most dangerous cities in the world. He was appalled, on playing the game, to see that all the street signs were in Arabic. Not Urdu. He talks about the effort put into making each follicle on each soldier's head stand out, into making their boot laces bounce as they ran, the millions spent developing this game, and how at no point did anyone decide to Google the language of Pakistan.

In *Jurassic World*, they refer to some pachycephalosaurus dinosaurs as pachys, or pakis – 'the pakis are escaping' one of the techs exclaims. The budget for the movie was $150 million. If I had to place a value on how much people would have to pay me in order to call me a paki, it would be more than $150 million. Words matter. Words are important.

The casualness with which someone I'm working with refers to 'two coloured girls'. The casualness with which a person having her photo taken with a nice view, and me obscuring the corner of it asks her husband to ensure he gets one 'without the Indian in it'. The casualness of being on the last train home, from London to Bristol, in the same car as the bar, listening to two drunk men in their early twenties shout at each other, 'n****r, we made it', repeatedly, with excruciating enthusiasm. They're just quoting rap, someone might think. They're drunk, they're harmless, they're being exuberant. Dickish, but exuberant.

Language is important.

Years before, I sat in an Indian restaurant round the corner. It's called Oh! Calcutta![1]. I found the exclamation mark alarming. The place was owned by a white guy. As I sat with my best friend and his then girlfriend, staring at the disco lights, I listened to Kula Shaker sing about 'Taatva', about 'Govinda jai jai, gopala jai jai'. I read the menu. One of the dishes listed was Chicken Chuddi, described as an exotic blend of authentic spices, tomato and peppers. It sounded so generic. What was an exotic blend, what were authentic spices, also – tomato and pepper? These were the biggest tastemakers aside from chicken in the dish? What was Chicken Chuddi?

Also, as you know, chuddi means pants.

I told my friend and his then girlfriend. They laughed at the whiteness of it all, ahahahaha, they said, cultural misappropriation is hilarious, they said in so many words. I felt mortified for the white guy owner, he had probably been duped by some guy he'd asked for a word that sounded 'Eastern'.

1   *Oh! Calcutta!* was a long-running, avant-garde, sexy theatrical sketch revue put together by Kenneth Tynan the theatre critic in the late sixties/early seventies, mainly famous for the fact that the cast was naked a lot of the time. The title of the show was taken from the title of a nude painting by the French surrealist artist Clovis Trouille, *Oh! Calcutta, Calcutta!* which was a pun on the French, 'oh, quel cul t'as' roughly translating as 'oh, what an arse you have'. It has nothing to do with India.

Maybe the chef was having a laugh with him. Maybe he was having a joke with his clients. I looked around. Everyone in the restaurant was white. It was a hipster student paradise. The mix of cod Eastern Britpop, minimal red lighting like a moody Ryan Gosling film and the prices, it felt like puppetry of food. The biggest crime. Not only was the Western balti curry now synonymous with my country's cuisine, but now we had white guys aping the food we made to fit in with the white guys.

I called the manager over.

'The Chicken Chuddi,' I said. 'You know chuddi means pants, don't you?'

He laughed. 'You having me on, right?' he replied. 'It's a specific blend of spices. Nice try.'

'It means pants,' I repeated.

He smiled, itching to get away.

I let him.

Language is important.

The door opens.

He stands in front of me. A boy, not yet 20, wearing a T-shirt that says GEEK on it in the all-caps of shouting pride. He holds a controller for a games console in one hand and a cider in the other.

'Hello,' he says politely. Nervously.

'Namaste,' I say, pressing my hands together in prayer. 'Hello.'

A car, a street away, pumps out a bhangra loop. The subwoofer bounces around my eardrum. I shake my head, turn around and head back across the street. Usually, when I leave for work, you're in the window, waving, propped up by your mum. Your smile is free. It doesn't know nuance yet. We should keep it that way.

A GUIDE TO BEING BLACK

VARAIDZO

With most people, their race is perhaps the only aspect of their identity guaranteed from the moment of conception. They'll be whatever race their parents are, and stay being that for life. For mixed-race children it's a little more confusing. We don't always come out looking like our parents, and often we'll be racialised differently to them. The process can take a little longer to figure out.

Because of this, I spent the first decade of my life unaware that I was black, and spent the decade that followed being not very good at it. They had a word for this in the playground, an 'Oreo': a kid that was black on the outside and white on the inside. I had 10 years of catching up to do, and it was showing, and I wished someone had written a guide to being black that I could have read and then just got on with it. Instead, I had to figure it out the hard way, through actually living.

Here are a few of the key lessons I learned, like what to do when you're the only black kid in a party when a Kanye song comes on, or how to decide which is the right hairstyle for you. It's the guide I needed when I was younger: this is the unofficial guide to being black.

1. Black is the New Orange: Explaining the 'One Drop' Rule

I first acknowledged that I was black in the back seat of my best friend Jenna's car. I was nine. Her mother was driving us, her older sister, and a couple of other kids that she carpooled, to their house for dinner. The older children had been having a debate over whether they were allowed to call someone Chinese if they *looked* Chinese but their country of origin was unknown. The word they were looking for, Jenna's mother informed the car, was Asian. Then she delved into a brief lesson on race.

'It's the same way our family is Scottish but yours are Irish, yet we're all still white, do you see?' she said, and Jenna, presenting further evidence to prove her mother's point, looked at me and declared, 'It's like you. You're English … but you're also black.'

Nine is a young age to discover such a thing. My first four years of life had not really included race. A better description would be that race was so commonplace as to make it obsolete as an issue. I had a white mother and a black father, an Indian godmother and a Japanese lodger. I'd been moved from London to Zimbabwe and back again. When we finally settled in Bristol, my group of friends in nursery resembled a Benetton commercial, all races and genders playing together after lunchtime milk. We owned the Rodgers and Hammerstein *Cinderella* on video over Disney's pretty white animation, and I thought nothing of the Filipino Prince Charming having Whoopi Goldberg and Victor Garber as parents.

This post-racial utopia dissolved when I was sent to a primary school in Bath and I was the only brown-skinned child in my year. Around the same time I developed an obsession with the colours red and yellow. My bedroom had pairs of red and yellow walls, and I exclusively used those crayons to scribble. I understood how these colours interacted, that if combined they created a new colour: orange. I applied this logic to my own family. With one black parent and one white, I was the orange to my father's red and my mother's yellow, not quite either but rather something altogether new. Does an orange thing ever stop to think that it might actually be red?

I never had reason to consider I was anything other than mixed-race.

Until the car journey. Jenna sat back in her seat and grinned, triumphant that she knew more about the world than the other children in the car.

'I'm mixed-race, actually,' I mumbled, trying not to draw the entire car's attention to what I was or wasn't. And Jenna, relishing her new found state of knowing everything, rolled her eyes and crossed her arms.

'Well, obviously,' she said. 'But you're still black. That's just what we'd call you.'

She was right, of course. As a term, mixed-race could never fully illustrate my experiences. It described nothing; the act of being not one thing or another. To be a mix of races is to be raceless, it implied, and yet that had never been my reality. My race was distinct and visible, the thing that defined me as different to the rest of my classmates. Mixedness alone couldn't describe this difference.

Blackness was something more convincing, more tangible. It spread out across my features in big lips and long forehead and hair that grew out rather than down. It filtered through me like a beguiling beckon, drawing security guards towards me when I entered a store and tricking my teachers into thinking I could outrun anyone. The world saw blackness in me before it saw anything else and operated around me with blackness in mind.

There was a drama to blackness, a certain swagger and verve, an active way of experiencing and being experienced that mixedness could not accommodate, one that I was committed to embodying fully.

There was one thing I'd never considered about mixing red and yellow: a drop of yellow into red paint won't do much to change the colour, but one drop of red into yellow and the whole pot is tainted for ever.

2. Political Follicles: Black Hair

Growing up under the wing of my white mother and with no other black children around me, most of what I know about blackness I learned through an autodidactic education. Nowhere is this more true than with my hair.

For the most part, I perceived my hair the same way I did my elbow. It was just there. I had no teachers to show me what to do with it. No experts to learn from. The best I could do with it was attempt to copy what I saw on television.

Sitting on the bath, a mirror in one hand and cold blue gel in the other, I tried to work out how to slick my baby hairs down into swoops and spirals to frame my face (this is what the TV showed black girls were doing with their hair in '06). Instead, I'd ended up frustrated and crying, with my curls crispy and my forehead sticky with the attempts of my unsuccessful gelling. What was this black girl magic that I hadn't inherited? What was the secret to this process that they had all learned and I hadn't?[2]

---

2   A toothbrush, it turns out, used like a mini brush especially for baby hairs.

I assumed these bathroom breakdowns were unique to me, the result of being a black kid in a white town. When I migrated back to London, I realised most black women have some variation of this story in their memory banks. It's not uncommon for black women not to have learned how to care for their natural hair until well into adulthood. Instead, we learn that Afro hair is difficult and that it doesn't grow. We learn that it looks unprofessional and that it will prevent us from getting jobs. Hairstyles designed to keep Afro hair neat and healthy, like locs and braids, are often considered too wild and wacky for professional settings. On one occasion, I remember my Afro was described by a teacher as 'distracting' to others in my class. So what can we black women do? Well, we straighten it and cut it and cover it and we pretend that it is not our problem.

Certainly, I've never felt validation like I did when I got my first weave. I had to get a train all the way to Bristol and beg my mum to pay for the hair out of my allowance. The women at the hairdressers brushed out my small Afro with the vigour of a mother scrubbing stains out of school jumpers. Then they took it in turns to cane-row my hair so tightly that my whole scalp stung, cocking my neck at impossible angles, talking amongst themselves in languages I did not speak whilst fighting to be audible over the sounds of MTV Base on the wall-mounted TV screen. There is no need for customer care in black salons. Not when you're paying for miracles.

It never occurred to me to complain about pain because afterwards, with this coarse dead hair resting below my shoulders, I felt beautiful. I entered the hair salon with three packs of long black human hair and I left as Beyoncé. Nobody could tell me otherwise. Wearing a weave was like uncovering a version of myself that I could finally see reflected in mainstream media. I looked like the black movie heroines and music icons I looked up to. I walked taller and smiled at myself when I looked in the mirror for the first time in my life.

Nobody knows the transformative power of a new hairstyle like a black woman. All too often, aspects of our personality become attached to the way we wear our hair. Or rather, certain hairstyles become attached to rigid structures of personhood. Sometimes, it feels like changing your hairstyle is changing your entire identity. The Afro is the hairstyle for black radicals whilst locs are for Rastafarians and hippies. I enjoyed wearing weave because I enjoyed being accepted, for donning the modern black woman's *style du jour*. It made me feel like I belonged.

Although my hair was different, the real change wasn't the hairstyle, but in my attitude towards feeling accepted. By conforming, I felt like I had a place in the world, and the feeling felt good. The real lesson is learning to hold on to that feeling no matter what your hairstyle is.

For myself, and I don't doubt for many others like me, learning to look after our natural hair is also to learn the lesson that our hair does not define us, and it shouldn't determine our sense of belonging either. It's removing the comfort barriers of conformity; straighteners, extensions and perms, and confronting the insecurities that lie beneath. Nowadays, whether my hair is straight and conforming or unbrushed and everywhere, I don't rely on a change in hairstyle for a change in attitude. I've learned how to look after my hair, both when it's in its natural state and when it isn't. But more than that, my hair taught me how to look out for myself.

3. That Which Cannot Be Spoken: The N Word

At some point, the inevitable will happen. It will happen at a rave, or a club, or a party, where music is playing and people are dancing. A song will come on, usually a rap song, and amongst my generation it will nearly always be a song by Kanye West.

This is when an elephant will sneak into the room, walking straight out of Kanye's mouth, dressed as a word that can't be spoken. They will notice it at the same moment they notice me: the only black kid at the party.

It's Kanye, so everybody knows the lyrics, and everybody is looking at me. I've got 30 seconds to a minute before the chorus hits to decide what to do. If I chant the word it will be a public confirmation of my blackness, a deliberate display that says this word is mine and mine alone to say. That I am allowed. That this is damn near a birthright. And in that moment of vindication it seems obvious that I'm going to sing along, because if rapping along to Kanye is one of the few privileges afforded to me as a black person, then of course I'm going to take it.

Except, there are a few other things going on here. For a start, by being in the room, I am the only reason why the rest of the party can't say it. I'm a big red stop sign in the middle of the dance floor, a symbolic reminder of why they shouldn't use such a word and who they will offend. Without me there, the word is just another rhyme in a lyric. It's a tree falling in a forest conundrum: if a white kid raps all the lyrics to 'Gold Digger' and there isn't a black person around to hear it, is it still racist?

Secondly, I've never grown up with the circumstances where this word has been used. Never learned the difference between the -er and -a suffix, never picked up on the nuances of context. Where Kanye comes from, vocabulary has changed, history has been re-claimed in linguistics. That Which Cannot Be Spoken means so much more: means brother means friend means fool means black. I only ever learned the white rule for this word, of which there is only one: this is a word that should never be said. By anybody. Myself included.

Growing up with all-white classmates, there was no context in which this word could be used. I attempted it once, around the age of 12, the same age I was trying out other swear words in my vocabulary to see how they worked. And this was the only one that didn't. My friend responded, at first, with confusion, and then with a face full of pity. As if she thought me unaware that this word's purpose was to be derogatory towards me and only me, as if she was worried she might have to explain what it really meant. I felt embarrassed, and so did she.

Even when, at 14, I finally joined a school with other black people in my classes, it never came out comfortably when we used it.[3] We said it because we could, because it was cool, because it was delicious to be entitled to something that everyone else wasn't. Not because it came naturally.

Which is my third point. My white peers knew that we had only learned this word, not through any culture of it being used, but in the same way that they had, through hip-hop and American films. This was Somerset. Even those of us who adopted it smoothly into our lexicon would be lying if they said they hadn't done it consciously. Just because we could say it, didn't mean we could pull it off. And because it becomes so glaringly obvious that this word doesn't saunter so comfortably

---

3 There were still only eight of us, a particularly high number in comparison to other year groups, and every single one of us was also mixed-race.

off of my tongue either, there is always a worry that white people will take me using it, me who was brought up by their rules, as confirmation that they can as well.

This is when duality hits me in the face. Is the problem that I grew up as a black face in a white environment? Or is the problem that I possess whiteness within me, that I came from a white household, and was brought up with the white rule books? I can't provide the answers of what to do in this situation just yet. All I can suggest is to cross your fingers and hope for a radio edit.

4. The World is a Stage: The Performance

For as long as black people have been visible to the Western eye, our collective role has been that of the entertainer. From being ogled at in the human zoos of the nineteenth century, to now, where our television sets still mostly show us in limiting, stereotypical roles: the thug, the hooker, the fresh-off-the-boat minister, there is much fun to be had observing our queer, primitive ways.

The only way to control this gaze is to indulge in the role of the performer. To entertain is a passive process, it happens whether we wish it to or not. Whereas to perform implies the intent to entertain. And as anyone who has been to a black family gathering before will know, we are excellent performers.

We learn this, as with any art of performance, from the generations before us. We learn specific ways to dance, to sing, to tell stories, to laugh and make others laugh, to cook, to rap, to make a beat with anything at hand; with our fists, our mouths, our bodies. It is so deeply embedded within our culture that we appear to know these things innately, and of course, we don't. We learn these things just as anyone could.

I was only ever around my black family during school breaks, so all of these things I perceived them as knowing innately I sought to learn in other ways. I turned to the internet to teach me, because it was the only access I had to black culture as a pre-teen. There were the obvious (and with hindsight embarrassing) Google searches: 'how to dance like Beyoncé', 'how to gel my baby hair', and 'what are the full lyrics to Dizzee Rascal – "I Luv U"'.

Then there were the lessons I picked up more subtly. I spent hours in black haircare forums, dominated by African Americans, and without noticing I was mimicking their grammar, their way of speaking, to fit in: 'are's' became habitual 'be's'. 'She does' could end up being replaced by the rather more decisive, 'she do'.

But this was the wrong kind of blackness to be learning. I knew nothing of America, had never learned this new grammar, these new words by ear. Being black, partaking in this performance, was not as simple as just knowing I was black from birth. I was engaging in it as a conscious practice. And the more I recognised this, the more inauthentic I felt. I was not performing. I was acting. This deep sense of paranoia crept in, that invisible forces were going to catch me out for faking my own blacknicity.

I debated whether being in these online communities from such a young age meant that this was an authentic way for me to be now, the same way a child picks up an accent when they move to a new place. Of course, it doesn't really work like that. Anybody is capable of going online and selecting access to blackness. From fashion houses adopting black hairstyles on their runways to white pop starlets claiming they invented black dance moves, anybody is able to mimic the art of black performance and mistakenly assume that they are included within it. Just because I picked up on a dialect, albeit one used predominantly in black communities, doesn't mean it was authentically mine. Its creation is rooted in a certain space and a certain time, one I don't intend to misrepresent myself as existing in. Their lived experiences inform their online words which have accidentally trickled down to inform mine. And as long as that stays the case, there is no reason for me not to let my lived experiences do the same. Because, after all, I'm black too.

While being black can be a shared experience, not all black experiences are the same. With my family, we share the experience of being black through being Zimbabwean, through food, through music. With my friends, the context is being young and black in Britain in the new millennium. When it comes to the world online, sometimes the shared experience is as simple as being a confused black kid who hasn't yet worked out where they fit in. And that's enough.

My authentic self is my default performance, the person I am when I'm not thinking or when I think nobody is looking. And sometimes this is a person who tries to dance like Beyoncé in her bedroom with her eyes closed, or listens to 'I Luv U' by Dizzee Rascal because that song is a certified jam, or says all the lyrics to a Kanye West song because she knows all the lyrics to a Kanye West song and isn't concerned, in that moment, about what they might mean. Sometimes she is none of these people. My authentic self stays black. She stays black when people are present and she stays black when people are not.

My blackness is both a performance and a permanence, it will exist with me despite my actions. And another part stays with me too, the part that dictates how I experience blackness: with the awkwardness and the puzzlement and often with the privileges of being a light-skinned black child who is ethnically white too. My mixedness plays as much of a role in the way I'm experienced as a black person as my blackness does.

Because the truth is this: there is no singular way to be black, no universal set of experiences that we all share, no stereotype that can accommodate the vast array of personalities and histories and ethnic backgrounds that black people possess. And though a guide would have been a gift at times, especially as a confused, adolescent outsider, all of that confusion was just a small part of my experience. There is no one way to be black. Our worst performance is entertaining the idea that there is.

MY NAME IS MY NAME

CHIMENE SULEYMAN

One September I wrote my name as it would be seen in Turkish letters in fountain pen across my desk. The teacher, a thin woman with high cheekbones, wiped it clean despite my protests that she look at it first – Şimen. I don't know where the desire to do so came from. My parents had never spelled my name like this, nor wanted to. But I had seen the Indian and Nigerian kids in my classroom become Bobby's and Ziggy's as the heritage of their authentic monikers was redesigned. Standardisation is the backbone of the Empire, after all. But survival is forgiving. And these were kids who knew that the blow of being called 'paki' on the climbing-frames could be smoothed away faster with a whiter-sounding nickname.

Years later, I remember the surprising tastes of the Bangladeshi food from a workman's café buried behind a bus lane in Stepney. The collective flavours of what we grew to know as 'Indian' food were, of course, aspects of three or four nations' dishes and muted for a British palate. On TV and online, famous chefs even now attempt their 'own' versions of such resonant dishes as jollof rice, or rice and peas, one going so far as to ruin the dish, and enrage Jamaican viewers, by using green garden peas instead of kidney beans. Over the years, on mainstream radio stations where N.W.A., Souls of Mischief, or Kendrick Lamar should have played, Vanilla Ice, Eminem, and Macklemore did and still do. If cultures were to survive in England it would be on the shoulders of bastardisation. This was clear to people like my parents, who understood this to mean that simplicity and effortlessness were of themselves the root of Anglicisation.

They had the foresight to see that Chimene would sooner be pronounced 'chimney'. That schoolchildren would sing 'chim-chiminee, chim-chiminee, chim-chim-cheroo' in front of thoughtless teachers. Instead, my name was offered to the English in phonetics: Shimen. They had quite literally spelled my name out. At home my name would appear on birthday cakes and cards as Chimene. On my birth certificate, passports, and bank card it plainly read, Shimen.

The name itself is not a Turkish one. Pierre Corneille wrote the French play *Le Cid* some many centuries ago about the tortured love between a Spanish man and woman: Don Rodrigue and Chimène. The story is essentially that of Romeo and Juliet and my parents had enjoyed the sound of the name, perhaps even that it belonged to literature and love. It is scarcely recognised that my name is a French one. It is foreign, and I am foreign, and it is within this framework that I move. With family and friends I am Chimene – layered in cultures and afforded the romance of such a name. With the state I am Shimen – conciliatory and afraid that my difference is a thing of difficulty for the British.

One evening my father drove me to yoga. It was a practice then new to me, and in the freshly painted walls of an old Finsbury Park clothes factory a white woman with long hair would fold and bend until we repeated her motions.

It was as I stepped from the car that my father said, 'Your grandmother used to work here.'

Here, my mother's mother would stitch clothes behind a sewing machine with Turkish women who had only wanted from life the privilege of work. Some decades later I was rolling a mat out, as one rolls the carpet of gentrification over our ancestors' footprints, onto the floor of a room of exercising white bodies. I remember laughing when the instructor closed her eyes and placed her mouth in a way to make the 'Aum' sound. Others followed and I thought how easy saying things came to them without understanding their essential nature.

Words, names, and their noises are careless in England. They are not put to use in the way that obstructed communities have learned to pronounce every violence put upon us as though it is sacred. We carry our trauma in every word that we say. The three religions that this chant spread across did not exist in the instructor's mouth. Spirituality cannot be borrowed. Religion belongs to the cultures we are brought up in, and cannot be studied and replicated without family. There is no 'Aum' without Indian dharmas, as there is no 'Allah' without Islam, nor 'Pull-up!' without UK Garage, or two hands coming together to form a W without Wu Tang. That is to say: You cannot have meaning without knowledge of the environment from which it stems. This woman was not speaking of the infinite, the world, the truth. What she meant was, 'This is a calming noise for you, this helps you focus, this is the end of the session.' It did not mean 'Aum'.

There is a wretched scene in Brian Friel's play *Translations*, where Irish place names are transcribed at the behest of English soldiers. Poll na gCaorach – meaning 'hole of the sheep' in Irish – becomes Poolkerry in English. Druim Dubh – 'black shoulder' – turns into Dromduff. Words with significance become sounds without any. To repeat a word as it has been told to you is not to be invested in its force. As is calling me Shimen without knowing that my name is Chimene.

The Cyprus my parents were born to used characteristics and nicknames in place of surnames. A defining feature – a bushy beard, a long moustache, a hunchback, limp, or loud voice would attach itself to your first name – Ahmet the Beard, or Crazy Hakan. Last names became signifiers for your place in the family tree. Mustafa may have a son, Hassan, whose name would be Hassan Mustafa. Hassan would then have a child, Zalihe, who would take her father's name as her last, to become Zalihe Hassan.

As one might name their child after a beloved deceased relative, the rotation of names are as much the rotation of souls. Will a child named after her departed aunt bear further resemblance to her namesake, they will wonder. See how she speaks with her hands just as her aunt did, they will say. She loves swimming as the woman before once did. It is reincarnation for the spiritually shy. Just as the Juniors, and Junior Juniors, of African American communities know the importance of preserving identity. Such is the way for those communities who prepare for their fathers' murders. My father and his father continued the tradition. Suleyman Recep bore my father, Recep Suleyman. On a spring morning in 1964, Suleyman was tortured first and then killed.[4] Walked by

4   Unrest in Cyprus began with the annexing of the island by the British Empire from the Ottomans. Struggles against the British for self-determination shifted from a colonial dispute to an ethnic one between existing Greek and Turkish communities on the island. On December 21st, 1963, Greek authorities launched an offensive against Turkish Cypriots, which continued until a ceasefire was agreed in 1967.

Greek soldiers to a pig farmer's house, his body was probed, cut, then desecrated with a severance that belongs to those who have learned to take. I have seen this sense of property in the eyes of men who step to their girlfriends, who walk into children's bedrooms uninvited, in the policemen who slam a brown or black body against a wall for a half-smoked zoot – no, often less. It is there in the white men and women who do not understand, to the point of frustration, why we still walk with the noose of our ancestors around our necks, as we cannot comprehend how they do not carry the indignity of their ancestors tying it there.

But tradition is an inescapable trait of our communities – those who cannot rely on land or home for their identity. Our parents, and their parents, and theirs before, have little more to leave us beyond their names, beyond their language. We have inherited the knowledge that community means to remain. When we cannot return to our homes – or are waiting for them to be taken from us again – we must get the hang of how to recreate it elsewhere. It is in the particular smell of rice, or aubergines, the pastry that survived on the windowsills of our mothers' kitchens. It is present in the familial catchphrases of a sentence once uttered decades ago, resurrected every mealtime, 'The koftes are burnt!' We have been shown to grieve beneath beautiful scarves tied around our hair, and to eat and drink water in back rooms with shut windows so we may not be seen replenishing a life that another has lost. We are heirs to their favourite chairs, and wedding rings, and the noose around their neck.

Ten years after my grandfather's death, Cyprus would be divided through its middle – the South for the Greeks, the

North for the Turks.[5] My grandmother was assigned a home so recently abandoned in war that her children and their partners bore the task of burying the 15 or so bodies scattered throughout the house. One blisteringly hot afternoon in the '80s my cousins and I threw a football against a freshly painted wall that left a mark above the door. Inches below were bullet holes. There were more in the doorframe of the living room and around the windows of a room to the side. On her bedroom floor, beneath a worn red Turkish rug, the ageing stains of blood spread across marble. We were children who found leg bones of unmarked men beneath the lemon tree. We were children who listened to our parents crack jokes about being prisoners of war as one might recount a story of a badly gone date.

One evening we set about digging the mound in front of our grandmother's house where we knew there to be a body. We went at it with spoons. Perhaps someone had a stick. Our parents carried coffee over our heads and crescents of watermelon as we played in such a manner. This was not neglectful. Remember that in the capital, sandbags still lined the streets. In No-Man's Land[6] windows stayed open from where owners had never returned to close them. Such a 'business as usual' response to war is a poison. I know that now. But it is also an oath to our family and countrymen that is born of belonging to something so remarkable. It is a kinship I do not have with the English despite being born, educated, and brought up by the streets of London – north, east, and south.

5   In 1974 the ceasefire was disrupted by Greek Cypriot militia, prompting an intervention from Turkey. Since, the Turkish Republic of Northern Cyprus has become a sovereign entity with no international recognition beyond Turkey.

6   The United Nations buffer zone has been in existence since 1974.

When the border was put into place the official records on the island began. It was more practical to document the lives of Turks now that whole Turkish villages were no longer burnt and buried alive, or churned through mincers like those neighbourhoods of Sandallar and Murat Ağa. During this time my father was obliged to register a family name and from the ashes came a new one – Şehitoğlu. 'Şehit' to mean martyr, 'oğlu' meaning son. Recep Suleyman now carried his father's name twice.

I tell a lie. He carried it three times. High on his shoulder were the stains of a 13-year-old boy who had inked the Turkish flag into his own skin. Know that for many of us to be proud of our nationality is a death sentence. That my father was then a 13-year-old soldier and the only provider for his mother and her five children. Know that brown and black children are not allowed freedom from maturity. How can we call a child 'the man of the house' and not expect him to mark his body with a target so he too might be killed and taken from this responsibility and almighty grief? Some 10 years later he found himself a prisoner of war for a second time. With his brother they tattooed their father's initial 'S' into each other's arms. Stroking my own ancestral noose, my first tattoo mimicked theirs – a sweeping tail coming from the letter, jabbing towards my chest like a sword. It is not antiques and money we are waiting to inherit from our families, but their skin.

In the days that belonged to my school years, friends gathered in my bedroom to study album covers and eat family-pack bars of chocolate. These were white friends, British in a way I could never be, and outside my bedroom walls were the deeply woven rugs thrown atop each other, the colourful mosaics of Ottoman-styled lamps, paintings of my father regal in a keffiyeh, the beauty of my mother peeking between the folds of a niqab emblazoned in oil paints on a wall. My mother had drawn with some dedication the intricate designs of Ankara buildings. My father had painted in thick strokes the mosques of an Istanbul skyline. Someone mocked that this was a 'house of chintz'. They all laughed, but if this was a joke I needed the punchline to be explained. I should have asked. I should have made them spell it out, 'The horse is not sad, it simply has an elongated head. The chicken wanted to be on the opposite side. Your parents' heritage is strange and cheap-looking to us and doesn't belong here.'

This house, unforgiving in its Turkishness, became a place I would, over the years, ask my mother to change. I suggested that the flamboyant walls be painted eggshell or chantilly lace. I proposed that the elaborate light fixtures be replaced. I wanted an English home, whatever that meant. I wanted the decor to be Shimen, not Chimene. After all, my father had left the name Şehitoğlu in documents belonging to North Cyprus wars, where in London he was once again Recep Suleyman for the purpose of keeping civics away from the colony. As far as I saw it, we had adapted so much already, why not take it beyond all recall?

My parents and I have always known a different language to each other. We have always had different accents. Though love has never been lost in translation, our frustrations of this planet have been. When I was 10, a man who worked with my father called for him on the house phone.

When I answered he said, 'Oh, I must have the wrong number. How can a child that speaks like you have a dad that speaks with that ridiculous foreign mess?'

The mess was not that my father pronounces 'hatred' to sound like 'hatriot'. Rather, that there is a whiteness that exists to be so tone-deaf it cannot make out our words, nor our lamp-fixtures, gods, nor our names – where all are as good as the dog-whistle without the Labrador.

I think back to that afternoon of my school years with a kind of burning envy. What must it feel like to come into someone else's domain and believe in one's right to stand so tall within it. To have confidence that your jokes and your jibes won't land a fist against your face, a bottle against your neck, a grab of your sleeve or cuff and have you thrown from the building, or the land, or the world. My fear of being taken from this galaxy was in fact so strong that I rushed the pronunciation of my own surname. Where I should have elongated the middle to an 'eyy' I instead rounded vowels so that they may be lost to the wind and reappear on the other side as Soloman. After all, Suleyman was the name of a murdered man. Şehitoğlu was the title of our punishment.

We have learned that our ways make us homeless and fatherless, just as there is a whiteness that is fearless to the point of tenure – unmovable and permanent. We have become chameleons navigating the land, answering to white slave names put upon black nations, searching for directions not to Coaquannock – the 'grove of tall pines' – but Philadelphia.

'Change your surname to an English one,' my mother suggested before I moved to New York earlier in the year, 'I'm worried they'll wonder what kind of Muslim your name belongs to.'

Outside my grandmother's house between the mountains, the tarmac, and the sky is the street name — Şehit Suleyman Recep Sokak. Some evenings I watched my grandmother's dark sunken eyes stare into the road name, gaze into the olive groves behind, and the rocks behind that, and the coral skies, and the heavens beyond. This was not a man's life on a sign post, nor in our name, nor on our skin – rather, his death. How can I say this without sounding like I have not missed my grandmother's smell, her gravelly cackle, and the Pepsi-filled fridge of her modest home, every single day since she has died – but I was thankful for her passing. I am not a woman who has faith in an afterlife but, should there be one, I hope it is kinder to her than the life she knew. The slab of concrete that marked her grave was quickly replaced with its permanent stone. We took hold of the temporary one, discarded in the overgrowth, and washed the soil from it. There are images we never forget – my father standing in his mother's grave, my father carrying her tombstone, her name, beneath his arm as he walked with it through the graveyard. My grandfather's grave remained in the South of the island, which may as well have been another planet. Finally on her tombstone there became a place for us to grieve them both. It read, 'Emetullah Şehitoğlu, wife of Şehit Suleyman Recep'. How many times and in how many places can we say someone's name and hope they eventually answer?

Understand this – we do not carry our fathers' names without bearing with them their suffering. We do not grow in London, New York, or Berlin with the bravery we are forever told our parents and their parents had. Such courage is almost a fallacy. That they were lionhearted is part truth, part fable, told by the strugglers to soothe our pain, before being given its stamp of approval by the whiteness that does not mind their martyrdom. Our ancestors were terrified. Do not forget that. Allow them the humanness of fear. Forgive me for saying that my name is a burden. Every version of it. How can I offer you the variations – Shimen Suleyman, Chimene Şehitoğlu – without explaining that there are not four words alone that make my title, but thousands? We are simply the martyrs who are too afraid to die.

I think of my tattoos and the process they have taken over the years. My second draws the words 'Bismillah ir Rahman ir Raheem', the prayer my grandmother often used to part ways. The third is the Ottoman tuğra, or signature, of Suleyman the Magnificent. The fourth, high up on my shoulder, is the Turkish flag my father had bled into his arm with a desire that it may either kill him or save him.

I once stood on the veranda of my grandmother's house – the smell of burning olive leaves, the tall grass, the pine trees – and wished the street were called something different. From the veranda there was no wind in the telephone wire. It stretched motionless from the street name and far up the road.

YELLOW

VERA CHOK

I am yellow. I'm a small, yellow-skinned female and one hundred per cent ethnically Chinese.

The longer I find myself in this country and the more aware I am of institutional bias, the more I feel the tensions between my Chinese ethnicity, my ex-colony Malaysian homeland, my British citizenship, and my 'American Dream' aspirational immigrant outlook.

> *I've heard that there's a kind of bird without legs that can only fly and fly, and sleep in the wind when it is tired. The bird only lands once in its life ... that's when it dies.*
> – from *Days of Being Wild*, a film by Wong Kar-Wai

In recent years, I've been hearing the term 'East Asian' rather frequently and I've felt uneasy. In the process of writing this piece, I'm realising that while I am technically East Asian in terms of ethnicity and descent, I'm not East Asian in the way some people might want me to be.

Hold up. 'East Asian'? What is that, really?

Wikipedia lists China, Hong Kong, Japan, Korea, Taiwan and Mongolia as East Asia. Mongolia was a surprise to me. When I was writing this piece, no one I asked, bar one, mentioned Mongolia. Wikipedia also threw up Vietnam, which though not in the correct location, is included in the 'East Asian cultural sphere' meaning that it is 'influenced by Chinese culture'. Hm. So are parts of Siberia or Manchurian Russia East Asian due to their cultural relations? In business, 'Asia Pacific' and 'ASEAN'[7] are other groupings of countries in that general geographical area. Who gets to label what? When I was growing up in Malaysia, I called myself Asian – I came from the continent of Asia, didn't I?

> *They are the real asians. The orientals are not really asian. They're just chinese.*
> – from 'Why do British people think Indians are Asian?', Yahoo Answers

China scares me. I don't speak any Chinese dialects, am unfamiliar with Chinese customs, and only use chopsticks under duress. My family, located in Malaysia, is part of the vast and widespread Chinese diaspora. I worry that if I ever visit China I would be shamed because of my obvious foreignness. In England, I have sometimes been asked to talk publicly about the sociopolitical landscape of China. As a British-born Chinese woman I know said, 'China is like Mozambique or Canada – a distant country but one where I happen to look

---

7   ASEAN is the Association of South East Asian Nations, established in 1967 in Bangkok by the five original member countries: Indonesia, Malaysia, The Philippines, Singapore, and Thailand, joined by Brunei (1984), Vietnam (1995), Laos and Myanmar (1997), and Cambodia (1999).

'Asia Pacific' is a loose term that usually refers to East Asia, South Asia, South East Asia, Australasia and the Pacific Island nations, but may also include countries on the coast of the Eastern Pacific Ocean.

like the locals.' I worry as much as the next white person about any possible threat to Western civilisation as I know it. In an interview for *Kin Podcast*, Episode 3 ('Oh Shit! I'm Not White') Dr Anna Sulan Masing and I talk about how, until we are reminded and put in our place, there are moments when we forget that we aren't white, male, or tall – things we grew up regarding as normal and desirable. In England, I am reminded often: I am yellow. Chinese.

It is Malaysia that I dream of, a land of coconut trees and equatorial heat, with its history of Malay kingdoms and a colonial legacy of Portuguese, Dutch, then British rule. My nostalgia is for the mountains, seas, and smells of this South East Asian country. My mouth is hungry for the shapes and sounds of Malaysia. Yet when I'm in Chinatown, attracted to anything that reminds me of Asia and gawping at the Chineseness of the space, or when 'East Asianness' and 'Chineseness' is ascribed to me, I find myself wondering if I would feel more at home if I surrendered to this neater role.

Being Malaysian Chinese does not make for neat explanations. Malaysia is ethnically diverse, with a population of Malay, Chinese, Indian, and indigenous groups. It is a rapidly changing, young country, having gained independence from British rule in 1957. As a child I was fuzzily aware of racial hierarchies. Simplistically, historical events led to the Chinese dominating trade, Malays farming and ruling, and everyone looking down on the Indian labourers and the indigenous population. Sweetly, propaganda in schools and on our screens held Malaysia up as a stable, harmonious, multicultural country. My closest friends weren't Chinese but when I got closer to the age when positive discrimination (that might help you get into colleges, win scholarships, obtain jobs, buy houses, etc.) might have counted against me, a family member quietly told me to re-examine my position in society. But even though I was beginning to experience the reality of interracial jostling, being a minority in Malaysia I felt nothing like I do now.

I looked to England as an extension of my home. My parents had been British-educated and my principal was an Irish nun. I read Enid Blyton and dreamed of midnight feasts. I hung out at the British Council – a boyish Chinese girl so sun-browned people thought she was Malay, looked after so thoroughly by a Sri Lankan babysitter she smelled of curry – mouthing along to Shakespeare on VHS cassettes. But as Malaysia grew less British I believed that in order to be the fullest, happiest, most free version of myself, I had to get to English soil.

In 1914, British subjects on the ship the *Komagata Maru* were not allowed to disembark in British Columbia because they were not white British subjects. Skin colour versus citizenship. It's not black and white.

When I arrived in England I felt the freedom of going about unseen and unheard, landed, as I had, in the largeness of London. But when I wanted to be heard, people look puzzled despite English being my first language. They still do, despite my not having a Malaysian accent. A yellow foreign body gets in the way.

Human speech is like a cracked cauldron on which we bang out tunes that make bears dance, when what we want is to move the stars to pity.
– from *Madame Bovary*, Gustav Flaubert

In his much-studied text *Orientalism*, Edward W. Said talks about Asia or 'The East' as being located in our 'imaginative landscape'. Said says that it is a place set apart 'geographically, morally, culturally' and that it is our distance from it that fuels our desire to know it. In the UK, 'East Asian' is replacing the word 'oriental' as the politically correct way to refer to people from the countries in that region. For many, 'oriental' keeps us mired in a romantic space, distant in both time and geography, and filled with exotic sensations. Ask a person on the street where or what 'the Orient' is and you're likely to receive a fuzzy answer. You might find an 'oriental' supermarket selling products from Turkey or another stocking Vietnamese sauces. Say 'East Asia' and what we might immediately picture is yellow people and lots of them. China, for example, has a population of close to 1.4 billion. That is 24 times as many people as in the UK. Our next gut reaction might be a flash of uneasiness. Do we associate them with cruelty, in war or against their own – think hara-kiri and unwanted baby girls, dictators and sneaky nuclear weaponry? Do we conjure up pictures of terrible smog and an unblinking disregard for the environment? Do we recall George Orwell's novel *1984*, where Eastasia, a fictitious superstate, upholds a political ideology called 'Death Worship' or the 'Obliteration of the Self'? Any of these associations, valid or invalid, might zip through our brains.

When we talk about race, the words 'black' and 'white' are familiar. 'Brown' too has come into play. I use the word 'yellow', offensive as many find it, because this is how I believe I'm seen. I use it because while we can't often tell what someone's race is, we do see colour. I use yellow because I'm not black, nor white, nor brown, and I feel I need a little flag to fly, and goodness me, what's this the band's playing? Passers-by catcall in Chinese or Japanese or use that well-known Vietnamese call-girl cry, 'Me love you long time!' referencing Kubrick's modern classic *Full Metal Jacket*. Sometimes, that's shouted in a Thai accent because we all know about the sexy ladies in Thailand, right? Who really knows the difference between Thai and Vietnamese accents anyway, right?

Oh! This talk about sex might have you hankering to dissect 'yellow fever' and the fetishisation of the exotic female body, but hold your horses. Notice first that Thailand and Vietnam aren't East Asian countries. Technically, they're South East Asian countries alongside Indonesia, Singapore, Malaysia, etc. Uh-oh. There seem to be yellow people who don't even come from East Asia. For my money, Thailand and Vietnam – we are familiar with their cuisine, right? – are countries with yellow-looking folk. I could include Laos, Cambodia, the Philippines, and Myanmar. How do we feel about including Nepal, Bhutan, or Kazakhstan? Hawaiians and Pacific Islanders are yellowish. There's also rather a lot of tribes indigenous to other countries who look yellow e.g. the Inuit of the Arctic or some Iban subsets on the island of Borneo. Anyone notice this before? Does it matter? I reckon it's OK, right? We don't spend much time thinking about the nitty-gritty of these distant countries or the specifics of their faraway people because they don't reach our daily lives. But. What happens when they're not so far away?

The label 'East Asian' has been helpful to inch us past the 'oriental' tag. It feels like a fresh new way to talk about the yellow folk in the UK today. But the earliest recorded Chinese settlement dates to the early nineteenth century. Yellow folk have made up a large part of the UK demographic and have done so for some time. Wikipedia gives an approximate figure[8]

---

8 'Approximate' because strangely, it doesn't take into account first generation immigrants. Data is fuzzy also because East Asians have historically only had the option of ticking 'Other' in ethnicity monitoring exercises.

of over 1 million British-born East Asians in the UK compared to 1.9 million black British (3%), and 3 million South Asians (7%). East Asians are the third largest ethnic grouping in the UK but are we only now *seeing* yellow people on British soil due to recent shifts in global economics? Yellow folk. So pale and silent.

Peter Andre's hit, *Mysterious Girl*, is in the air...

Why did an old white English man in a Nottingham pub shuffle up to me and shout, 'Chinese!' to the room? Why did a young black man in Brixton murmur Chinese words to me on the street? Are these examples of racial abuse, misguided sexual advances, an assertion of male power over female, or a combination of all of the above?

In 2013, 2.4 million heterosexual interactions on the Facebook dating app 'Are You Interested?' were analysed and showed that 'all men except Asians' preferred Asian women'.[10] ALL. The fetishisation of the Asian female body is highly problematic. Sexual submissiveness, sexual voracity, and voicelessness is a particularly tricky and damning combination. When I googled 'Asian babes in films' (sorry!), IMDb – the key database for film and television – threw up a list called, 'Asian women White men romance movies'. The Asian women in these films worked very hard to keep

9 Note that this is the American usage of the word Asian, which includes East Asians, South East Asian and those from the Indian subcontinent. It is a particularity of the UK to use the word to refer to just the Indian subcontinent. For a discussion on sexual fetishisation, the American definition of the word Asian seems more useful.

10 Please note that my examples here are from a heteronormative perspective but the experiences of Asian LGBTQ+ and the intersection of sexuality, gender and race would certainly shed more light on how we classify and interact with people.

their white boyfriend, mostly to no avail, and many of them died as a consequence. Googling the less provocative phrase, 'Asian women in films' still gave me the list 'Asian American stereotypes in Hollywood movies'. In instances where I've seen Asian women in traditional,[11] hard-core pornographic films produced by Western and Japanese companies, they are the opposite of silent. They are screaming either due to extreme pleasure or extreme pain via violence. Violation scenarios are common.

Everyday Feminism's piece, '5 Ways "Asian Women Fetishes" Put Asian Women in Danger' is a basic, but on-the-nose, list. According to the piece up to 61 per cent of Asian women in America experience physical and or sexual violence from a partner in their lifetime, and over 30,000 Asian women are trafficked into the States per year.[12] I'll hazard a guess here: the fault lies not in the women but in the attitude towards us. A South East Asian woman I know said that the feeling of being objectified seems core to being an Asian woman.

Powerlessness is a particularly heavy weight to fling off. In order to be attractive to men of any colour, we are expected to be small and pliable. I know there is an alternative stereotype – the cold, automaton, dominatrix, *femme fatale* Asian woman – but we don't seem to be mail-ordering as many of them lot. There was a point in the past when I stopped dressing 'prettily' because when I was out

11 'Traditional' as opposed to feminist, queer or ethically made porn.

12 Yes, most data available on yellow women is American. Recall how basic information on the number of East Asians in the UK is difficult to find. Perhaps this says something about how the UK's third largest ethnic minority group is (dis)regarded.

with ANY white man, no matter his age or looks, I was talked over and looked down on. It was assumed that I was his escort or mail-order bride. A friend of mine meeting her white boyfriend for dinner was asked to leave a restaurant because they thought she was soliciting. I am sex positive and advocate sexual freedom of expression with consent, but I am cautious around any violent male desire to conquer/colonise a passive Asian body, especially if that male is white.

Look up American performance-maker Kristina Wong. Her grotesque but smart comedic work both disrupts the objectification of the Asian female and experiments with sexually objectifying the stereotypically emasculated Asian male. Asian American Eddie Huang's memoir, *Fresh Off the Boat*, has been transformed into a family friendly US TV series, but the rather more serious book addresses the sexlessness of the Asian male head-on: *We're allowed to play ONE role, the eunuch who can count. You seen* Romeo Must Die! *Jet Li gets NO PUSSY!*

It's no overstatement to say that Aziz Ansari's TV series *Master of None* is a game-changer. How many times in media have you seen an Asian male have a sexual life? *MoN* opens with Ansari's character in the throes of sex. His sexual relationships are depicted as 'normally' as a white male's, and he has an Asian friend, played by Kelvin Yu, who is held up as a hottie in the series. This is television history, and I hope that it is this kind of TV that takes over our hearts and minds. If you happen to spot an Asian in UK media today, they are more than likely to be reinforcing racial stereotypes. Sex and power are central to the way we understand the world and both male and female Asians are very low down on the power scale.

Despite shyness and society's strong message on what makes

a nice English (ha ha) girl, I feel compelled to discuss sex and the way in which we construct and perform sexually attractive selves given our constraints. Not doing so is an extremely isolating experience for me. My feelings of humiliation – unwarranted, I know, but hard to shake – from being hypersexualised and generalised about on a daily basis because of my skin colour and gender, seem abated in the not unpainful act of exposing my shame. My body as a site of violence.

Can this Little China Girl (RIP Bowie) ever step out, speak out and tell you, baby, just to shut your mouth?

> *[The oriental woman] never spoke of herself … never represented her emotions, presence or history* – Said, *Orientalism.*

Remember the old white man in the pub and the young black bloke on the street who publicly projected Chineseness onto me? How did they know that I'm ethnically Chinese? Oho. Now I don't know about you, but when my prompt is 'East Asian' not only do I think 'yellow', I think 'Chinese'. Perhaps it's the sheer number of Chinese folk – 50 million – who live outside China. There are Chinese takeaways in most towns in the UK. Chinese people make up roughly half of the total East Asian population in the UK, so yes, a yellow person on the street is most likely ethnically Chinese. Well done to the Chinese-spotting blokes! But in race monitoring exercises, yellow people – Chinese or not – have, historically, been thrown into a pot called 'Other' and data on life in the UK is sparse, and we're so silent we don't shout about the racist abuse we encounter, right?

> *Hey, look, it's Jackie Chan!*
> *Oi, chink! What are you staring at? Ching chong, ching chong!*

– a selection of insults commonly shouted at yellow people

I did not know that Chinese people are more likely than any other minority ethnic group to be subject to racial harassment and property damage ('The Fourth National Survey of Ethnic Minorities'). We don't see this on our screens. Violence against yellow folk doesn't spring to mind when people mention hate crime. I think of African Americans being shot in the street over nothing. I remember documentary footage of a Muslim woman being knocked out on the street. Chinese folk across the UK are abused, not only frequently but repeatedly – Chinese takeaway workers are sitting ducks. Owners and their families are often the only yellow family in town. A BBC *Newsbeat* (January 2015) article discussed the under-reporting of these hate crimes: it's because we're spread out across the country, and because hate crime dispensed little and often is rather difficult to prove or stop. I wonder if it's because the sexiest, most quotable statistics I could find easily on the internet[13] sound dated, dull or inconsequential unless you step back and consider what the evidence seems to indicate as a whole but can't prove quantitatively, i.e. that proportionally, Chinese people experience higher levels of fear and violence than any other minority group in the UK. Violence is only as visible as we are. Who knew that after WWII, some 2,000 Chinese seamen in Liverpool who had helped in the war effort were deported 'home' without warning? This violation was so swift and hidden that for decades their British wives and families

13 Sue Adamson et al., *Hidden from public view? Racism against the UK Chinese population*, Min Quan report, (The Monitoring Group, 2009).

thought that they had simply been left. There are a few articles online now, but only if you know what you're looking for.

What with the whitewashing of history and the darkness surrounding slavery and oppression, I don't feel as if I own, or am allowed to own, 'real suffering' because of the colour of my skin. Instead, I bear a different kind of badge, one I'm supposed to be pleased about: 'model minority'. Is yellow too pale a colour to shout about?

Yellow. What unites a Chinese, Vietnamese, Japanese, Korean, Thai, Taiw... *anyone* yellow in the UK? It's not our wildly disparate cultures nor our real or imagined homelands. It's hidden histories, made-up sex lives, violence invisible to others. In forms, the plurality of our immigrant narratives is boxed up as 'Other' but we are here. I see you.

KENDO NAGASAKI AND ME

DANIEL YORK LOH

Being a memory play, it is dimly lighted, it is sentimental,
it is not realistic.
In memory everything seems to happen to music. That
explains the fiddle in the wings.
(Tennessee Williams, *The Glass Menagerie*)

So begins Tom Wingfield, the narrator character in Tennessee Williams's *The Glass Menagerie*.

On any given night when *The Glass Menagerie* is performed, though, Tom Wingfield transports the audience back to 1930s USA, where a 'huge middle class of America was matriculating in a school for the blind' – whereas, ladies and gentlemen, I give you 1970s Great Britain: a place that many believe was a land of joyous liberty before the totalitarian oppression of The Political Correctness Brigade committed the heinous Stalinist crime of actually making it a bit difficult to take the piss out of ethnic minorities, gay or disabled people, and only ever regard women as either battleaxes or sex objects.

Like Tom Wingfield's memories of the 1930s, everything about the seventies in my mind seems to happen to music. No 'fiddle in the wings' though. Instead it's a soundtrack of Gary Glitter and Rolf Harris introduced by Jimmy Savile and Stuart

Hall to an almost constant chatter of sexist smut and racial jibes dressed in dodgy Y-Front underpants. A world where younger readers will have to imagine no Sky TV or BT Sport and where all football matches kicked off in unison at three o'clock on Saturday afternoons and the only live match you ever saw on TV was the FA Cup Final once a year.

A world where a lonely half-Chinese schoolboy in the West Country found a curious 'hero' in the inveterately cheating shape of what appeared to be a villainous Japanese wrestler called Kendo Nagasaki.

Because Kendo Nagasaki was a fellow 'oriental' (the acceptable term of the time) and far from being a dull passive silent one, Kendo Nagasaki was a badass.

In the seventies we watched *World of Sport* on a Saturday afternoon. *World of Sport* was what was known, I believe, as a 'sporting omnibus' programme. It began around midday on a Saturday, showed what mainly seemed to be fairly obscure sports such as skiing and bowls (no disrespect intended), and went all the way through to teatime when we would eagerly catch the football scores on the hilariously primitive 'vidi-printer' before turning over for *Basil Brush* and *Doctor Who*. *World of Sport* was introduced by a plummily spoken smoothie called Dickie Davies, who had the cheesiest seventies 'tache you can possibly imagine, compensated for by an endless and seemingly genuine enthusiasm for this cornucopia of sports that no one on the planet seemed much interested in.

What we really watched *World of Sport* for, though, was the wrestling. Usually on in a two-hour block and showing a succession of fights, the wrestling was *de rigeur* Saturday afternoon viewing in our house.

Nowadays it seems to be common belief that professional

wrestling is staged pantomime and not a competitive sport at all. I for one will make no attempt to either confirm or debunk this, although whenever I've seen the supposedly 'genuine' Olympic wrestling it seems to consist entirely of two men in leotards grappling tediously on a mat while being awarded points for undetectable (to the layperson's eye) displays of 'skill', lacking any of the blood, thunder and, yes, theatre of the pro wrestling I grew up watching.

Certainly I don't know of any professional wrestler who has, fessed up in public to the sport being fake. It's entirely possible they sign some form of 'secrecy contract' (like the Magic Circle perhaps) but when I have seen interviews in the press or on TV with professional wrestlers they fiercely deny there is anything 'staged' about their craft at all. I've even seen a couple of interviews where wrestlers have offered to put their press interrogators in head or arm locks to ascertain for themselves whether the sport is faked. If any professional wrestler is reading this, then please rest assured I am completely willing to take your word that it is a genuine competitive sport with no need for physical demonstrations as proof.

At the age I was at the time, it made not a jot of difference whatsoever whether it was 'real' or not and I was thrilled, every Saturday, to the exploits of the great characters of professional wrestling with ludicrous monikers such as Giant Haystacks (he was indeed giant), Big Daddy (whose sole but popular tactic was to butt his opponents with his sizeable belly), The Dynamite Kid (he was supposed to be quick … I think) and, er, Mick McManus.

Whether it was actually panto or not there were certainly heroes and villains with much booing and hissing as well as some hilarious slapstick anarchy, the two-fighter-per-team 'tag' matches in particular usually descending into riotous chaos with fighting continuing into the auditorium as the crowd bayed and roared. It was thrilling, hysterically funny, full-blooded entertainment, and made dismal provincial winter afternoons that much more bearable.

Before Kendo Nagasaki there was another 'oriental': a Japanese wrestler who appeared briefly. He was chubby with a bum fluff moustache and didn't appear to win any fights at all. He was mercilessly baited by the crowd despite appearing only to resort to the traditional wrestling villain's stock-in-trade 'dirty tactics' when it was painfully obvious he was getting thoroughly beaten. I have no memory whatsoever of his name but he was referred to by the commentator (who also seemed to despise and ridicule him) simply as 'The Japanese', as in 'oh, The Japanese is cheating now', etc.

But he was nothing like Kendo Nagasaki.

By now, the Chinese/Japanese thing was getting thoroughly confusing. I'd finished at one school full of white kids calling me a chink and transferred to another school full of white kids calling me a chink and singing songs about 'Chinese and Japanese' having 'dirty knees' (it rhymes, geddit?).

Sometimes I got angry with the singing chanting white kids and tried to hit them or throw things at them. As a result of this, as well as singing chanting white kids calling me a chink or a Jap and hurling allegations at me about the cleanliness of my knees, my world suddenly seemed to fill up with red-faced white adults shouting loudly at me that I needed to learn not to lose my temper when white kids were calling me a chink or a Jap.

I grew up surrounded by white people. At that school, there was me and my brother, plus two black kids who were also brothers. Their names were Godfrey and Geoffrey and the four of us seemed to cop racial abuse off the entire school all day every day.

Of course, the Golden Rule that all 'minority ethnic' people learn when we're growing up in Britain is that we're simply not supposed to get angry about any of this. To do so is to invite all kinds of accusations about having a chip on both shoulders and so forth. Occasionally one can join in with the rest of the majority populace and vent one's spleen about politics or inflation or the bus being late, but we soon learn we're supposed to be 'reasonable' about racism.

Even now, the 'victory' we 'politically correct killjoys' have 'won' has come at a price, in that we're rarely allowed to point out the indignities of having one's race/gender/orientation/disability used as the butt of jokes without being implored to 'get a sense of humour, for God's sake'.

I can remember just a couple of years ago being invited on to a Radio 4 programme to discuss the broadcaster Jeremy Clarkson's use of the racist slur 'slope' when referring to a Burmese man on a sloping bridge (geddit?); I was assailed, in a preliminary pre-programme interview (it's a serious business you know), by a BBC journalist in the pressured tones one imagines an impatient farmer using to herd a particularly recalcitrant bovine animal into a field, repeatedly asking 'So, Daniel, are you *outraged* by this? Are you *outraged*?'

Confused by this and suddenly feeling unsure of my #AngryEthnic credentials I took a pause during which I could hear said Beeb journo breathing impatiently down the phone. I was shopping in Hammersmith Primark at the time (I'm ashamed to say) and took the call on my mobile phone, so you can only guess how surreal this 'outrage assessment' felt. Eventually I responded 'I just think Jeremy's a dick, basically'. Evidently disappointed by my insufficiently humourless chippiness, they relegated me to the closing 45 seconds of the discussion, to which I contributed after decamping to my favourite Hammersmith Indian restaurant (Shilpa in King Street if you're interested), where I attempted to sound articulate and measured whilst surrounded by chapattis and chutney that were admittedly far more enticing than the prospect of being outraged by the rather tired antics of a millionaire who hangs out with the Prime Minister, likes to drive fast cars, and who uses the n-word despite allegedly trying everything in his power to avoid doing so. The seventies though was the veritable heyday of political incorrectness and it was where I spent a somewhat traumatic childhood. I also had one of those haircuts that Chinese kids the world over appeared to have at the time that seem to have resulted from placing a bowl over the child's head and cutting the shape round it. Life was difficult.

From the ages of five till around 10 my 'anger' became a major issue. After being shouted at by white adults for losing my temper over being called a chink or a Jap, I would then be sat down by other white adults who would try to get to the bottom of why I was so 'aggressive' when I was called a chink or a Jap. I saw white child psychologists who actually gave me tablets – presumably to enhance the serotonin in the brain that prevents one from taking offence or feeling humiliated by gangs of white kids calling one racist names loudly and repeatedly.

At this point I was being called 'Chinese' and 'Japanese' so much I was beginning to think that 'Chinese' and 'Japanese' was literally all the same thing. I learned later of course that they are two very different and separate cultures and that the two countries have even fought wars against each other. Sometimes I wonder about a world where a solitary white kid is abused in the playground by a gang of 'ethnic minority' kids shouting 'English, German, giving us a sermon' (well, the principle's the same).

'Chinese' was what I was though, as informed by my nonplussed parents. Actually, let's qualify that: *half*-Chinese. Outside my own family I barely met any other Chinese people. The term 'East Asian' doesn't appear to have been invented at that juncture in history and the collective umbrella term for us arguably-yellow-arguably-dull-brown/olive-people-with-funny-shaped-eyes was 'oriental' – a ludicrous colonial expression, which literally means the 'furthest point east'. The mysterious 'orient' began life in the Ottoman Empire, i.e. Turkey. As civilised white men murdered, pillaged and plundered their way further across the globe, 'orientals' were found in the 'Middle' East and as the intrepid colonials went further still, 'oriental' came to sum up everyone and everything east of India. 'Oriental' has connotations of bamboo and flutes and red sunsets. It should only really be used to describe carpets, as the word has an inherent exoticism that I'm not sure a boy growing up in Wiltshire can ever fully embody. In the US 'Asian Americans' have rejected the term 'oriental'. Here, the Chinese (at least) have positively embraced it, because we appear to be a pragmatic species and aren't known as the 'model minority' for nothing. So at this confusing point of second generation immigrant experience, I accepted that I was an 'oriental' and found a 'role model' in another 'oriental': Kendo Nagasaki.

There appeared to be very few 'orientals' on TV in the seventies and the ones that were haunted me to such an extent I almost found myself wishing they weren't there. Along with 'chink' and 'China' I would be taunted with cries of 'Bruce' (Lee, naturally, though in the Land Before Home Entertainment one rarely actually *saw* Bruce), 'Kung Fu' (a TV series starring David Carradine as the supposedly mixed-race Eurasian martial arts expert with legendarily rubbish slow-motion fight sequences), 'Grasshopper' (there was a blind, bald Chinese guru in said *Kung Fu* series who would appear in flashback and advise Carradine in a ludicrously exaggerated cod-Chinese accent which many white people at the time loved to imitate), 'Hawaii Five-O' (being set in Hawaii and being an American rather than British show, it actually had a reasonably inoffensive Asian side-kick character), 'Hong Kong Phooey' (a cartoon series about a Kung Fu kicking dog in a silk dressing gown), 'Fu Manchu' (Sax Rohmer's legendarily racist cartoon Chinese villain further immortalised in a series of films starring Christopher Lee, one of which seemed to be on literally every Sunday afternoon) and 'Cato' (a character in the Peter Sellers Inspector Clouseau films who appeared for 10 minutes in every movie and got the living shit literally kicked out of him and who many white men of a certain generation seem to adore beyond all reasonable ken).

Given how few 'orientals' there were on TV at the time it was also astounding how many of them were portrayed by white men. I can vividly recall wondering whether Chinese men just didn't do acting or whether white men just loved dressing up and looking silly. Even my favourite TV programme in the world, *Doctor Who*, got in on the 'yellowface' act.

Yellowface is a form of theatrical makeup used by performers to represent an East Asian person (Wikipedia).

1970s *Doctor Who* was a very different beast to the one that adorns our screens now. There was no soppy soapy romance, no hopelessly po-faced self-aggrandisement, no superficially flashy CGI and no bombastic manipulative music. It was just cardboard sets, men in rubber suits, rattling good scripts (er … usually) and a maverick outsider travelling in time and space (what could be more attractive to a boy who was bullied at school?).

However, in one crucial area, New *Doctor Who* trumps Original *Doctor Who* hands down. The modern version positively teems with diversity of all kinds. 'Old Who', I'm afraid to say, was populated almost entirely by white people with some very occasional but fleeting ethnic stereotypes bunged in. For a remit with the whole of time and space as a palette, this is a bit crap frankly.

Somewhere in the mid-1970s, the luridly titled *Doctor Who* story, 'The Talons of Weng-Chiang' graced six consecutive Saturday evenings. A handsomely mounted Victorian Sax Rohmer homage that did, however, manage to feature, in the very same story, arguably one of the worst giant rats ever seen on TV, as well as one of the very worst examples of yellowface as a gang of silent, sinister and inscrutable (it's amazing how easily and often those words flow together) goons (the only appropriate description) appeared, led by an English actor called John Bennett sporting ridiculous false eyelids that looked like you could sit on them, skin made up yellower than a lump of cheese and speaking in a hopelessly mishmashed Chinese/Japanese hybrid accent that would have had Henry Higgins completely stumped. Not nearly so much though as the fact that the BBC still carries a website page somewhere that heaps lavish praise on Mr Bennett's staggeringly silly turn, opining that, unless they knew, a viewer might be hard-pressed to tell that the English thesp wasn't in fact Chinese. Not unless they were under the impression that Chinese people had eyelids made from recycled skateboards and talked like Yoda in *Star Wars* when he's been on the ketamine, I think.

There appeared to be no 'oriental' comedians to take the piss back and, unlike black people, we 'orientals' didn't even have any 'oriental' pop stars. There was a Japanese bloke who played bass in the video for Rod Stewart's 'Do Ya Think I'm

Sexy?' which, being Number One for what seemed like forever at the time, did at least mean that this one almost-Chinese cool-looking dude was on *Top of the Pops* every week.

And that was it.

And then along came Kendo Nagasaki.

Kendo was a proper badass. In wrestling parlance, a 'heel' as the sport's 'antagonists' are traditionally known (the term has possible biblical origins apparently). He won all his fights, dispatching his hapless opponents with consummate ease though a combination of breathtakingly agile flourishes, athletic kicks and gloriously Machiavellian skulduggery. Kendo (in my memory play) wore florid silky martial arts gear, all dragons and flames and bamboo-style lettering. He was sleek and quick, cunning and sly, made elaborate entrances to the ring where he acrobatically warmed up, revelling in the booing and baying of the crowd whom he arrogantly baited (and did so again after his inevitable victories) in what seemed, to a racially abused schoolboy, the ultimate act of ethnic defiance.

In short, Kendo Nagasaki was an out-and-out dirty villainous cheat that the crowd, viewers, commentator and other competitors loathed beyond all seeming limit – except that this fiendish 'oriental' won bout after bout with his despicable and blatant dirty tactics, appearing to positively revel in the fact that no matter how much everyone involved seemed to will it, he simply would not be beaten.

Now, 'kendo' is a form of Japanese martial art descended from ancient swordsmanship and 'Nagasaki' is of course the Japanese city famed for ever as the one that was controversially flattened by 'Fat Man', the second US atomic bomb at the tail end of World War II. So the name, as well as being completely nonsensical, was arguably offensive. But this was the 1970s, remember, when we watched publicly subsidised paedophiles on TV.

So Kendo Nagasaki was a dubiously named gangsta badman. Kendo also wore, as part of his rather florid orientalist costume, a mask. A mask with (naturally) epicanthic eye slits, that covered his entire face and made him appear even more of a villain. There was a strange wrestling rule about masked wrestlers: they could only have said mask removed when they were defeated in the ring.

But that was never happening to Kendo Nagasaki. He was quicker than everyone else, could do 'proper' kung fu (unlike that David Carradine slow-mo bollocks), and was adept at getting in cheeky little punches when the ref wasn't looking, as well as carrying on fighting when his opponent was on the deck and even laying out the ref when occasion demanded.

And I found myself silently willing on this masked man of the East as the only strong assertive role-model on TV who I could somehow relate to, albeit tenuously, despite the fact that everyone else in the entire country (the ones who watched wrestling anyway) appeared to despise Kendo Nagasaki.

And then, after what seemed like years, the fateful day arrived.

Kendo was defeated (by Mick McManus or some other bland wrestling good guy). And it was no simple KO. A wrestling 'great' like Kendo Nagasaki required the whole 'two pinfalls' – a pinfall being a move where a wrestler holds his opponent so both shoulders are on the canvas for three or five seconds (I forget which) – to finally end what was a simply glorious unbeaten reign. But this day Kendo was outsmarted, out-thought and outfought, though not out-cheated, Kendo managing to the last to go down with some defiant underhandedness.

But go down he did as he was pinned to the canvas one last time, the ref counted off and the crowd howled in jubilant primal triumph.

And then came the moment when the victor got to unmask the notorious Kendo Nagasaki as the audience bayed with glee ...

Kendo knelt ...

A hand tugged at his mask. I steeled myself, comforted by the fact that soon we would see Kendo's proud Asiatic features gloriously unbowed.

The hand tugged further, pulling Kendo's mask up and up and ...

Off it came ...

To reveal ...

A white man.

!!!!????!!!!????!!!!

Another bloody white man.

White with blue eyes and blonde hair.

A cherubic-looking blond white man.

And a half-Chinese boy turned off his TV in stunned silence.

NOTE: A mere glance at the likes of Wikipedia and YouTube appears to reveal that I've probably got Kendo mixed up with another masked East Asian-themed wrestler imaginatively called 'Kung Fu' who wore rather more florid outfits than Kendo's which appear disappointingly prosaic when viewed now. There's also a clip of Kendo being unmasked by Big Daddy mid-bout and him being a balding white man with brown, not blond, hair.

It's all very confusing, but like *The Glass Menagerie* this is a 'memory' play.

An ethnic 'memory' play.

With no fiddle in the wings.

WINDOW OF OPPORTUNITY

HIMESH PATEL

When I was four years old, I tried to jump out of my bedroom window.

No, I wasn't ending it all before academia drowned my youthful optimism in a sea of social awkwardness and HB pencils. I was trying to be a Teenage Mutant Ninja Turtle.

I was obsessed with the cartoon, watching the same video over and over again at Jackie the babysitter's house. Seeing how much I loved the show, she let me keep the tape and Mum used it to keep me immobile as she worked around the house.

One afternoon, she was working in the kitchen and called for me. I didn't respond. She went to the living room to investigate, where the video was still playing but I was nowhere to be found. She called for me again. Nothing. She headed upstairs to find me, crouching on my windowsill, ready to jump.

I know how this may seem, but even at the age of four, I had enough of a grasp on physics to know that jumping down to the ground from that height wouldn't end well. I'd thought it through. You see, underneath my bedroom window was the porch roof, which was flat and [hopefully] sturdy enough to hold my weight.

The script was written.

We were running up. The director was ready to call 'action'.

And ... a hand grabbed my collar from behind and yanked me back inside.

The video soon disappeared and my bedroom window was locked.

In December 2012, I was invited by the Runnymede Trust to take part in a panel discussion on race in UK film and broadcast media, at London's South Bank University. I was five years into my time at *EastEnders* and the organisers believed that young budding actors would be interested to hear my opinion on the matter. As the evening progressed, I began to feel more and more out of my depth. The other members of the panel (including one Riz Ahmed) were articulate and informed. I found myself without a point to make. I felt like I was out of the loop. In the years since that evening, the subject has become unavoidable, and rightly so. Lenny Henry's BAFTA Television Lecture in 2014 and Danny Lee Wynter's Act For Change Project are spearheading a movement that's aiming to redress the balance. I began to wonder how I had managed not to notice such a huge schism in my industry even though it directly affected me.

I think it has something to do with where I grew up. Rural Cambridgeshire, for all its tranquillity, isn't the most multicultural of places. The story of how I ended up there begins long before I was born.

In the 1960s, a lot of Indians who had settled in Kenya began moving to the UK, some taking advantage of British passports, others fleeing from increasingly severe immigration laws. My grandfather (or Dada, as I call him) lived in Nairobi, working for a company called Lamson Paragon. He was on the factory floor, making business stationery. By 1968, his two eldest sons and his eldest daughter had married and moved to the UK, leaving him in Kenya with my grandmother, their youngest daughter, and my dad. He asked Lamson Paragon for a transfer to Britain and the powers-that-be said yes.

So in 1970, my dad, aged 16, found himself in the sleepy Cambridgeshire town of St Neots, home to the factory Dada had been transferred to. It transpires that my family were the unwitting pioneers of multiculturalism in St Neots – as far as Dad can recall, they were the only South Asian family in their immediate area, perhaps even the whole town. I assumed that Dad and his family must have felt ostracised. I was wrong: Dad can't recall ever feeling that way. Whereas the segregated immigrant communities in the big cities were bearing the brunt of xenophobia, no one in St Neots seemed to have any problem with my family joining their community. This positive experience my dad had as a young adult, accepted into British society with open arms, would echo down the years and shape my own experience decades later.

During the harsh British winters, my grandparents escaped back to India. It was during one of these trips, in 1976, that my dada noticed a young girl sat on his bus. He saw her talking to a friend, laughing and smiling. He kept seeing her almost every day and wondered who she was, which family she came from. He made some enquiries and eventually found out. Fortunately, they had some family in common, so Dada sent a marriage proposal to this mutual relative, who passed it on to the girl. Or as I like to call her … Mum.

It took a while for my parents to meet though.

At the time she received the proposal, my mum was studying in India and Dad was studying in the UK. For this reason, the first time around they both said no. Then, in November 1978, my mum's family moved to the UK and my dada, so sure this girl was the perfect partner for his son, reopened the lines of communication.

As luck would have it, there was a mutual family wedding taking place and the families conspired to have my parents meet during the nuptials. The first day, the plan failed miserably. No one told Mum or Dad that they had to look out for each other and Dad, being the appointed wedding photographer, was far too preoccupied with lining up the perfect shots for the happiest day of the couple's life. So on the second day, the families attempted it again, this time informing the concerned parties to keep an eye out for each other. Alas, neither of them actually bothered to do so and attempt number two also failed.

Frustrated, Dada decided to take everyone and go over to Mum's house in London.

They arrived, introductions were made ... and then the woman who would be my mum and the man who would be my dad were shoved into a room to talk. They ended up talking for 45 minutes, a pretty long time by most standards.

By January 1979, they were engaged. I asked them both what made them say yes to each other.

'I don't know,' Dad said.

'No, seriously,' I replied.

'Whatever expectations I had were fulfilled. I found someone I could get on with. Something clicked.'

'Mum?'

'I met with quite a few guys before your dad,' she explained. 'In hindsight, I've always had a strong personality and I never did what was expected of me. But your dad was different in so many ways.'

It's true, Mum did go against the grain of what was expected of a girl of her generation. Her father afforded her a good education, a rarity for girls in India at the time and this, coupled with her sheer determination, has had a profound effect on the course of my life.

Dad agreed to get married on the condition that it wouldn't be until he finished his studies, of which he still had a year remaining. Still, they were married in the eyes of the law on April 19th, 1979, and the Hindu ceremony took place a year later, on April 27th, 1980, after which Mum moved into the family home in St Neots. Dad's studies led to a job as a dental technician and Mum eventually found work at an insurance brokers. Their life together had begun.

The next decade brought a lot of changes. In 1983, my sister was born. Then, in 1985, Dad's brother-in-law told him about a shop that had come up for sale in a village called Sawtry, 16 miles up the A1. Being a shop owner himself, he advised that buying the shop would be the best thing my parents could do. After much deliberation, they decided to go for it.

I wondered whether they did it to take control of their lives, become masters of their own fate. Mum, however, says they simply took an opportunity that was afforded to them and did the best they could. Although they had my sister to look after at this point, they weren't thinking of an ideal future in which they'd be rich business owners with children who wanted for nothing. They were simply putting one foot in front of the other, learning as they went. All that was certain was that the more hard work they put in, the better the reward would be.

In 1986, they moved from the family home to the flat above the shop. Dad continued to work nine to five at the dental technician's, taking over the shop in the evening so Mum could look after my sister and do the housework. This work ethic is what forms the foundation of my life and it's knowing how hard my parents work that continues to humble me. Mum often tells me what happened when they first turned a profit of £1,000. They'd never physically seen so much cash in their lives and it was theirs to spend, but they weren't entirely sure what to do with it. So they wrapped it in a plastic bag.

'Perhaps we should hide it in the oven?' Mum suggested.

'Yeah, but if we forget it's in there we might burn it,' Dad replied.

They ended up hiding it in the drawer underneath the cooker.

In 1989, Dad gave up working as a dental technician to join Mum in working full-time at the shop. Business flourished – their hard work was paying off.

1990 was a year of contrasting emotions for my parents. In August, my dada passed away. Two months later, I was born. By now, they'd moved to a house in Sawtry. I spent the first nine years of my life there. It was a fairly lonely existence. None of my school friends lived nearby and I didn't know anyone in the area. The time spent alone here was what fired my imagination – making up for the lack of a world outside, I built imaginary worlds in my head. I wasn't just playing football in the driveway, I was playing a match at Wembley. After watching *Toy Story*, I used my old baby monitor to see if my toys were coming to life (sadly they didn't, but toys are clever like that). When I did finally make friends down the road, it turned out to be the beginning of my career as an actor – I managed to convince them that I was an American kid called Michael. This continued for some time. One of the kids was actually American and even he fell for it. I have no idea why I did it and shortly after I began this performance art piece, we moved house. I don't think they ever found out.

We moved to another village nearby, where Mum and Dad

had bought a house with a shop downstairs. The village was a tight-knit community of around 350 people (a stark contrast to 5,000 people in Sawtry) and soon enough everyone was a friend or a familiar face. The shop had been shut for over two years so my parents garnered a lot of affection simply for reopening it. Regular customers became family friends, I attended church services and played in village cricket matches. The annual village panto was a huge boost for my confidence as an actor.

For Mum and Dad, it was the closest they'd felt to home since they left India – they both originally came from tiny villages in Gujarat. Despite moving to a country 4,000 miles away, they found themselves calling a tiny village home once again. I, on the other hand, was still finding my definition of home. At the time, it meant countryside, a small community and ... not many ethnic minorities.

Yet Indian culture remained a huge part of my childhood. Behind closed doors Mum only spoke to me in Gujarati so I'd learn the language. Bollywood was my introduction to cinema and the soundtrack of my childhood. Hinduism was also at the core of our household, but this is one of the aspects of my identity that left me conflicted. I was brought up and identify as a Hindu and there's no doubt that some of my earliest memories are linked to this – the smell of incense sticks and the learning of prayers that we recited at the shrine in the living room. Still, I don't know a lot about Hinduism and the philosophical intricacies of what is known to be the oldest surviving religion. Surprisingly, my mum feels the same way.

Growing up in India, she recalls faith as being a very personal thing. Each home, whilst observing the basic tenets of the religion, would favour a certain deity. She can only recall community worship at her village mandir during annual festivals, such as Navratri, Holi or Diwali. Her experience of Hinduism was of a very lenient, polytheistic religion that meant different things to different people. Having said that, I'm aware of a lot of traditions that began to clash with my liberal perceptions as I grew up – the separation of male and female seating at some weddings, funerals and festivals; the expectation of a girl to be married by a certain age (which carries across several religions) – this sort of thing made me begin to question the validity of my faith.

The ethnic demographic of my village was echoed by most of the schools I attended and especially the school where I eventually settled to do my GCSEs and A levels. I was one of two Indian guys in the entire school and the overall student population wasn't particularly diverse. Due to this being my general experience, I never saw it as an issue and I guess it wasn't – it was a pretty honest representation of the local population.

As a teenager, I struggled to fit in, but not for lack of trying. Like everyone else at that age, I followed closely what my peers were watching and listening to. So I was drawn towards bands like Arctic Monkeys, Muse and Kasabian, watched *Doctor Who*, *Harry Potter* and *Lord of the Rings*, whilst studying Shakespeare and Bertolt Brecht. Meanwhile, at home, I was still listening to Bollywood music and watching Bollywood films. My sister, who was having a cultural epiphany of her own at university, introduced me to the music of Nitin Sawhney and Niraj Chag. Yet, because no one else knew anything about these things, it was never of any interest to them.

I remember telling someone at school about *Rang De Basanti*, a Hindi film I'd seen that had a big effect on me. I wanted to lend him the DVD, but he didn't seem particularly interested. A similar attempt to introduce someone to Nitin Sawhney's music was briefly humoured and then passed by.

Looking back, this dismissal of my Indian cultural reference points must have caused me to start burying that side of my identity – if it wasn't relevant to my social growth, what use was it? Talking about any of it just drew blank looks and an awkward end to the conversation. It gradually became a very personal part of my life, rarely shared or spoken of with anyone else. Until now.

I've always been something of an outsider and at this point it's a bit of a chicken and egg situation – I'm not sure if I'm just naturally this way, or if being ostracised at an early age made me so. Either way, my teenage years at school kind of enforced the feeling. Although I made some friends, I never found a group that I got into trouble and came of age with. I kept my head down and did my work. I only really came alive in drama lessons – acting was the only thing I was confident doing. It didn't matter who I was in real life, because on the stage I could be anyone and I seemed to be good at it. Even when everyone else had seen *Bugsy Malone* and I hadn't, it didn't stop me being a part of the play. The difference in cultural background didn't seem to hold any sway here. This was what first drew me to acting – here, my propensity for imitation and jumping out of windows was actively encouraged. I could be anything that I wanted to be.

The summer before starting A levels, my life changed when I got the role on *EastEnders*. A whole world opened up to me, not just as an actor but as a person – I made lifelong friends and finally felt accepted into a family outside my own. I was riding high on the fact that I was getting to do what I loved for a living. I was working with actors I had admired for years and I was part of a show that was sewn into the fabric of British society – it was an absurd privilege for a kid from a tiny village in Cambridgeshire.

I stayed in my village for five years after starting on *EastEnders*. Keeping my family and my home near me during this time helped keep my feet on the ground – until I moved to London I still did the paper round for my parents. Outside of the job, very little changed in my life. I moved to London in 2012 and it seems strangely appropriate that it was then that I had my first brush with the issue of race on screen. London's awoken me to just how incredible multiculturalism can be and how dishonestly we're representing that in television and on film. At the same time, I began to analyse the part I've played in on-screen diversity.

Although the Masood family on *EastEnders* were specifically Pakistani Muslims, I think they were widely regarded as a kind of generic representation of a South Asian family. There were intricacies regarding their faith and how it impacted on their lives but I, as a Gujarati Hindu, could always relate to the stories my character and the Masood family were part of, and I know that there are people from various South Asian backgrounds who felt represented by the family. What I loved most about playing Tamwar was that his unique qualities had nothing to do with his ethnicity or religion – he was just like anyone else and perhaps that had a part to play in my forgetting that I was representing a huge section of our society.

Recently, I was reminded of how impactful our media can be. The Monday after the Paris attacks, a scene that we'd shot two months earlier was broadcast. In it, my character reads a Surah from the Qur'an to his girlfriend and explains to her what being a Muslim means to him. 'Be kind to people … and love them.'

In the wake of the weekend's events, it seemed to strike a chord with a lot of viewers.

This is why I became an actor. It started because I wanted

to pretend to be a mutated bipedal turtle. It became a way of escaping from the drudgery of everyday life and now I've come to see it as a responsibility. Storytelling is the most powerful way to promote our understanding of the world in which we live and the vessel to tell these stories is our media. Britain is filled with people from all corners of the earth, each with a wealth of stories to tell; sometimes, race, culture ethnicity are a key part of the narrative, sometimes not.

In discovering so much about how my family arrived here in the UK, I discovered how rich their story is with the culture and traditions of their homeland, but at its core it's a universal story about love and life. My heritage, while inherently linked to my ethnicity, only makes up a part of the role I play in society – day-to-day I'm just another face in the multicultural population of twenty-first-century Britain. If we share the gifts that people have carried across continents and acknowledge them as part of the fabric of our society, from the national curriculum to the mainstream media, we could be on the cusp of a paradigm shift in our understanding of the world.

I must have been about six when I had my first sleepover. My friend Adam had come over and we stayed up till the early hours talking about god knows what. When we finally grew tired, I looked out of my bedroom window and found myself transfixed.

Through the same bedroom window that had been locked to me, I saw my first sunrise.

It was beautiful.

IS NISH KUMAR A CONFUSED MUSLIM?

NISH KUMAR

On September 18th, 2012, I was sitting in my house. This is a common occurrence. 'Sitting in my house' is one of the things I'm best known for, amongst my group of friends, along with 'Bob Dylan trivia' and 'being asleep'. That month was a period of relaxation for me. In August I had performed a run at the Edinburgh festival of my debut stand-up show *Who is Nish Kumar?* A show that one critic had described as 'a comedy show'. The writing and subsequent execution of it had left me in a state of physical, emotional and financial exhaustion, so I had given myself a couple of weeks off in September before I began looking for a new office job so I could continue to support my dream/delusion of being a full-time comedian. My aim that month was to sit around and play a football management computer game. This may well be the least athletic endeavour of all time. It's worse than computer games where you pretend to be a footballer; at least those involve the simulation of exertion. This game requires you to do the admin for imaginary footballers. Still, everyone needs a hobby and that was mine.

Anyway, that morning I was about to return to the fictitious dugout as Manchester United manager Phileas Q Superfly (they let you choose your own name) when I opened my laptop and decided to quickly check in on Facebook. My friend, the comedian Jack Barry, had written on my wall. I clicked on it excitedly as Jack is always good for a laugh, whether it's onstage, in conversation or inside the internet. He had written the following:

'Don't know if I'm the first one to show you this but this just popped up on a meme website I was on. Apparently you're an angry Muslim in the US.'

I was, as you can imagine, utterly baffled. Below the text of his message was a link to a meme website called Quickmeme. com. The link led me to a picture of my own face. This was a surprise. If you're not expecting to see your own face, it's always a surprise. I have no idea how twins get anything done around each other. The picture was a publicity shot that we ended up using as the poster for my aforementioned Edinburgh show, and above it was the title 'CONFUSED MUSLIM'. Around the picture, in a white font with a black outline, was text that read:

'Angry that Christians insulted my prophet, cannot insult Jesus as he is a prophet too.'

At this point my confusion had escalated from bafflement to mild panic. I had not been informed that this was going to happen. I had no idea what any of this meant. I really didn't know what a 'meme' was. It's a point of pride to me that I stay resolutely oblivious of much of contemporary culture. I try to pretend this is because I'm too cerebral to be concerning myself with all this nonsense, but in reality it's probably a manifestation of my own intellectual insecurity. As is my tendency to overuse polysyllabic words.

My flatmate quickly explained to me that people on the

internet share pictures with each other and they all change the caption to variations on a single theme. So he showed me one of 'surprised man' and there were loads of different captions speculating as to why this man was surprised.

But here's the thing – I am not a Muslim. My parents are Indian by birth, and as for their religious classification, my father would identify as a Hindu while my mother prays to 'all the gods, because that way I'm covered every which way'. I try to inform her that I'm not sure you can trick God, but she's convinced she's found a loophole. I wasn't offended that anyone would think I was a Muslim. There's no reason to be. In all honesty, I was offended that they hadn't recognised me as NISH KUMAR 'comedic genius and star of stage and screen' (citation needed).

Also I was pretty used to it. There's a huge Muslim population in India, as you all probably know, so people assuming that an Indian is a Muslim isn't the strangest thing in the world, despite the fact that the majority of Indians are Hindu. However, it's more likely for me. My family is from Kerala, a state in the south of India, which has a long history of immigration, dating back to the sixteenth century when Vasco Da Gama led a Portuguese delegation there. This immigration appears to have crash-landed on my face. I have a face that people seem comprehensively unable to place. I'm regularly confused for being pretty much every ethnicity other than my own (Indian).

Most strangers assume I'm from the Middle East, which isn't a problem, aside from when those people work for US customs or are themselves from the Middle East. A few times a year, in London, someone will approach me and start speaking to me in Arabic because they think they've found the reassuring familiarity of someone they share a language and culture with, in what is otherwise a strange and foreign land. I then have to dash those dreams. I used to say, 'I don't speak Arabic' but now I say 'I'm Indian', only because I don't want them to think that I am Arabian and haven't bothered to learn the language. I don't mind people thinking I'm an Arab, I just don't want them thinking I'm a lazy one.

So it wasn't a surprise, necessarily, that people would think I was a Muslim; it happened fairly regularly and I had no problem with it.

But this was a different kettle of shit.

I had no idea what this was supposed to mean. Was this a knowing joke from one Muslim to another? After all, it takes some rudimentary knowledge of the tenets of the religion to know that Jesus is a prophet in Islam. That's the kind of knowledge you don't often associate with racists, a group not known for their attention to detail. Or was this just Islamophobia with my face plastered all over it. What if people thought that I was behind this?

There were three possible alternatives and none of them were good.

1. It was a person being Islamophobic. I was therefore being racially abused and not even correctly. The only thing worse than racism is inaccurate racism. It was hurtful to me and to people who are actually Muslims.
2. It was a knowing joke made between some Muslims, of which I was now, unjustifiably, part.
3. People would think that I was involved and it was somehow part of an attempt to reinvent myself as some kind of non-white racist comedian, like a non-ironic Borat.

You might think that I was overthinking things. I would inform you that, overthinking is inevitable as a comedian. It's an occupational hazard, like being punched in the face if you're a boxer, or being roundly despised if you're a member of Coldplay. In reality, no one cared, and hardly anyone even saw the meme. That didn't stop The Good Guy (me) from boarding the Neuroses Train to Crazytown.

Here was my central concern – the great thing about joking around with your friends is that you understand each other's intent. If you make fun of your friend, there is a pre-existing understanding of your shared values and assumptions about the world. It's what comedians try really hard to do onstage. We try to establish our personalities and our beliefs so that the audience trusts us enough that when we do make a joke about a contentious subject, there's a reason for it, and it's not just crass or an expression of prejudice.

But on the internet jokes appear untethered, and out of context.

Context is all-important in comedy. Journalists and audience members will often ask you to tell them your favourite joke, but very often it's all about who tells it. It's the singer not the song. The material of a stand-up comedian is intrinsically bound up in that person's onstage identity. Nowhere else is this problem better summarised that in 'Diversity Day', an episode of the American remake of *The Office*. In the show, the hapless boss Michael Scott (played by Steve Carell) is hauled in front of a racial diversity seminar for performing Chris Rock's seminal 'N**** versus Black People' routine in the office. Scott is entirely oblivious to why a white American repeating that routine verbatim would be a problem in any circumstance, much less in an environment where he is the manager. In his frustration he says:

'How come Chris Rock can do a routine and everybody finds it hilarious and groundbreaking and then I go and do the exact same routine, same comedic timing, and people file a complaint to corporate? Is it because I'm white and Chris is black?'

This scene summarises the significance of context and intent in a much better way than the thousands of tedious blog posts and think pieces on the same subject, including the one you are currently reading.

Incidentally, it's become very fashionable to say that the US *Office* 'only really gets going in series two', which is absolute rubbish. The first episode is not great, as it's a direct remake of the UK original, but the rest of the series – including this episode – is excellent. I'm aware it's strange to stop in the middle of an essay, in what is otherwise a credible and excellent book, to talk about a sitcom that ended in 2013 but I just think it's a point that's really worth making. Anyway – the message here is context is key and Steve Carell is great.

So I was now the Confused Muslim. I wanted to contact someone, but there was no one to contact. Quickmeme was just the host website, there was no way of tracing who did it originally. The anonymity of the internet is a real problem. It facilitates the culture of 'trolling' – it's easy to say anything to someone when you don't sign your name to it. That's why 'KINGOF69ING' can spout whatever hateful nonsense he wants without fear of reprisal. In my case, it meant that someone could steal my face, and I couldn't do anything about it. I felt like Nicholas Cage in *Face/Off* before he steals John Travolta's face. Or maybe it's the other way round. I can't remember – whichever one the good one was.

In any case, the picture was a publicity photo and so was supposed to be put into the public domain. This wasn't what we had intended if I'm honest. They say all publicity is good publicity, but I'm not sure the term 'all' covers 'publicity that doesn't have your name on it and somehow could make you look like either the victim or perpetrator of a low-level hate crime'. If they did, then I salute the inventor of that phrase for the specificity of their foresight.

Without any way to trace the creator, it fell to me to establish how they had got my picture. No one had sought permission so, how had this happened? I googled the phrase 'Confused Muslim', hit the images tab and then saw a picture of my face. Then I worked backwards by clicking on the picture. It was a link to a review of my Edinburgh show. It quoted a line from my show where I described myself as 'one of the few people that's regularly confused with being both a Muslim and a Jew'. That meant that the Google algorithm, or whatever the technical term is, had picked on two words from that sentence when you searched for 'Confused Muslim'. Incidentally the other pictures on the search were Omid Djalili and Jesus Christ. What incredible company to keep. I've always seen myself as the mid-point between those two (this is obviously a joke, I don't want to start getting angry emails from ardent fans of Omid Djalili). This also means that if some other idiot decides to balance things out by doing a 'Confused Jew' meme, it'll probably be my fucking face again.

I posted the meme on my Facebook wall and my Twitter page, to friends and sympathisers of my comedy (I can't quite bring myself round to the idea that I have 'fans', I prefer to think of them as people who tolerate, rather than actively enjoy, my humour).

I had expected people to react with incredulity and outrage on my behalf. However, my expectations were quickly confounded. Instead of being passive, the internet – or at least my miniscule section of it – went to work defacing the entire meme. People started posting things like 'This is a comedian called Nish Kumar' and 'Is the Confused Muslim meme, isn't a Muslim'. A couple of my friends used it to settle some scores: 'Nish Kumar owes me a fiver'. Sadly as these are all anonymous I have no way of knowing who that fiver belongs to so will never return it. It may have something to do with those texts my friend Ed keeps sending me saying 'you owe me money'. I guess we'll never know, and in any case, I've already spent that fiver on sweets.

I often think about the person who created the meme. I imagine that they're pretty frustrated. The great thing about doing memes about cats is that cats don't tend to have the internet and ruin the meme by having their friends write things like 'Mr Whiskers did not sanction the use of this photo'. And if they do we've all got much bigger problems than my face being stolen.

There were no reprisals, or at least none of the kind that my family were worried about. When I told my mother she speculated that I'd be banned from America. I had to inform her that the CIA were probably not spending their time trawling through Quickmeme looking for suspects, otherwise Guantanamo Bay would be full of cats and that guy who sang 'Chocolate Rain'. On the plus side, if they were, it certainly would have livened up the second series of *Homeland*.

My dad was worried that it would offend religious extremists. I had to inform him that they were too busy being offended by absolutely everything in the world to worry about me. The only people I'd really been worried about offending were ordinary Muslims, who have nothing to do with terrorism and spend their time having to deal with reprisals for the actions of lunatics that have nothing to do with them. My friend, the comedian Tez Ilyas, has reassured me that they discussed it at the last big Muslim meeting, and I'm fine. However, I suspect Tez to be lying about the existence of these meetings as he always smiles as he mentions them. Then when I ask him about why he's smiling, he claims he's 'remembering a joke that he heard at the meeting and I wouldn't get it because I wasn't there', which seems pretty plausible.

The meme itself served as the inspiration for my 2013 Edinburgh show *Nish Kumar is a Comedian*, a show which most critics agreed was 'another comedy show by Nish Kumar'. Within the comedy community, it is generally agreed that the second show is the hardest one to write, a phenomenon musicians refer to as 'second album syndrome' and further evidence that all comedians just secretly wish we were as cool as musicians. The consensus was that I was given a pretty substantial hand by the meme, with one of my friends claiming 'the internet is writing your show for you' – an opinion with which I found it hard to disagree. Ironically, more people probably found out about the meme through me talking about it in my show than if I had just kept my big mouth shut. I had managed to spin a minor internet-based incident into a moderately successful comedy show, like some kind of poundshop Dave Gorman.

If you visit the website, you'll see that the meme still exists, as a monument to the strange, brief period when I was the 'confused Muslim'. That seems like as good a place as any to leave things – what with that being the name of the meme and all. It gives a nice sense of circularity and strikes a definitive tone. To be honest the rest of this all seems a bit unnecessary. I'm sure they'll edit it out of the finished book, in any case.

FORMING BLACKNESS THROUGH A SCREEN

RENI EDDO-LODGE

I have just finished writing a book about whiteness. This was a book about whiteness as a political force, how it settles like a blanket on our comprehension, how it seeps, and strangles, and silences. I wrote about whiteness from the perspective of an outsider, who – despite my university-educated, well-spoken relative privilege – has always been locked out of whiteness's exclusivity clause. Dissecting political whiteness is paramount to understanding how racism operates in Britain. So often positioned as invisible, neutral, and benign, whiteness taints every interaction we'll ever engage in.

But now I am at a loss. And although I am not a fan of binaries, spending so much time staring into the face of whiteness has forced me to ponder my blackness.

My blackness as a whole, defined not in opposition to a dominant majority, nor constructed as an undesirable 'other' by racialised forces intent on denigrating it. To ponder *my* blackness. Not the blackness that is tacked on to the phrase BAME [black, Asian and minority ethnic] for flimsy equality and diversity purposes by public sector organisations beholden to the Race Relations Act. No. Blackness defined by black folks. The celebration of melanin. For as long as I could comprehend the world, I only knew I was black because I was sure I wasn't white.

Now I want to talk about blackness, our representations of it, how we understand ourselves through the eyes of someone else. How, when I was growing up, the positive black-led and black-owned representations of blackness weren't to be found in the British Isles. Instead, they were being imported from the United States. With globalisation, this is par for the course for all aspects of our pop culture. Yet when it comes to blackness, American-centric media contributed to an erasure here.

It was a kind of displacement that went hand-in-hand with Britain's collective forgetting of black contributions to British history. The black history I learned in school was about the United States. I learned in school that on December 1st 1955, Rosa Parks was arrested for refusing to give up her seat at the front of the bus, setting off a chain of events that resulted in a bus boycott in Montgomery, Alabama. But I didn't learn that less than a decade later, a similar bus boycott took place in Bristol,[14] roughly 106 miles west from the stuffy south London classroom I was learning these facts in. British black history, positioned across the Atlantic, was as real to me as *The Simpsons*, and that was a tragedy.

I had an incredibly strong sense of heritage. Being a third generation Nigerian immigrant is not something your extended family will let you forget. I knew where I came from, but I struggled to see where I was presently at. I needed anchoring,

14 The Bristol bus boycott, led by youth worker Paul Stephenson, saw a city-wide boycott of the bus service in response to an informal colour bar that stopped black people being employed on the buses.

but the legacy of blackness I kept seeing was characterised as thoroughly American.

As a nineties child, I came of age before social media had really taken off, before normal girls were DIY-ing their own media in their bedrooms, creating blogs and YouTube channels, and reassuring their peers that black is beautiful.

I relied on television. My life was pretty sheltered. I ricocheted from the small council flat that I shared with my mum, to my school around the corner, and occasionally to a childminder. I was the only black child in a class of 30 in suburban south London. I have memories of my little white girl classmates trying to convince me that because my skin was black, my tongue was black too. I have memories of an art teacher encouraging my class to draw our 'beautiful blue eyes' whenever we got the crayons and sugar paper out. Everything around me was so starkly white that I began to believe that I would turn white sooner or later. I was quietly being written out of the narrative of humanity in my immediate surroundings.

I needed to find a blackness that was vaguely relevant to a tall, skinny, London-born-and-raised Nigerian girl, and that wasn't to be found in after school and Saturday morning television. When you're young, you translate yourself through representations of people who look like you. And when those characters look like you, but were of a different continent, and a different culture, it invited a kind of cognitive dissonance.

The first black family I saw on television was on *The Fresh Prince of Bel-Air*. For many late-eighties and early-nineties babies, the Banks were the archetypal black family, that all black people should be aiming to be. They were affluent and upper-middle-class, well-dressed, and incredibly well-educated. They even came complete with Geoffrey, the (black)

British butler. It was a complete transgression against the reality of the majority of black families' lives in America at the time, let alone black families in the UK. Even today, 20 years after these episodes first aired, white households in the States hold on average 16 times more wealth than black households. Despite the continued growth of the black middle class in the US, at the time, the Banks family were a total fantasy. And that was OK, because light-hearted entertainment is supposed to help us escape from the drudge of reality.

The Fresh Prince was as much about class as it was about race. The whole point of the show was examining the social *faux pas* that came about when lower-class Will went to live with his upper-class family. From west Philadelphia, to Bel-Air in Los Angeles. It was class that provided the most laughs, from the clashes between Will's relatives and his friend Jazz, to the withering looks of Geoffrey the butler.

As well as *The Fresh Prince*, I was peripherally aware of the Huxtable family on *The Cosby Show*, although it was a little bit before my time. As far as I can tell, the set-up was essentially the same. The Huxtables, based in Brooklyn rather than Los Angeles, were another wealthy black family breaking stereotypes. Like *The Fresh Prince*, the show had its affable, loveable patriarch, traditional family values, and more morals of the story at the end of an episode than you could shake a book of Aesop's Fables at.

But, whilst casting blackness in a positive light, the black American characters I watched were not allowed to be complex. Everyone was good deep down. If they misbehaved, it was never out of ill will, and any intra-family disagreements would be cleared up before the end of the episode. Perhaps this black-led programming was responding to programming that had gone before it that represented black people as a monolith

– lazy, uneducated and stupid. These were simplistic, narrow, and binary narratives that didn't afford us any humanity. It was predictable (and understandable), then, that the black-led response did just the opposite.

I watched black nuclear families – successful, moral along conservative Christian lines, educated and wealthy families – who deeply loved one another despite the light trials and tribulations they might endure throughout the span of a 23-minute episode. And I got it. After centuries of racist depictions of blackness, from blacked-up actors in theatre to blackface minstrels, black programme makers wanted to put their best foot forward, and not let the side down. They probably thought that in order to encourage successful black families, they had to show them in the first place. Almost 200 of *The Cosby Show*'s episodes were written by Bill Cosby himself, whilst the legendary TV and music producer Quincy Jones was at the helm of *The Fresh Prince*.

But this defensive, albeit understandable, response was just as binary and just as simplistic as the overtly racist depictions of blackness before it. It would take another couple of decades of fighting regressive stereotypes until black characters could be afforded the same kind of complexity, humanity and sometimes downright mundanity that depictions of white male characters had enjoyed for centuries.

And of course, the lionisation of the small 'c' conservative, wealthy and successful black family in these television programmes was nothing more than naked respectability politics. This was the logical conclusion of these faux positive representations of blackness, and it couldn't have been more obvious when the now disgraced, but then widely celebrated, black patriarch Bill Cosby delivered his 'Pound Cake' speech to an NAACP [National Association for the Advancement of Coloured People] event in 2004. This was the speech that launched his career as a conservative cultural commentator, and considering that *The Cosby Show* was initially based on Cosby's stand-up sketches, it wasn't surprising that respectability was a consistent theme in his work.

'Ladies and gentlemen,' said Cosby to his audience. 'These people set, they opened the doors, they gave us the right, and today, ladies and gentlemen, in our cities and public schools we have fifty per cent drop out. In our own neighbourhood, we have men in prison. No longer is a person embarrassed because they're pregnant without a husband. (Clapping.) No longer is a boy considered an embarrassment if he tries to run away from being the father of the unmarried child. (Clapping.)

'If you knock that girl up, you're going to have to run away because it's going to be too embarrassing for your family. In the old days, a girl getting pregnant had to go down South, and then her mother would go down to get her. But the mother had the baby. I said the mother had the baby. The girl didn't have a baby. The mother had the baby in two weeks. (Laughter.) We are not parenting. Ladies and gentlemen, listen to these people, they are showing you what's wrong. People putting their clothes on backwards – isn't that a sign of something going on wrong? (Laughter.)'

Ever the conservative traditionalist, Cosby blamed black people for everything, spouting rhetoric more commonly found behind closed doors at posh dinner parties. 'Those people are not Africans,' he said. 'They don't know a damned thing about Africa. With names like Shaniqua, Shaligua, Mohammed and all that crap and all of them are in jail.

'Now look, I'm telling you. It's not what they're doing to us. It's what we're not doing. Fifty per cent drop out. Look, we're raising our own ingrown immigrants. These people are fighting hard to be ignorant. There's no English being spoken, and they're walking and they're angry.'

Cosby's pound cake speech revealed the class hatred of respectability politics.

Respectability politics is the dogged belief that if black people just shape up, dress better and act right, racists would suddenly have a dramatic change of heart, and stop their racist ways. Respectability politics puts all of its faith in racist gatekeepers (telling us that we must change to appeal to their inherent, good-natured humanity), and puts none if its faith in black people living under the weight of poverty and discrimination, scrabbling, trying to make a life anyway they can. Poverty is narrow and limiting. People work within the confines of it. That they have to do that is not the problem. Poverty itself is the problem.

So, how could a lanky kid from London go about asserting black Britishness after a childhood full of seeing blackness through a conservative American cultural lens? I searched for a bit of authenticity amidst the onslaught for many years, eventually cutting off all my hair and hoping for the best, letting it grow back in tight curls, and spending time getting used to them. These were the bits of me that I had tried to erase, in pursuit of looking like the pretty, light-skinned American black women on the TV. I am loath to write about a monolithic blackness, because I know it doesn't really exist in that way. So I settled on exploring my own. To be an immigrant, good or bad, is about straddling two homes, whilst knowing you don't really belong to either. It is about both consuming versions of blackness, digging around in history until you get confirmation that you were there, whilst creating your own for the present and the future. It is up to you to make your own version of blackness in any way you can – trying on all the different versions, altering them until they fit.

BEYOND 'GOOD' IMMIGRANTS

WEI MING KAM

Years ago, my mum would sometimes call me and my siblings to the kitchen excitedly.

'Why, what's going on?' I'd ask.

'Look!' She would point at the TV, and someone Chinese would be on it.

'Oh my god,' my baby sister would groan. 'Why are you always so excited? So they're Chinese – so what?'

We rolled our eyes at each other, and trooped back to our books and Gameboys, perennially embarrassed and uncomprehending, leaving her to watch whoever the fellow East Asian was, like they were a celebrity.

A decade later, my mother's excitement seems more like surprise. I've noticed our long, gaping absence from the cultural landscape and come to recognise the mix of shock and curiosity at seeing a face like mine onscreen, a rare acknowledgement of our existence in the UK. *Look*, my mum was saying. *We're here*.

It often doesn't feel like it.

The Chinese in the UK have been called the 'hidden' or 'invisible' community,[15] given that we are perceived as

---

15 'Chinese diaspora: Britain', *BBC News*. http://news.bbc.co.uk/1/hi/world/asia-pacific/4304845.stm

ostensibly successful, assimilated into British society and self-reliant. In America, we're called 'the model minority'. We do education, food, medicine, finance, and all sorts of other things well, according to popular belief in the West.

As a journalist, Katy Lee's career choice doesn't follow the conventional well-worn stereotypes.

'My dad did want me to work really hard at school,' she says, grinning at me over Skype from her flat in Paris. 'He did want me to make lots of money when I grow up ...' We both start to giggle at the inevitability of parental anxiety. 'He's disappointed that I'm a journalist making not very much money, instead of a banker or whatever.'

Katy has worked for the international news agency Agence France-Presse for five years, moving from London to Hong Kong and then back to Europe. Her educational CV reads like this: high-achieving grammar school; Cambridge; City University for Broadcast Journalism. Half-Vietnamese, half-English, she caveats our conversation by saying that her experience has been tempered by being half-Asian. Despite that warning, her observations all feel very familiar.

'Even as a kid, before the *Tiger Mom* book was a thing,' she says. 'I was vaguely aware that as an Asian kid, I was expected to work hard at school, and that came as much from general society as it did from my dad.'

Ah, Amy Chua's *Battle Hymn of the Tiger Mother*. The hard-working, naturally-clever, silent East Asian is a pervasive stereotype, but the horrified furore around Chua's parenting memoir shows that beneath the Western awe at Chinese educational attainment is a profoundly uncomfortable fear of a seemingly alien culture. Headlines such as the BBC's 'are strict

Chinese mothers the best?'[16] jostled with claims that such parenting leads to a lack of creativity, and people predicted that Chua's children would become friendless robots.

Katy is unimpressed by this.

'It fitted very nicely into a narrative that already exists, that they already had a vague idea about,' she sighs. 'You know, [the idea that these] parents will do anything for their kids to get good grades, they're really cruel, this is exotic, so strange, it's so different from how we behave.'

We both observe that pushy parenting isn't limited to East Asian people, and she says, 'I think a lot of white parents do this, and this is what pisses me off about it.'

Integrate well. Move upwards in society. Be praised – until people worry that you're doing too well, and then they remember that you're foreign. This is perhaps best illustrated by an educational study published by Routledge in 2005, where various teachers attributed success to inherently 'Chinese' qualities while simultaneously hinting that these qualities were 'enclosed', 'denying children individuality' and in opposition to Western cultural ideas.[17]

Political relations play a part in this too. When I bring up China's economic rise, Katy nods.

'I think Britain is going through an identity crisis at the moment. Reactions to things like *Tiger Mother* are like "Who are these people, are they going to take over?"'

It's a shrewd assessment of the contradictory views that the UK has of Chinese people, and one that Jiaqi Hou agrees with.

16 'Are strict Chinese mothers the best?' *BBC News*. http://www.bbc.co.uk/news/magazine-12249215
17 Louise Archer and Becky Francis, *Understanding Minority Ethnic Achievement in Schools: Race, gender, class and 'success'*, (Routledge, 2006), 44.

'Labels can be easily removed. It's not controlled by the minority community itself, and it's related to the international political environment,' he says, when I ask him about the model minority stereotype. 'Anything can change, labels just show how vulnerable the communities are, because today they can be a model minority, but tomorrow they might not be.'

Jiaqi is the project manager of The British Chinese Project, a non-profit organisation that aims to engage the Chinese community in the political process and strengthen its social standing. When I meet him, the BC Project's advisor Cohan Chew and their media director, Jun Kit Man, they take me into a meeting room and sit across the table. It's very businesslike, and I get the feeling that Jiaqi has been asked many of the questions I put to him before.

For such an allegedly successful minority, the level of Chinese political engagement is among the lowest in Britain. The Electoral Commission found in 2006 that 30 per cent of British Chinese people weren't on the electoral register.

'The reasons are very, very complicated, it's not simply [as people] say, that Chinese people are shy, reserved, that they haven't got used to speaking out and being vocal,' Jiaqi says, with a hint of weariness. 'We have a lot of Chinese candidates, but unfortunately, most of them won't be selected to safe seats. So that dramatically reduces the chance of them winning. If we are looking at those Chinese who have never registered [to vote], or have never voted, language barrier is always the first reason.'

He goes on to talk about the large number of people working long hours in catering, who don't have the time for politics, and the ugly history of Chinese exclusion from other forms of employment.

A pause, then very firmly: 'These are all related reasons, it should not be thought of as simply culture. I strongly disagree with anyone who has that opinion.'

The lack of interest in wider civic participation that the low voter registration suggests, is compounded by a pervading distrust of police. In 2013 the BC Project published a report on the Chinese community's relations with the police, and 43.8 per cent of those who did not report a crime selected 'do not think the perpetrator will be caught' or 'do not see any point in reporting', as reasons for their inaction and apathy.[18] Statements from the respondents included feeling that the police reacted too slowly after reporting the crime, and, worryingly, 'many felt that the police failed in their responsibility to make them feel safe and were instead "intimidating".'[19] None of this sounds like a completely happy community.

When I ask Jiaqi if he feels their concerns are being taken seriously, he tells me, frustrated, 'A friend of mine got robbed in her apartment and all of our friends, we called the police, but they said, "We don't have police patrolling that area, we can't do anything".' He continues, 'So basically after an hour the police finally went there, but only because we had more than 50 people calling for the same issue.'

Not much seems to have changed since Min Quan's eye-opening report on racism against the Chinese in 2009. A part of The Monitoring Group, Min Quan's study was prompted by the 2005 murder of Mi Gao Huang Chen outside his takeaway in Wigan in an attack by more than 20 white youths. The reaction of the investigating officer in the case was a classic example of systemic racism. '[He] denied the murder

18   All-Party Parliamentary Group on the Chinese in Britain, *Chinese Community and Policing Report 2013*, (British China Project), 16.

19   *Chinese Community and Policing Report 2013*.

was racially motivated and dismissed [Mi Gao's partner] Ms Jia's accusations of police incompetence as "sheer nonsense".'[20]

Despite repeated warnings about racial harassment, the officer also described the murder as 'unforeseeable'.[21] Min Quan's study notes that, 'Eileen [Jia] remained isolated. In fact, her ethnic origin seemed to work against her. As a Chinese person she was stereotyped as being self-reliant; and not in need of the kind of support offered to other families of murder victims.'[22] She left the UK shortly after the trial.

The case is an extreme example of police indifference towards racial abuse suffered by Chinese people, but the report makes it clear that it is far from isolated, saying that 'there are perhaps even higher levels of racial violence or harassment than those experienced by any other minority group.'[23]

Unsurprisingly, it's not just outright abuse that is an issue for the British Chinese. A paper on inequality for the Joseph Rowntree Foundation in 2011 found that 'inequality levels are also extremely high. Despite the high median levels of resources, poverty rates are above average for both adults and children.'[24] But the illusion that the community as a whole is prospering is, for some East Asians, something to be embraced.

20 'Girlfriend blames police as "racist" killers jailed', *The Guardian*. http://www.theguardian.com/uk/2005/dec/17/ukcrime.race

21 'Takeaway murder teenagers named', *BBC News*. http://news.bbc.co.uk/1/hi/england/manchester/4424766.stm

22 Sue Adamson et al., *Hidden from public view? Racism against the UK Chinese population*, Min Quan report, (The Monitoring Group, 2009).

23 Sue Adamson et al., *Hidden from public view?*

24 Lucinda Platt, 'Inequality within Ethnic Groups', *JRF Programme: Poverty and Ethnicity*, (Joseph Rowntree Foundation, 2011), 14.

This attitude was epitomised by a piece by Clarissa Tan in 2014 in the *Spectator* [25] in which she proclaimed confidently that, 'Britain has many challenges ... racism isn't one of them.'

She goes on to say, 'The danger with crying racism at every turn is that it conceals real problems ... an Ofsted inspector recently raised the issue of working-class white schoolchildren being overlooked and without representation versus ethnic groups ...'

Nothing, of course, about the fact that despite being among the highest achievers in our schools, Chinese male graduates in 2004/5 could expect to earn 25 per cent less than white male graduates. [26]

That particular ceiling is only one of many she ignores. 'I have been welcomed and accepted in this country, and – uncool as this may sound – I feel grateful for this,' she says, towards the end of the article. It seems like a very low bar for gratitude.

'Thinking about the model minority thing,' I say, 'there will probably be some people I talk to who think, "Oh it's a good thing!"'

Viki abandons her sushi completely.

'No it's not! People who think that think, "It's positive racism", which is the most ridiculous phrase I've ever heard in my life.'

Viki Cheung works in publishing. We're sitting in a Japanese restaurant in Chinatown on a Sunday, attempting to

---

25 'Britain has major problems – racism isn't one of them', *The Spectator*. http://www.spectator.co.uk/2014/02/how-racist-is-britain/

26 Yaojun Li, Fiona Devine, Anthony Heath, 'Equality Group Inequalities in Education, Earnings and Employment', Equality and Human Rights Commission, (2008), Executive summary, iii.

chat in between the endless plates being brought to our table.

'You're treating all East Asians as a homogenous mass,' she continues. 'We're all individual people, why is this such a struggle to see that?'

I mention the absurd dichotomy that the phrase 'model minority' indirectly suggests. She nods. 'Yes. In the same mouthful as saying, "East Asians are the model minority because they're quiet and hardworking", [you imply] black people are apparently loud and lazy.'

I ask Viki if she feels she has to push back against stereotypes. She considers this for a second, and replies, 'I am far more outspoken at work than I ever thought I would be, on work issues. I'm aware that if I'm not it's contributing to the "quiet, sensible [stereotype]".' I nod, understanding. There are very few East Asian people in publishing. 'And I'm going to have to be even more me to combat that, especially because I'm a woman. I would rather be thought of as opinionated.'

Even as I think about how much hard work that sounds, she says, 'It was an active choice I made. It's a choice I made a long time ago, but I amped it up since coming to work in publishing, which is a very white industry.' She shrugs. 'I'm a very outspoken person anyway, it's not a facade in any way, it's just a more me version of me, out of necessity because I don't want …'

Viki stops for a few seconds. 'It's a really heavy lot of things that I have to think about to not be stereotyped. And I have no idea if my efforts are even working.'

Sensible, quiet, shy … some things just follow us around. The idea of not complaining being an admirable trait, is something that struck Katy Lee during our Skype chat.

'I do think it's interesting that this idea of being a model minority is tied up with essentially being quiet,' she says. 'Just sitting back, not complaining about stuff, and getting on with making money. Being quiet is considered a really good quality.'

Especially when it comes to the rights of others to make racist jokes at someone else's expense.

The week before we chatted, it was announced that Janette Tough, a white actor, had been cast as a Japanese designer in *Ab Fab: The Movie*. Amidst the fury that the decision unleashed, newspapers published opinion pieces (by writers who weren't East Asian) on the row. Helen Lewis in the *Guardian* wondered why drag wasn't considered as bad as yellowface. The *Telegraph* managed to comprehend that blackface is 'fundamentally racist', and yet decided that Ab Fab's yellowface was merely mocking a nation. 'No country is immune to satire – and nor should it be,' they concluded.

Be quiet. Stop complaining. Let us have our fun. Don't be so sensitive. You're normally quiet, aren't you?

Katy sighs with disappointment.

'The yellowface thing is a really good example. I think I was listening to some comedians the other day [they were talking about] what accent it's acceptable to do and saying, "Well, like obviously you can't do a Jamaican one, but like I think Chinese is pretty OK," and well no, it isn't!'

'People expect me to be a good worker. Professional etc., I think this is because of the stereotype that we are smart and nerdy and thus seen to be a hard worker.'

I stare at the email and grin. I found Rebecca Yip's blog through her YouTube channel a few weeks ago. Both are called *Asianchemnerd*. Her family is from Hong Kong, and she moved back there from the UK to do her chemistry PhD a year ago. After reading about her reasons for doing so ('I had some awful times with racist people [in] secondary school'), I emailed her asking for a chat.

'Born in UK but ethnically Chinese, everyone looked at me to be an outsider,' she wrote back. She doesn't, unsurprisingly, escape systemic prejudice in academia either. 'Generally, professors tend to be white men. I feel that we do have to prove ourselves more than a white man.'

She mentions a racist incident in the UK involving her boyfriend, who is Indian. 'I want to bring up my family in a place that is safe, and they feel welcome and they can feel like they can reach their full potential, without holding back because of their race.'

In the UK, she says, there will always be something holding them back.

As I watch her Chinese New Year video, I wonder: how many other people like her leave this country to find better things?

'I do feel that there're better work opportunities elsewhere. What I want to do personally, I want to work in Britain. I'm British and I want to work here.' Paul Courtenay Hyu, otherwise known as 'Chinese Elvis', is giving me the lowdown on life as a jobbing Chinese actor in the Curzon Soho café.

I mention the steady stream of British black actors honing their potential in America, and he nods.

'Well it's happening to a very small extent with the East Asians. Elaine Tan is over there and she's working her arse off.' He adds in a satisfied tone, 'And she is the main person in our episode of *Doctor Who*. So there are two Chinese in it, and she's got a Geordie accent, and pretty good too, I have to say. And I do my Yorkshire accent.'

He mentions Singapore and Hong Kong as other places that British Chinese seek work in.

'They're more like the kung fu guys, the ones who can do stunts. A lot of Singaporeans go back to Singapore because it's just better [than the UK]. Anybody who has a right to work there seems to go back quite often ...' He reels off a list of other actors who work in Singapore. 'Adrian Pang hasn't been back for about fifteen years and I don't blame him, because he's just staying busy, whereas here we're scrabbling for shit.'

He mentions very casually that he went to drama school with an actor from *The Hobbit*. I gape at him for a second, and he grimaces at the memory of seeing his old classmate in the trailer.

'The majority of us British actors – apart from Ben Wong, literally apart from him – we haven't had the opportunities that all our white peers have had,' he says. 'So whilst we might in the 80s have had the equivalent talent and potential, they've had a chance to develop it, and we're just sat there stagnating going ...' He grabs a Curzon café menu and puts on what white people call a Chinese accent, then mimes being a waiter. 'Ohhhh we talk like 'dis, a Chinese menu for one?' I wince, and he slaps the menu down on the coffee table. 'That's what we've done, so we aren't as technically on top of it as we should be. That's an unforeseen consequence of not getting the same opportunities.' Paul picks up the menu again, exasperated. 'You have to be better than you should be in order just to keep up. Women say that, don't they, you have to be better just to stay par. I think that's what we suffer from as well.

'We pay our taxes, we deserve something, it's only fair. We pay our fucking BBC licence, we deserve to see somebody on *EastEnders*! Surely after 30 years of East-fucking-Enders we must have had a Chinese family on it ... at least once ... for six months?'

* * *

He's not the only person thinking this. Everyone I spoke to for this essay voiced annoyance or puzzlement at the lack of East Asians in British media who weren't stereotypes. From illegal immigrants in *Casualty* to Triad members in *Sherlock*, hardly anyone writing for the British screen (or book) seems capable of imagining British East Asians as British. If we're not villains à la Fu Manchu, we're delicate women who need saving, usually by white men (Gemma Chan in *Sherlock*), or comedy material.

Even Katie Leung of Harry Potter fame, arguably the most famous British Chinese actor we have, recently expressed frustration at how limiting her roles are. 'More and more when I see a script that requires a Chinese accent of any kind, I flinch a little bit,' she said, in an interview with the *Herald on Sunday*.

News coverage, rare though it is, is hardly better, going between the extremes of criminality or some comment on the model minority story, usually to do with education.

We're not seen as human, because we never get to be complex individuals. Our defining characteristic is generally our foreignness. Even news reports about education carry an undertone of fear of a culturally alien other and of being usurped, both here and internationally. Being a model minority is code for being on perpetual probation. Hostility towards the 'yellow peril' is never far from the surface.

It's easy to cling to a position of privilege when it acts as protection from the ever-present danger of being seen as outsiders, but playing to the myth of the 'good immigrant' does not lead to real equality, or even acceptance. Breaking out of the 'model minority' box and looking beyond that status towards humanity and freedom is the long game.

'YOU CAN'T SAY THAT! STORIES HAVE TO BE ABOUT WHITE PEOPLE'

DARREN CHETTY

A few years ago, I taught a Year 2 class in east London. I had built up a good bank of multicultural picture books and resources and shared these with the class whenever seemed appropriate. When it came time for the class to write their own stories, I suggested that they used the name of someone in their family for their protagonist. I wanted them to draw on their own backgrounds, but was worried about 'making an issue of race'. When it came to sharing their stories, I noticed only one boy had acted upon my suggestion, naming his main character after his uncle. He had recently arrived from Nigeria and was eager to read his story to the class. However, when he read out the protagonist's name another boy, who was born in Britain and identified as Congolese, interrupted him. 'You can't say that!' he said. 'Stories have to be about white people.'

Let me back up for a second.

I've spent almost two decades teaching children aged between four and 11, in English primary schools that serve multiracial, multicultural, multifaith communities. Over that time, I have come to notice that whenever children are asked to write a story in school, children of colour[27] will write a story featuring characters with 'traditional' English names who speak English as a first language. This has been the case across the schools I have taught in with barely an exception. Yet, I don't recall it ever being discussed by teachers in these schools or on any of the courses on writing that I attended over the years.

My own attempts to open up conversations about what I have noticed have had some success but have also been met with angry responses from a loud minority of teachers. In one case, I recall being asked, 'Why are you making an issue of race when children are colour-blind?'

The question contains an assumption, namely that children are 'colour-blind'. I think this might stem from a belief that children do not attach any significance to racialised identities, particularly in twenty-first-century multi-ethnic urban classrooms, because we inhabit a post-racial world. If children were writing stories where the race[28] of characters was varied and random, there might be some merit in claiming that children are colour-blind. However, even the strongest advocates of racial colour-blindness do not argue that all people are white ... and English. They argue that race no longer matters. If that's true, why are young children of colour and young white children writing exclusively about white characters?

I'm confident the boy who said that stories had to be about

27 I use here 'children of colour' and 'people of colour' to refer to those who are racialised as 'other than white'. Originating in the USA, this term is used increasingly in the UK. Alternative terms include 'Black Asian and Minority Ethnic' (BAME), racially minoritised and 'Global Majority'.

28 I view race as socially constructed and agree with Gary Younge that it is 'a nonsense' that nevertheless affects our lives and thus should be talked about.

white people was being sincere and indeed, in the ensuing class discussion there was a fair bit of uncertainty about who could and couldn't be in stories. I was surprised and confused by this. Why did my students without fail write stories about children from very different backgrounds to themselves? And why were these characters always white? Why hadn't my efforts to offer a culturally diverse reading diet made clear to them that stories could be about absolutely anyone?

At the time, I don't think I realised what I was up against.

If you are a teacher, try this with your class. Ask them to write down their favourite 25 children's book characters. Then ask them to count how many of those characters are white (and look for other patterns too, such as gender and disability). If you're not a teacher, ask any child you know. Or maybe ask the staff in a bookshop to show you the picture-books with a black boy, or a mixed-race girl or a Muslim child as the protagonist. I tried this once and received a lot of help in searching from a clearly panicked shopkeeper – but very few books.

Booksellers like Letterbox Library provide a service valued by many parents and teachers in going the extra mile to locate books featuring people traditionally under-represented in children's literature. Of course, booksellers can only sell books that get published. And the stories I hear from people in publishing and from authors leads me to wonder if some UK publishers share the same confusion I observed in that Year 2 class. Namely, an uncertainty about the place of stories featuring people of colour and the place of people of colour in stories.

A South Asian author told me that she was advised to change her name for a book cover in order to broaden its appeal, and another writer was advised that unless they were writing an 'issue' book, their book-cover protagonist should not be black, as this would result in fewer copies being purchased. Whether or not such advice is based on evidence – do white book buyers *really* shy away from buying books because they feature black characters? – it seems that this concern with race and commercial viability certainly troubles this idea of 'colour-blindness' or 'post-raciality' in the UK.

Not only that, it means that, as a teacher, I have fewer books at my disposal to demonstrate to BAME children that stories can be about people like them.

Chimamanda Ngozi Adichie recalls that the stories she wrote as a seven-year-old in Nigeria were based on the kinds of stories she read, featuring characters who were 'white and blue-eyed, they played in the snow, they ate apples'. According to Adichie, this wasn't just about experimentation or an active imagination, 'because all I had read were books in which characters were foreign, I had become convinced that books by their very nature had to have foreigners in them and had to be about things with which I could not personally identify.'[29] We learn so many things from reading stories, including the conventions of stories such as good versus evil, confronting our fears and that danger often lurks in the woods. The problem is that, when one of these conventions is that children in stories are white, English and middle-class, than you may come to learn that your own life does not qualify as subject material. Adichie describes this as 'The Danger of a Single Story' – a danger that extends to stories which, whilst appearing to be 'diverse', rely on stereotypes and thus limit the imagination.

Children's literature professor Rudine Sims Bishop offers

29 'The danger of a single story', Chimanda Ngozi Adichie TED talk. https://www.ted.com/talks/chimamanda_adichie_the_danger_of_a_single_story/transcript?language=en

a useful metaphor for helping us think about what is at stake here. Whilst acknowledging that 'good literature reaches across cultural and ethnic borders to touch us all as human',[30] she argues that books can act as both mirrors and windows for children. 'Windows' offer us a chance to look closely at a view of the world we may not have previously seen. Those windows might take us out to escapist fantasy or provide a view of lives we have not previously seen. These are notions familiar and vital to writers, teachers and those of us who care about stories. But Sims Bishop adds that books might also mirror our lives in some aspects and that children from the dominant culture tend to have books as mirrors whilst children who have been historically 'ignored – or worse ridiculed' do not, and that this communicates important messages about the extent to which 'they are valued in the social context in which they are growing up'. Recognising that a window can be a barrier, Sims Bishop later added the idea of the sliding glass door as 'a way to suggest that a book can offer … a lived experience for a reader'.[31]

It was a concern over the lack of stories that allow all children to see themselves in the fiction they read – books as mirrors – that motivated Verna Wilkins to establish Tamarind Books, first as an author and then also as a publisher. Wilkins recalls her son coming home with a self-portrait in which he had painted his face 'bright pink'. She recalls the conversation:

'Is this you?' I asked feebly.

'Yes,' came the confident reply.

'Are you that colour?'

'No. The teacher gave out flesh colour to everyone!'

---

30 Rudine Sims Bishop, 'Reflections on the Development of African American Children's Literature', *Journal of Children's Literature*, 38:2, (Fall 2012).

31 Ibid.

'Oh. Fine. I have a lovely brown crayon and we can fix that right now.'

'No!' he said. 'It has to be that colour. It's for a book!'[32]

My classroom story is remarkably similar to Wilkins's story of this conversation but took place over 20 years later. I certainly don't want to diminish the huge impact that Tamarind has had on children's publishing but I'm confident Wilkins would agree with me that there's a need for more like her in children's publishing, as campaigns like #WeNeedDiverseBooks are arguing. Wilkins made the decision to focus on books with everyday representations of black children rather than what she terms book about 'issues'. Wilkins has good reasons for doing this but it does mean that stories like hers with her son, and mine with my class, which invite us to explore ideas around childhood, racism and the arts would probably not be published by Tamarind, however well-written.

I've written elsewhere about how the books that often are recommended as dealing in some way with racism do so through metaphor and animal allegories.[33] There may well be benefits to this – not least the avoidance of further portrayals of children of colour as victims – but this also means its hard to find portrayals of children of colour thriving in a world where racism exists. A much-discussed example is J.K. Rowling's 'Harry Potter' series. The books are seen by many as arguing for inclusivity and tolerance, tackling challenging themes such as racial purity and oppression. These themes are explored through fantasy figures such as wizards, giants and elves. At

32 Verna Wilkins, 'The Right To Be Seen', Patrick Hardy Lecture, October 29th, 2008.

33 Darren Chetty, 'The Elephant in the Room: Picturebooks, Philosophy for Children and Racism', *Childhood and Philosophy*, Vol. 10 No 9, (2014).

the same time, amongst the teachers and pupils at Hogwarts, there are very few people of colour and no clear explanation of why that might be. So a story that has so much to say about racism on an allegorical level at the same time depicts people of colour as marginal without exploring their marginalisation.

Malorie Blackman has shown that compelling stories that do not shy away from racism can be written for children with her 'Noughts and Crosses' series, whilst also demonstrating that there are so many stories beyond racism to be told about children of colour. In 2014, in her role as the presiding Children's Laureate, Blackman spoke out about how diversifying the characters in children's literature would benefit all readers. In a piece for Sky News, which itself became a news story after she was misquoted in the original title, Blackman is quoted as saying,

'You want to escape into fiction as well and read about other people, other cultures, other lives, other planets and so on. But I think there is a very significant message that goes out when you cannot see yourself at all in the books you are reading. I think it is saying "well, you may be here, but do you really belong?"'[34]

Clearly, not everyone agreed. However, despite receiving racist abuse online Blackman vowed not to be silenced, and mainstream newspapers ran stories about children's literature, diversity and marginalisation.[35]

I don't think such marginalisation is limited to children's books. As well as books, the children I taught were learning about stories from film and television. One popular show

---

34 'Call for more ethnic diversity in kids' books', *Sky News*. http://news.sky.com/story/1323753/call-for-more-ethnic-diversity-in-kids-books

35 'Malorie Blackman facest racist abuse after call to diversify children's books'. *The Guardian*. http://www.theguardian.com/books/2014/aug/26/malorie-blackman-racist-abuse-diversity-childrens-books

amongst pupils I've taught over the years is set in the very area of England where we live. When it was launched in 1985, *EastEnders* was lauded for its inner-city realism and diversity.

Creator/producer Julia Smith declared that 'We don't make life, we reflect it.' She also said, 'We decided to go for a realistic, fairly outspoken type of drama which could encompass stories about homosexuality, rape, unemployment, racial prejudice, etc., in a believable context. Above all, we wanted realism.'[36]

In 2009, the BBC compiled a list of the 100 *EastEnders*' characters with the most 'doof doof'[37] cliffhangers – an indication, albeit an imprecise one, of who has the main storyline. As the BBC website says, 'Impact after all is the bedrock of the perfect cliffhanger.'[38]

According to the 2011 Census, inner east London boroughs have populations that are somewhere between 45–71 per cent BAME. So, how many of the top 50 most impactful characters in this programme, set in the East End of London and aiming for realism, were BAME?

None.

Many of the children I was teaching watched *EastEnders*. Given the chance they'd talk about current storylines. Perhaps, as well as learning about dramatic plotting they were learning that people who looked like them and their parents were 'supporting cast' not 'lead roles'. Perhaps this again comes

36 Christine Geraghty, *Women and Soap Opera: A Study of Prime Time Soaps*, (Cambridge, Polity Press, 1991).

37 Doof Doof refers to the drums that kick in as the theme tune plays at the end of the show.

38 'Who has the most doof doofs?', *BBC*. http://www.bbc.co.uk/programmes/articles/1wZjwgr7519fmWF6m10wgz1/who-has-the-most-doof-doofs

down to questions of audience … for whom are these stories produced? What do the creators assume, rightly or wrongly, about their audience?

In her essay *Playing in the Dark*, Toni Morrison argues that 'the readers of virtually all of American fiction have been positioned as white'.[39] Karen Sands O'Connor, a professor specialising in Black British children's literature, says of West Indian writers who came to Britain, 'In order to be writers, they had to tell their own stories; in order to be published authors, they had to do it in a way acceptable to their mostly white British audience.'[40]

So who is the reader for children's writing in a classroom? I think that's probably a complicated question – but in a very literal sense it is the teacher. Teachers read their students' writing and teach them about the kind of things they hope or expect to see whilst reading.

After reflecting on my experience with my Year 2 class, the following year – whilst teaching Year 5 – I was emboldened to experiment. What would happen if for just one lesson I insisted they write about a character from a similar ethnic, religious and linguistic background as themselves – just as I sometimes insist they try to include a fronted adverbial, a moral dilemma or a tricolon?

First we discussed ourselves in terms of, amongst other things, language, family migration, physical appearance including skin and hair, religion, hobbies and clothes. Then I asked the children to write a character who was similar

---

39 Toni Morrison, *Playing in the Dark: Whiteness and the Literary Imagination*, (Harvard University Press, 1992), xiv.

40 Karen Sands-O'Connor, *Soon Come Home To This Island: West Indians in British Children's Literature*, (2007), 140.

in some but not necessarily all of these categories. As I modelled this process for them, I realised that previously I too often defaulted to 'traditional' English names and white characters when writing in class. Now, I tried to draw on my own experience, creating composite characters from family members and applying some of the writing techniques we'd noted in our class reading.

Then they wrote. Clearly, many of them enjoyed the lesson and many produced their best piece of writing. Here are a couple of examples:

Bang! As I stormed to head teacher Mrs Paula's office my head filled with fear. Fear of exclusion!

Mrs Paula was a short, slim, young white woman with red ruddy cheeks. She was a stern woman who hated disobedience and inappropriateness. As I stroked my black hair, my smooth lips crumpled and my creamy brown face turned red with worry.

Michael

Maryam Patel was a twelve-year-old girl, whose parents were Indian, but she was born in Britain. She was a fairly religious person. However, Maryam thought one does not have to wear a headscarf to be religious. She loved her red straight hair. Her hair was as red as blood. She had decided to dye her hair as she hated her dark brown hair. She loved football and the club she supported was Liverpool. One day I will play for the Liverpool women, she thought.

Nabila

I want to avoid making huge claims here. However, I do sense a greater emotional engagement with the story from the children and the beginnings of an authorial voice in both Michael's dramatic first-person opening and Nabila's character description. Nabila is not writing the 'single story' stereotype of Muslim girls. She is writing something far more interesting. There is genuine characterisation in the paragraph not just a short list of features, which I often encounter. More than that, there is some insight in this nine-year-old's writing – and I think that is precisely because she is using her own life as inspiration for her creativity whilst drawing on her reading of fiction. Her descriptive paragraph comes after a lesson looking closely at descriptions by a range of children's authors, which is where the idea of including the protagonist's thought or principle as well as a simple physical description emerged. As her teacher, I tried to get her to focus on a range of structures for describing a character and then give her clear encouragement to draw on her own experiences and those of the people she knew well.

I am not claiming any expertise here, rather sharing a story from my teaching. In many ways I have only scratched the surface and I've tried to include other voices in this essay for those who want to go deeper. I developed my practice from one of just offering a more diverse range of stories in the classroom to modelling writing that drew on my own background so as to signal to my students that they may do the same. I made time to have discussions with students that developed our language for describing skin colour and hair texture and recognised the diversity in the classroom and the lack of diversity in the stories we were writing. I shared examples of how writers explore character's thoughts and feelings so that stories become specific, memorable and something that resonate with us as human beings. I'm not suggesting teachers should always do this but rather that they try it and then review the results; perhaps along with the children they teach.

When I initially wrote about this issue, many people commented saying either that I'd articulated something they'd felt but not said, or that I'd made them see something they'd previously not noticed. A few people were clearly annoyed by it or just dismissive. But many began telling their own stories, often tales of frustration with classroom environments and children's literature – as former children, as parents, as teachers. Perhaps in the telling of these tales, of being the antagonist battling against omission and absence, we can become protagonists, writing ourselves into a richer, multilayered narrative – beyond a single story.

Speaking to Nabila, she told me she had never written about an Indian heritage and/or Muslim character before. Nobody had ever told her she shouldn't. But at the same time, nobody had ever explicitly given her permission. Subsequently, she wrote two further full stories about 'Maryam Patel'. The third instalment described Maryam's trip to India.

Trust me, it was a good read.

An earlier version of this chapter appeared on Media Diversified.[41]

---

41 'You can't do that! Stories have to be about White people', Media Diversified. https://mediadiversified.org/2013/12/07/you-cant-do-that-stories-have-to-be-about-white-people/

ON GOING HOME

KIERAN YATES

I'm looking out of the window midway through the eight-hour journey back to my homeland and thinking of the countless diasporic tales of going home I've read over the years. I consider how the sea has inspired a thousand clichés, about never feeling quite whole, of experiencing an identity cut into neat, disembodied pieces. Staring out it suddenly becomes so clear why we contribute our experiences to a canon saturated with tales of diaspora drama. From Rushdie's 'imaginary homeland' to Naipaul's 'sugar cane and sugar cane', to each reference of a billowing sari in the wind, it's ironic how fraught literature has been with Kipling-esque throwback exoticism. But for any writer, the poetry of crossing oceans to rediscover our home is irresistible, and perhaps for many of those writers who were rarely given opportunities to champion their homes it was too tempting to draw from the multicoloured utopian visions of lush green jungles and air scented with milk and honey. As a fragmented world allows for more nuance now it's obvious that in reality, it's the details of these experiences, not the grand clichés that really reveal the most about ourselves and our journeys.

It's been eight years since I've returned to Punjab. Last time, I was a student, which enabled me to swerve questions about marriage and career, but now I'm officially an adult everything will be up for scrutiny. I'm making mental notes about how best to sidestep the lines of questioning in the courtrooms of family living rooms and kitchens, as we pass over Turkey. I see the mountains below and think about when my granddad made this journey over 40 years ago in the opposite direction, on a Boeing 747 to London Heathrow.

The Britain that accepted him, the place I call home, is now experiencing a period of rejection. The last year has seen a depressing attack on many immigrant communities, as the aggressive rhetoric of adhering to 'British values' has catapulted itself into political and social policy. Cameron specifically targets Muslim women for their poor language skills, the tabloid media demonises refugees on a daily basis, and the rhetoric encouraging us to prove our allegiance to the country's best interests, makes the place I call home feel less safe for people who, largely, look like me.

As the tannoy announces in both Hindi and English that we can unfasten our seatbelts, I consider how the demonising of language is a depressingly familiar narrative – these new plans (that actually pop up every few years) proposing the enforcement of English lessons, as a way of promoting integration under the guise of celebrating British values.

In reality, proposals like this create even more forensic side-eyes that you notice when you're speaking your mother tongue on the train to Kings Cross, or forget yourself in a quiet café and finding yourself speaking Punjabi too loudly on the phone to your cousin.

I know that language can be painful, and so too do a generation of immigrants who have arrived here through different pathways. For them, language is the great battle to fight, and for many it's a war you always feel like you're losing. Even when you get the language, unless you shed your accent, you're continually reminded of your difference. For Indians, our accent has almost become a universal in-joke. The Apu-*thank-you-come-again* novelty, the ingrained Western truth that 'everything sounds funny with an Indian accent!' is an imprint of cultural worth. French accents are sexy, intelligent; Americans (in rap, anyway) cool and culturally appropriated; Indians are comedic – a fact that made the 'One Pound Fish' guy a brief chart hit thanks to tongue-in-cheek purchases from middle England. Whenever I think of his 'novelty act' that 'the nation' loved, I'm amazed that even as recently as 2012, that colonial spirit of finding humour in difference lived on in the hearty laughs of people using my granddad's accent to be entertained. His Indian/British accent was a map of where he'd been and what he'd seen. He travelled from our village in Bahowal to Delhi, to Southall, to Calgary. His voice mirrored those journeys, a living imprint of his memories, and revealed the things he didn't about himself.

Language acquisition is of course a result of age, prior education, resources, and access, rather than a simple time-plus-effort equation. A fact that the current dangerous political rhetoric erases with its snappily presented policy; it's difficult to argue with. Who can protest against the idea of more resources for immigrants? The only problem with this is that those who speak the language of their homeland first, before the language of the coloniser, are made to wade in thick, asphyxiating shame. That they should fall victim to the threateningly punitive 'learn-or-get-out' deal that political rhetoric is ramping up, is obvious. For anyone who has actually seen someone learn a language, it's safe to say that the school of 'well you live here, just learn the language!' thought isn't quite as easy as that. And remember, even when you get it, people will still take the piss.

Next to me is my one-year-old cousin. He is flicking the tray compartment up and down repeatedly, fascinated. My mind is immediately back to my nanaji, who had never travelled on a plane before his journey to London, and I think of how he must have been fascinated by this tray and the cup holders and the plastic cutlery and the window shutters, and how he must have craned to see these same views below.

After a nine-hour drive I'm in the pinde, in my home village of Bahowal. This is where my family comes from, where generations of us have lived, worked and died. My cousins are staring at my sari in adoration. I'm embarrassed at how unnecessarily extravagant it is. My grandma is enjoying the attention I'm getting, but my cheeks are red and I'm terrified of my relatives thinking that I revel in this uncomfortable showboating.

We spend three weeks in this village, disconnected from the internet, showers, unable to walk around unchaperoned. I struggle with the details. I'm scared of the high-speed scooters my cousins whizz around on, which are victims to the untarmacked roads. My reticence to just fearlessly hop on one with my sari on makes me look like some kind of nanny-state soldier trying to enforce Draconian traffic safety and I'm heckled until I finally just shut up and submit. The buckets of water I collect from the well are the exact height of my knees and every time I walk with them, I knock them over, spilling water everywhere, to the entertainment of the neighbourhood children who come to watch me every morning. Even my long, perfectly pointed acrylic nails give away my cushy life, devoid of manual labour, and every time flour gets stuck in them when I'm in the kitchen, making chapattis, I can hear my grandma tutting next to me. My attempts to realign myself with a traditional Punjabi identity fall flat and I'm getting it wrong over and over.

My Punjabi identity back home is a fairly typical second generation one. It's Hoshiarpur football T-shirts as streetwear in London, Bhangra and grime playing out of your cousin's BMW, sending pictures of you in Air Max 90s and a sari to a WhatsApp group. Being a British Asian in 2016 is about being in on the joke when in comes to reclaiming parts of our identity you're supposed to feel ashamed about.

I wear sari tops in the rave, blast Bhangra in the car, make friends with corner-shop owners and teach co-workers about Vaisakhi, delicately explaining to them why saying 'Salaam Alaikum' to a Sikh is a misstep. I grew up revelling in being a typical Southall girl, finding familiarity in the shaved eyebrows of my older male cousins, before moving to a white community where people didn't get me and I noticed just how different I was. Being dragged out of my comfort zone enabled me to discover a new kind of British identity and eventually my family got used to my weirdness, that I wanted to be a writer, that I had white and black friends, that I wanted to stay in reading *Harry Potter* instead of going to the Mega Mela on the common.

At home, the coding is pitched right and I've learned how to navigate my identity in white spaces, in family spaces, in my own. But here, in this village, my specific adoption of Punjab through my own lens is scrutinised by my family and found lacking. They don't understand my jokes, my observations, my London-twanged Punjabi.

This becomes particularly apparent at times, like when my masi catches me on the roof of our house where I've escaped with my sister (it's the only place you can get any privacy and I'm so bored of the local gossip and eternal tea-making below). I'm making a video of a faux toothpaste advert, spinning around as I bite into some sugar cane and flash my pearly whites into the camera (my grandmother swears by sugar cane as the answer to pristine white teeth). I'm winking into the camera and making 'ColCane' taglines in an Indian accent, and my masi berates me for acting like a child. She doesn't understand me, what I find funny, why I'm so weird and different. She constantly compares me to my cousin, who looks like a Kardashian, works as a teacher and has just had an arranged marriage to some heartthrob doctor son. They are cooing over pictures of her while I'm spoken about in tones of puzzlement and sympathy. I overhear my uncle's wife noting that she heard me listening to 'black music' in the bathroom (Fetty Wap) and that I was probably 'messaging a boy' (untrue, no data) and that I always wake up too late (true, but jet lag?).

Going back to the pinde flags up all the things I can't do properly – my rotis aren't round enough, my hands aren't steady enough to apply mendhi, my teeth are too weak to pull sugar cane. While my job as a journalist requires me to artfully draw out other people's voices, I'm unable to give myself one that doesn't present me as pretty inadequate. I am what my favourite cousin calls a 'proper paki' when I'm at home, owing to my love of 'freshie' interior details, Zee TV and old-fashioned songs – but here I'm a fraud, 'a proper coconut' (as my other cousin calls me), too modern to gain favour with the simple tasks, and too strange to be adored by my masis. Despite this, I love every minute of my inadequacy, and it's the intimacy of the unsaid – that they describe me as beautiful when I'm not there, that they worry when I'm out of sight – that allows me to grow roots.

Our next stop is in Delhi.

My 15-year-old cousin in Delhi who reminds me of a desi Paris Hilton illustrates that there is a different code here. Her opening question on seeing me is, 'What's your favourite cosmetic product?', spoken in a city-dwelling modern Delhi drawl that I recognise from Bollywood, aping Karisma Kapoor.

It signals that being humble about what you have isn't the state of play here.

As I arrive, she sees me in my thick, unfashionable suit of heavy embroidered gold thread and as she stands in designer pyjamas, I can see she's visibly disappointed.

'Why are you wearing that?' she asks me.

The answer is that I endured the hellish car trip in said suit to look respectful – my tracksuit is in the boot – and it now seems that I've been scratching my neck on this heavy chuni for the last 10 hours for nothing. When we arrive, my other younger cousin, who is almost 10, runs out to greet me excitedly – somehow, it's been relayed through family Chinese whispers that I'm a fashion journalist and she's expecting a Chanel-clad, high-fashion, vogue catwalk model. What she sees is my matted hair and shapeless, outdated (as her sister has just let me know) suit and she's confused. I'm wearing my nani's sandals and I can see her looking at my dusty, unmanicured feet.

Her mum, my ex-model masi, looks at my eyebrows. I had them threaded before I left, by my Topshop regular, but by now they're unruly and grown out, and I haven't trusted anyone to do them here through fear of getting them too thin (like my last trip). It's unfathomable to my masi why I have bad eyebrows and the trio stare, amazed at my terrible make-up. In a post-desi YouTuber world it's incomprehensible to my cool teen cousins that I would arrive un-contoured and un-highlighted.

I try to explain that 'I'm sorry I look very tired, it was a long journey', and they're nodding but in a way that suggests that they would probably look immaculate had they done the same and that I'm too lazy to care how I look.

All in all, I don't think I'm quite what they were expecting.

Over the weekend my cousin takes me through her selfie wall, which has over 100 colour print-outs of pouting selfies she has taken. We bond over our love of Zayn Malik, she's disappointed at my lack of knowledge about Shruti Arjun Anand, a make-up YouTuber, after I told her I was 'into make-up' (I am, but not on a par with her forensic knowledge, bordering on maniacal) and her mum berates me for feeling uncomfortable asking their servant to make me food.

My unironic love of Bollywood classics and Honey Singh are judged quickly and expertly by my aunty in Delhi, a middle-class ex-model who cites Indian 'cinema' as an interest and has five Fair'n'Lovely products in her bathroom. At one point I spread a thick layer of the lightening cream on my face for Snapchat declaring my fairness and she's staring at me, wondering what's funny. I know the rules but I don't quite impress, and before I know it, it ceases to matter because we're en route to Delhi airport, on our way back home.

The taxi driver as we were driving to the airport opened the doors and on hearing me speak boomed, 'Ah! You're from London?!'

The accusation hung in the air and after a second I had to begrudgingly acknowledge that I was. Opening your mouth reveals more than you might like about who you are and where you come from. We've created routing responses for the monotonous, bordering-on-parodic regularity with which we are asked where we're 'from', and in India you are forced to admit, that it's London.

His son was from here and while my mum was on the phone and we darted across the city, we spoke about Modi and Britain and Zayn Malik and Kajol and Adidas tracksuits and his love of Fruit Pastilles and my inability to make round rotis.

I realised that this was where I understood myself, in snatched conversations, in connections, in the beauty of the throwaway details that it's my job to discover. It's why I was a born journalist, asking questions about the world and myself while always feeling just outside it. I will always be fascinated by seemingly inconsequential details and while my difference makes me strange back home in Britain – where people like me are made to feel like outsiders – in India, reminding myself that I have a stake in two worlds is what makes me able to love and respect them and absorb the details that simultaneously empower and disempower me. Knowing when to speak and knowing when to silently observe is a code that thousands of immigrants before me have learned to manoeuvre to their own end. For me, it will always be on the page where I find my voice most comfortably. I celebrate those who are more articulate than me, standing proud, and proclaiming their additional identities.

Walking onto the plane, as the hum of Anglo-Indian accents on each seat shuffles through the air alongside the many bags, I prepare to stow away my own language now I'm returning to my home in London, an adult again.

Returning home isn't so much reinforcing the crippling clean-cut duality of my identity, like writers have historically professed to feel, it's about how just how anomalous I am in both worlds. The plurality of my strangeness – of being split, of being Indian, too fresh, too Western, too bizarre, too independent, isn't as welcome as I hoped.

I see coming back to my village as significant, thanks to my privilege of being able to leave. But also because I can simultaneously cherry-pick my favourite aspects of my culture for anecdotes back home and social media, and keep the private, painful reflective ones for myself. This is what so many second-and-third generation immigrants experience visiting their homeland. We fine-tune the ability to find the nuances funny, deflecting the crushing weight of displacement and diaspora drama that becomes part of our everyday.

As we board, and I take my last look around the airport adverts of cosmetic creams selling 'lighter, brighter' skin, I think of every time I've made a joke about Fair'n'Lovely cream that has fallen flat because white colleagues have looked so horrified.

I learned quickly that there are certain jokes the white community can't ever really find funny because the punchline means wading through gasps of horror or sympathy, or worse, lengthy explanations whenever you make a quip about skin lightening, arranged marriage or hate crimes. Learning the comedic levels of rooms is part of the immigrant experience, and even going home reinforces how learned and Western mine is. I know when to keep quiet; keeping quiet is all part of the displacement and I think of how keeping your head down is a crucial physicality of the immigrant experience. When people bemoan this generation constantly craning their heads downwards on their phones, I can't help but think of all those heads looking down, avoiding trouble, not wanting to draw attention to themselves or their differences. Of my granddad and his friends keeping their eyes fixed on the floor – perhaps people just didn't notice it back then.

I feel the shudder of the plane's wheels hit the ground and I'm jolted, physically, back into action. My phone is accepting three weeks of WhatsApp messages and now the announcement is made in English first. The Bollywood film I'm watching is cut short and I'm looking out on to the gangway and the rain hits the tarmac and I wait in my seat, indulging in this no man's land of the plane before I'm forced to leave. The wind hits my face and I understand how people define these moments as poetic examples of duality – cold from hot, grey from colour. But for me, there is no neat duality, no cleanly sliced elements of my identity that are in opposition. There is no hollow insecurity about rootlessness because those additional details and stories I've learned are additions to our identity, not losses. Being aware of inadequacies or seeing your own strangeness through different eyes, gives us a wholeness that allows us to see the world with humour, nuance, and complexity. The notion of fragments is not what defines me – the gift my grandfather gave me was that his life as a good immigrant allowed me, generations later, to recognise the power and strength of that experience. We've never really been split, never been cut in half, we've just been silent about how we've been empowered because we haven't always felt it, have been too busy being good immigrants, not making a fuss, and quieting down when people felt uncomfortable. Rewriting the narrative of retracing our journeys has, for me, derailed those ideas of losing our internal battles of identity and cemented a simple fact – we've never had anything to lose, only everything to gain.

FLAGS

COCO KHAN

Letters, they were the key. As long as you could find a letter stating the address of the flat you'd found yourself in, you could call a taxi and sneak off without waking him, indeed without anyone ever knowing you'd been there.

That was a trick I learned with Felix – Felix with the peroxide hair so blonde it could (in the right light) appear to be a continuation of his porcelain skin. Blue-eyed Felix in the patent Dr. Martens and the MA1 jacket. I remember him distinctly: six-feet tall, ravenous roll-up smoker, aloof in demeanour but animated quickly by discussions about sculpture, which he was studying. I met him a few times, at various art shows – mutual friends, cursory chit-chat, nothing special.

When Felix and I eventually had sex, it was based on very little conversation. I like to imagine that it was my raw, potent animal power that did it – that the shirt with stains from breakfast made his heart skip a beat; that he watched me from across the room hovering around the canapé table and his loins stirred; that he once saw me pull up my ill-fitting jeans while balancing not just one, but two plastic cups of warm white wine and thought *now that is a woman of true brilliance*. But I suspect the free bar at the after-show party had something to do with it.

We had sex in the dark because the light bulb burst as soon as we switched it on. He offered to fix it but I said it didn't matter. After, Felix slept soundly but I tossed and turned. As dawn broke, light began to filter into the room, and for the first time I came to see, to learn, something personal about him.

He had flags, lots of flags. Union Jack flags everywhere, all over the room. Reality had jolted and the world was vibrating from the impact. Suddenly, the room felt blindingly bright, and claustrophobically small. One flag was tacked to the door, another took the form of a desktop mug crammed full of pens. Hung up on the rails was a button-down Union Jack shirt that felt like it had been pulled from a costume cupboard and, to my alarm and bewilderment, the very bed we lay on – a red, white and blue striped spread.

Between the shock, confusion and increasing alcohol withdrawal, my body began to turn. Only a shrill ringing filled my ears now, while piercing shards of glass made themselves present inside my head. *Who? Who? Who?* I kept asking myself, *Who is this person? Why wouldn't he mention them, didn't he know how they'd make me feel? Was that supposed to be a part of it? Is this a game, a fantasy, some imperial-themed kink that I didn't know about?*

The flags, the boots, the jacket – a terrifying thought began to dawn on me. *A skinhead. He's a skinhead, a stealth skinhead with hair. I thought he was an art student, that it was fashion not fascism …*

I pulled the covers off my body, quietly and slowly, and after putting on my dress, I gathered up my belongings and left.

By the time I hit 16, I felt I had gleaned everything about relationships I possibly could have from my immediate surroundings. E12 was a working-class neighbourhood, mixed racially but with more South Asians than most, and despite being part of London, it had a distinctly small-town feel – comforting and suffocating in equal measures.

From the adults in my community, I learned that sex was something to steer clear of unless it was within marriage (or you knew how to keep it a secret). From the kids at school – mostly other brown kids like myself – I learned that sex was something to steer clear of, unless you were a boy (or you knew how to keep it a secret). From Bollywood, I learned that men with handlebar moustaches are evil, that men in white linen flares are good, and that women were damned if they do, and damned if they don't, whatever the situation. In the background of all of this were the independent women of Destiny's Child and the guiltless hedonism of *Sex and the City*, which we weren't supposed to watch, but knew how to keep it secret.

Back then, I lacked confidence but felt at least that I was wise to the world. I was certain that, unlike many of my teenage friends who found themselves in difficult situations, I had a view of the bigger picture even though I'd had no practice. I understood men were allowed to be reckless and hurtful, but it was women who'd get the blame. It was always women who were made to hide. Strange how something so banal and everyday had become so powerful.

There was my best friend, Praveena, who, when she was 17, fell for an older man. He was 32 at the time, but she was young and naïve, not suspecting that this love could have been somewhat predatory. Praveena and the Predator had made a sex tape, which, in retrospect, should have been handed in to the police. Somehow this tape made its way into her brother's possession – and then her father's – and Praveena was told she would never be allowed out of the house unsupervised again until she was married.

For a long while, I would cover for Praveena and say she was studying at my house, when in fact we were out at some under-18's club night. Over the years, my own overprotective mother began to loosen up, and understood that I was a sensible girl who didn't need constant monitoring – not least because I kicked up quite the fuss if I was. Soon, she began to cover for us too, answering the house phone and speaking to Praveena's mum in Urdu – *yes the girls are studying hard, very hard indeed*.

I learned a lot from my mum. She came to the UK in an arranged marriage that was unhappy for many years. She divorced her husband, struggling to raise two children singlehandedly, and when she eventually found love, bore another child: me. My father didn't work out, and he had the privilege of returning to his old wife, scar free. I only found out many years later quite how burdensome it had been for my mother – people, sometimes even close relatives, made her feel ashamed for falling in love, and, I suppose, unwittingly, for bringing me into this world.

Although she never publicly approved of Praveena, or later, me, I know she had a quiet sympathy – a sympathy for women who dared to take a chance.

'I've decided to give it a go, this whole sex thing, I want to have a pop.'

'Right. Okay.'

I was talking to Stacey, my study buddy from Sixth-form College. Stacey was 18, and as fiery as her wavy red hair. She drove a distinctive purple Nissan Micra, which clashed marvellously with her appearance. She was always nipping around in that thing, getting speeding fines, making blowjob gestures at any rubberneckers at traffic nights. Stacey ended up dropping out of college when she fell pregnant. She and her entire family moved out of the neighbourhood before the baby was born – rumour had it, her boyfriend's father had paid them to leave, to hide them away somewhere.

'So where should I start?'

'You don't have to start, it just happens doesn't it? You just have to let it.'

For Stacey, maybe that was true. I wasn't – and never have been – the girl who walked into a room and made heads turn. I was always that little bit too short, too fat, too dark. Besides, I didn't want sex to be something that just happened to me, like a tragedy.

'Anyway, don't you want it to be special?'

'If I'm waiting for someone who is actually hot and awesome to just rock up and say they want me, I'm going to be waiting a while. Look, I don't want to go to uni next month as a virgin – I'll have my own place – I don't want it hanging over me; get it over with so I can have some fun. Mate, I'm a safe-sex evangelist, I know what I'm doing. Honestly I'm not going to make the same mistakes as everyone else but I don't see why I should miss out, life's too short.'

'Well, what about Sandeep? He's cute, you said you liked him. You can borrow my car if you want, just make sure you don't bring it back gross.'

'Is it bad to say that I really hope I'm good? You know, in bed. I really hope I'm a natural. I mean, how am I supposed to know what to do?'

'You don't have to know. They know. You just follow their lead'

'How do they know?'

'They just do, don't they? Dirty mags, I guess. And they talk, they're always talking about shagging. Listen, you'll be fine. Practice makes perfect.'

* * *

When I came back to London after university, I was cockier than ever. I'd learned a lot in those four years away. I'd learned how to flirt, how to party exceptionally hard, how to orgasm, and how to tell any man who was selfish, pressuring, or downright unwelcome to fuck off without a second thought.

I'd read a lot of books, fantastic books from heroic women who ventured into the darkest corners of humanity and returned with messages of equality and hope; working toward a day when sex would no longer be about power, about stealing something from someone else, but instead about shared joy. I wanted to have that joy in my life, on terms that suited me, and felt it was possible. I enjoyed my independence and my close female friendships; I wasn't scared to grow attached to the right man and some chance dalliances did develop into more formal relationships. As for the rejections, well they were all part of growing as a person.

I had life in the bag. I'd laugh thinking about the younger me, curled up like a pretzel in a Nissan Micra, so threatened by the hard cock in my hand, whispering soothing nothings at it as though it were a wild animal that could attack me at any moment. And the laughs kept coming, for years. The nocturnal life – bars, clubs, parties – were already silly enough without the unexpected thrill of meeting someone. I took great pride in regaling my friends with female-focused bedroom tales, stories that had no doubt been around for millennia but never seen the light of day. How else were we going to make sex equally ours if we didn't talk freely about it?

So I'm on top of this guy like a cowgirl champion. My belly's there, it's hanging out, and I'm like, swish-my-hair I don't care. But then, I'm not even joking, I start to get vertigo, like actual Alfred-Hitchcock-James-Stewart spinning around like a Spirograph vertigo. Do you think too much wine can induce vertigo? Cowgirl, down! Dismount!

Then, one day, it was talking freely that changed everything.

'So am I your first?'

'Was I that bad?!' I said laughing.

'No no, I mean, white boy. Am I your first white boy?' he grinned widely.

'Afraid not. I've had all the races, and before you ask, yes they were all better than you.'

He smiled genuinely. 'You're my first. I've only ever been with white girls so I'm glad I have.'

I hadn't thought a great deal about the colour of my skin, or theirs, but now I couldn't get it off my mind.

Is that why they want me?

I asked myself that question every day for weeks and months after that, and not just about the white boys, but the black boys, and even Asians like me. At first, I ignored it. What was the big deal? How different was it really to any of the quick judgement calls we make on who we fancy? But I felt uneasy, and I couldn't shake the feeling. I wondered if he went back to his friends and told the 'I shagged an Asian girl' story over the 'I had a great time last night' story.

I felt defeated.

I decided I had to take control of the situation. I tried for a while to wear it like a badge of honour, imagining myself as some kind of sexual crusader, breaking down stereotypes with the power of banging. I took it seriously, like it was the Olympics and my nation's hopes rested on my shoulders. I took time to learn new sexy moves, and pulled many muscles attempting some impossible tantric pose that no modern human being could possibly do. On dates I would tolerate the vaguely insulting stereotypical questions, patiently answering,

'No, I have never been promised to a man I've never met. Actually I can barely cook at all.'

Perhaps worse were the apologisers. The ones that were like, 'I just want to check, is this okay with you?' before watching an episode of *Homeland*.

Eventually, I couldn't take any of it anymore.

The first time I was called a paki, I was at primary school. I must have been around seven years old – eight maybe – and I was in the lunch hall queuing for school dinner. Somehow, an argument had broken out between me and another girl in my class, Amy. We were arguing about something completely meaningless (as children will do) when it came out. I'm not sure if she even knew what she was saying; she looked surprised as the words passed her lips – 'you are a paki'.

It was like time had stood still. Even at that age, I knew this was a step too far; up shot my hand, *Miss! Miss!* I called a dinner lady over. Now, this dinner lady was more a dinner nan; a grey-haired, older woman, who must have been hard of hearing because, when I told her that Amy had called me a paki, she replied in complete earnestness, in her thick East End accent, and said: *she called you a packet? A packet of what, love?*

After that, I didn't hear the word again until I found it spray-painted on the side of our house: 'Pakis go home, NF'. I always found it mildly amusing that they signed their name. Why? As though we wouldn't know who it was? Just in case we mistook it for the racially themed high jinks we brown people were always up to.

Days later, my older brother and some of his friends frogmarched a scrawny, trembling white teenage boy to our house. He was the culprit and he was here to apologise.

'It was a dare,' he said. 'I didn't mean it, I'm sorry.'

'Let him go,' said Mum. 'Can't you see he's crying? He's just a child.'

He couldn't have been more than 13, he had those awkward teen proportions where the hands and feet are huge, but the rest of the body hasn't caught up.

He was a skinhead but he wasn't scary. Indeed, there was something strikingly clown-like about him – huge cherry-red Dr Martens, strangely high-waisted trousers, braces, shirt buttoned up to the top. As he scooted off he turned back to me before he'd disappeared around the corner and, raising his arm, did a Nazi salute. Then, he was gone.

I didn't expect to see Felix ever again, but he was hard to miss. He was tall, and his hair was unmistakable. He didn't seem pleased to see me, but he did remember who I was, which was something. Maybe I *was* the only non-Aryan he lured back to his flag dungeon after all.

We exchanged courtesies, talked sculpture, he rolled up two cigarettes, put one behind his ear and held the other out to me, saying, 'I can't remember if you smoke or not.'

Outside, we sat on the curb and smoked. He joked that I could have left a note and I explained truthfully that his whole flag get-up was nothing short of terrifying.

'As if you wouldn't have just fucking stayed, and actually asked me about it.' He paused, catching the expression on my face. 'I do understand. I know the flag's a bit, you know, sensitive, and maybe I should have said something. I'm sorry if I intimidated you. No, I definitely should have said something but hey, I was drunk and distracted by the hot girl in my room.' He leaned over and bumped his shoulder against mine. 'You know there wasn't a moment when I was hanging those flags and I thought, Well I wonder what would happen if there was an Asian person in this room? To be honest I didn't think there was going to be any girls in that room at all.'

'So you're not extremely right-wing with a Kryptonite for weird but-notably-babe-ish Asian girls that is secretly tearing you up inside?'

'Ha, no. My dad was a punk in the 70s – and not a racist one – so we always had flags in our house. I brought them to the flat because they remind me of home, that's all.'

A queue was beginning to form at the door now. The bar was getting busier, the music sounding louder and louder each time the door swung open.

'I guess I should apologise too maybe. I'm sorry I didn't give you the chance to explain. I had this really weird experience a few months before we hooked up where this dude basically told me he was happy that I was Asian and it really freaked me out –'

'Yeesh'

'– I don't know, did he want me to be grateful or something, that he chose me? Did it make him feel better about himself that he was a cool, right-on guy? You know, I just want to have some fun, while I'm young and I don't have a mortgage or kids or whatever, but there's always something, some bullshit thing, that turns whatever could just be really cool, into something horrible. And you know, I do want to keep meeting people and having fun, whether it's a one-off thing or something more, I'm open to what life wants to give me. But that comment, it's just ruining it for me. I'm always thinking, does this person actually want me or am I a brown-shaped thing that will do? It's a real mood-killer to say the least. I wish I could just find a way to know for sure'

'Can I make a suggestion?'

'Is your suggestion getting a taxi and going back to your punk palace, because if it is, I'm up for it?'

'Ah see, I don't think my girlfriend will like that very much. But, I was going to say, why don't you try *talking* to the guys, getting to know them for real—'

'I've tried that and it's even worse, so many stupid, shitty questions—'

'Well then, don't keep talking to them if they're douchebags. If you want to engage 'cos they're nice but a bit daft then cool but if you don't want to, then don't. It's not your job to try and correct everything. We should go inside, the bouncer is getting angry.'

'No, I think I'm going to go home. Would you be really offended if I said I hope I never see you again?'

'Why?'

'Because you're great and I feel annoyed at myself for disappearing.'

His eyes smiled. 'Okay, well tell you what, I'll disappear now, and we're even. Just make sure you remember what I said.'

'Sounds good.'

I gathered up my handbag and put on my coat slowly, watching him as he put out his cigarette. He shook my hand, formally like at the end of a job interview, and with a perfunctory 'yes, sir' nod clicked his heels together theatrically. He walked through the entrance and turning back just before the door closed behind him gave me a wink. Then, he was gone.

CUTTING THROUGH (ON BLACK BARBERSHOPS AND MASCULINITY)

INUA ELLAMS

If Africa was a bar, what would your country be drinking/ doing?
– @SiyandaWrites

Last year, Botswanan writer Siyanda Moutsiwa tweeted a 'classic writing prompt' designed for workshops on character interaction. 50,000 tweets later, #IfAfricaWasABar was trending. The answers came in thick, fast, vicious, tragic, insightful, insulting and illuminating. It shed an unashamed light on African geopolitics, on what Africans thought of other Africans, what they thought about Europeans and finally, on a project I had started two years before.

#IfAfricaWasABar Europeans would spike all the drinks then sell antidotes to everyone at a later date.
– @ChetoManji

When I became an immigrant and left Nigeria aged 12, my father and I began cutting each other's hair. We lived in Dublin, where whenever I followed my white Irish friends to get their haircuts, I'd see panic cross the faces of their barbers who had little or no experience of cutting African hair. I learned not to ask. I'd sit, watching the business conducted in almost absolute silence. Everything changed when we moved to Peckham in London and I came across the familiar bastions of masculinity that are African and Caribbean barbershops. Late into the night, light would pour out of glass-fronted shops stuffed full of Afro/Caribbean men holding court and I dived back into that world. I discovered conversation of the broadest nature, from football to parenting, Creole languages to nutrition and I started writing 'Barbershop Chronicles' – a play about what African men inside them talked about. A month into it and I wanted to go bigger, to see if conversation on the continent mirrored conversation here, to see what indigenous Africans thought about us in the diaspora, and what Africans thought of other Africans. I left England and travelled to South Africa, Zimbabwe, Kenya, Uganda, Nigeria and Ghana and #IfAfricaWasABar brought my findings into sharp focus.

South Africa

In 2013, two days after Nelson Mandela died, I arrived in Johannesburg. Africa's most respected statesman, mythic and legendary figure, most esteemed father, had passed and the country was in shock. The men I spoke with talked of nothing else. Their emotions ranged from loss at his death, to disgust at his portrayal, to frustration that he died without seeing his 'rainbow nation', to suspicion at backroom deals he might have made for peace. They believed South Africa was still gripped by apartheid and mentioned a study released the previous year, which found that 40 per cent of white South Africans didn't think apartheid

was wrong. Millie, a writer and art director I met, explained that
the demons of the regime were never exorcised. After it was
abolished, the generations of men who had been emasculated,
called 'boy' under the regime, who came forward with stories of
kidnapped, maimed or murdered family members, were told to
forgive and forget. The Truth and Reconciliation Commission
was set up in such a way that all the perpetrators had to do was
come forward and apologise. Not many came forward, and of
those who did, not many apologised.

'They never got to get mad and no one was held accountable,'
Millie said. 'This is why crime is so violent in South Africa,
why we are the rape capital of the world.'

Millie believed deep-seated mental health issues have
only calcified and festered and this frustration is taken out on
women.

Andile, a travelling IT Consultant, talked about how
alcoholism was rife in the 'coloured' community he came from.
His ancestors worked vineyards for white South Africans and
were not paid in money or food, but in barrels of wine, which
left a thirst for alcohol in his blood. Every single member of
his family suffered and complete abstinence was his only cure.

I met Shoni who took me to Yeoville, the most multi-ethnic
neighbourhood in sub-Saharan Africa. Walking, we heard
a mixture of tongues: languages from Cameroon, Ghana,
Zimbabwe, Tanzania, Nigeria, Malawi, Jamaica, Trinidad and
Zambia spliced with South African ones: Zulu, Afrikaans
and Xhosa. The following year, a spate of xenophobic
killings would grip the nation. Marching mobs, protesting
immigration, would kill seven black immigrants from other
African countries, echoing 2008's outbreak where 67 were
killed. At the time, I knew nothing of the events of 2008 and
couldn't have predicted the future, but I left South Africa

with the impression that it was a melting pot of ideas: deeply African in traditional ways, yet so deeply marked by inherited British elitism that it looked down on other African nations – even as it sought to unify its 12 tribes under one identity.

#IfAfricaWasABar South Africa would be drinking all kinds of alcohol and begging them to get along in its stomach.
– @SiyandaWrites

Zimbabwe

I was meant to travel to Harare, but hadn't been granted a visa. I resolved to interview Zimbabwean barbers and clients in Jo'burg. They were everywhere: when sanctions were placed on Zimbabwe because of President Mugabe's violent land reform programmes, three million Zimbabweans fled to South Africa. Dwain, a musician, explained that this, and Zimbabwean conservatism, were the reasons why he left – there wasn't a market for the music he wished to make. Now, everything had changed.

After I explained the project, he guessed I wasn't granted a visa because of my job.

'Uncle Bob … (the affectionate name for Robert Mugabe),' he told me, 'doesn't trust writers from the West. They always lying, exaggerating about him.'

He added that I'd have had problems finding barbers and clients anyway because dreadlocks are BIG in Zimbabwe: men are growing, not cutting locks. In 1980, after bloody battles defeating imperialism and British Rule, Bob Marley sang at their Independence Day celebration. That sowed a legacy and culture of Rastafarianism, which Dwain said, 'is all about spirituality, consciousness and self-pride. This is why we respect Uncle Bob now … he stands for consciousness and self-pride.'

I thought back to Mandela's burial, which had been aired live on South African television. Of the politicians, heads of state, presidents, vice presidents, royalty and dignitaries in attendance, Mugabe got the loudest, longest, most rapturous applause.

'This is because South Africans recognised he succeeded where Mandela failed: getting land back.' Dwain believed that Zimbabweans were natural farmers. In the neighbourhood in which he was born, most grew their own food with their bare hands. 'This is why losing land to colonisers was a big deal, why winning it back meant so much.'

Dwain introduced himself as one of the 'born frees' who grew up in a free Zimbabwe. He had turned from hip-hop to Chimurenga music. Chimurenga is the Shona word for 'struggle' harking back to the battles and liberation of the seven tribes of his country. As he spoke, the pride of surviving those times shook like a knife in his voice, sharpening his words.

> #IfAfricaWasABar Zimbabwe would be telling stories about how it fought the bouncers to get inside.
> – @TheGaryCahill

Kenya

I landed in a half-empty Nairobi, three days before Christmas. Though English and Swahili are the official languages of Kenya, Sheng, which I'm not versed in, is the language of gossip. It was difficult to find barbers and clients I could speak with, but after two days I found Ian.

Ian asked, 'Who discovered Mount Kenya?'. I said I didn't know. 'Kenyan textbooks will tell you that a German missionary, Johann Krapf, discovered Mount Kenya. How is that possible when my ancestors had been grazing cattle there for centuries? There are 42 tribes in Kenya, you think not a single one of us looked up and thought *That's a very big hill, let's go check it out*. We need to reform our entire educational system and teach an Afrocentric syllabus.'

The conversation turned to two new government laws. One he called the 'Madonna Law', after the pop star famously adopted a Malawian orphan, introduced tougher regulations for foreigners wishing to adopt Kenyan orphans. Allegations of child-trafficking were rife. The second was regarding business, demanding that 30 per cent of government contracts be awarded to women, young and disabled people.

'Already, she, I mean women, are running around Nairobi with big ideas and contracts, but she doesn't have the capacity to do the job,' he said.

He feared that domestic Kenyan life would suffer, society would crumble and men would loose their standing in their own families. He felt Kenya was not prepared for this change. As he spoke, I got the fleeting sense that the 'she' he mentioned was none other than his own wife. We talked for four solid hours after the shop had shut, and he seemed reluctant to return home.

Two days later, I journeyed to a barbershop in the 'Calif' neighbourhood, where evidence of new businesses were everywhere.

In celebration of Barak Obama's Kenyan roots, there were buildings named 'Barak Bakery', 'Obama's Corner', 'Obama's Barber' and 'Yes We Can Limited'. Conversations were wild … everything from Kenyan witchcraft versus Nigerian witchcraft, to love-potions, adequate punishment for rapists, 'acceptable' bestiality, cross-border travel, and the strength of the Kenyan shilling against the Ugandan shilling. There was also pride in Kenya's ability to attract Chinese investments, who, the barbers commented, were becoming the forty-third tribe of Kenya.

If the South Africans were searching for their identity and Zimbabweans proud of liberating theirs, the Kenyans were celebrating new wealth, enterprise and global recognition.

> #IfAfricaWasABar Kenya would be the loud 'new money' drunk, telling everyone about his cousin Barack who done made it in the States.
> – @ShikoNguru

Uganda

I travelled to Uganda next. Compared to South Africans, Kenyans were a chilled-out folk. Compared to Ugandans, Kenyans were absolute firecrackers. Ugandans seemed to stride with a deep and lengthy leisure through all aspects of life, such that at the airport, I felt like I was merely queuing at a supermarket.

In the first few days, the taxi driver from the airport and Patricia of the British Council painted a picture of the linguistic landscape in Uganda. The driver said that whereas 100 per cent of Kenyans speak Swahili, only 30 per cent of Ugandans did. He spoke proudly, as though it elevated them above the Kenyans. Patricia added that during the Liberation War between Uganda and Tanzania, Idi Amin distrusted government officials who'd been educated in England and spoke English better than he did. He deposed a lot of them, gave their jobs to those he trusted and insisted duties of office be executed in Swahili. Those years were brutal and after the war Swahili became synonymous with military dictatorship, so, the people rebelled and chose English as their official language but spoke mostly in their tribal tongues.

My contact was Dre, a soft-spoken, loose-limbed starving artist who had an interest in etymology. He explained that of the 56 tribes in the country, the Buganda (hence the country's name) are the largest.

He told me, 'Baganda' is the plural for 'Muganda', which is what you call a lone Bugandan, and 'Luganda' is their language.

Easy.

I tracked down a shop with a magnificently welcoming barber called Simon. Where the South Africans searched for their identity, Zimbabweans proud of liberating theirs, Kenyans were celebrating wealth, the Ugandans overwhelmingly spoke of romance and its complications.

Simon was flabbergasted when he discovered that as a Nigerian, I didn't have two girlfriends and almost kicked me out of his shop when I admitted I didn't have a single one.

He had two, suspected that not only did they know of each other, they were fine with it. Jackson, a handsome 22-year-old model chimed in, detailing his girlfriends, but the most in-depth conversation was with Mark, who explained that neither did he believe in nor 'love' his wife. He believed in 'Godly' love – love for orphans, animals, the disabled etc., but romantic or 'Human' love deposed objective thinking, which he believed was foolish and dangerous to marriages.

Weeks before, the government had passed a law giving the death penalty to homosexuals and weeks later, the death penalty clause would be substituted with life imprisonment. At the time, when I raised the topic, the clientele echoed the sentiment that it wasn't the Ugandan way, that it threatened the dowry system, which was still part of society.

Mark, who did not 'love' but deeply respected and cherished his wife, had paid sixty cows for her. The men explained that marriages were the only opportunities fathers had to gain back some of costs of raising a child; husbands paid for daughters. If men married each other or women married each other, there'd be no one paying for anyone and wouldn't everything fall apart?

> #IfAfricaWasABar Uganda is the guy getting really angry that two girls are kissing across the room.
> – @ImranGarda

Nigeria

Because I was travelling to my own homeland, I did no preparation whatsoever. I expected to naturally synchronise with its barbershop culture, for it to embrace its prodigal son. As soon as the plane touched down in Lagos, I noticed two things. One, West African heat must be some brand of hellfire – unrelenting and merciless compared to the East's – and, two, the people.

Nigerians are crazy – a different breed of African man. Never before has the East–West divide been so apparent to me. The sheer breakneck speed of Lagos life and the feeling that everything is happening simultaneously … isn't a feeling. It is real. There are 371 tribes in the country, 500 languages spoken, which makes sense of why so much doesn't quite work in Lagos.

I stayed on Victoria Island among the rich elite. During the first three days, my internal compass evaporated under the heat and the poor directions I was given. When I finally found barbershops and collapsed into the chairs exhausted, I discovered the barbers refused to talk unless I paid them, and rich clients thinking themselves too good to converse, remained resolutely silent.

Wole, the lone contact I had in the theatre industry, took me to the spots he knew but they were either staffed by non-English speakers or barbers who, without payment dismissed the project. On one of the dejected rides back to the hotel, I asked why 'This House Is Not For Sale' was spray-painted on so many properties. Wole explained that Nigerian conmen had perfected a way of breaking into and selling properties when their owners holidayed. The writing on the wall was the only sure way of safeguarding homes.

'419 ...' he added – the moniker for Nigerian con men – '... refers to section 419 of the Nigerian Criminal Code which deals with obtaining property by false pretences.'

On my last day, I poured my woes into the open ears of Wallace, the driver who taxied me to the airport. He patiently listened, feigned annoyance that I hadn't called him and without missing a beat, did his best to portray barbershop culture on the mainland where he and the working class lived. It was a whole other world. Men come specifically to talk, food hawkers come by to feed clients, and because of the constant lack of electricity, boys in the hood come to charge their phones. In the darkness of Nigerian nights, they're the only places with electricity, they glow, literally, like beacons of the community where 'men come to be men,' Wallace told me.

As the plane took off, I remembered something Wole said. 'There are phrases you see when arriving in major cities, "Welcome to LA" a billboard will say, "Welcome to London" another, but ours reads "This is Lagos".' It is a statement. Its subtext is "Enter at your own peril", "Sink or Swim", or as Wallace put it: 'Hustle or die'.

I can't fault that mentality, it is relentless and enterprising.

#IfAfricaWasABar Nigeria would own it.
– @MduThaParty

Ghana

On landing in Accra, I noticed the country felt like the older, calmer, wiser brother to hot-headed Nigeria, as though it had harmonised its 70 tribes where we had failed desperately. Because there is a healthy rivalry between the two countries, as a Nigerian, it pains me to say this.

The first two days were spent with Aunty Mary, a friend's mother, who embraced me as her own, and the rest of the week I stayed with a mentor and his family, so perhaps the cumulative effect of their domestic lives slowed me down. I was no longer a travelling bachelor. I was a surrogate son in one house, a new uncle in the other. Whatever it was, something had changed. I found barbershops easily and the best one within walking distance of the house. The conversations were not of business, politics, infidelity or crime, but of family, language and fatherhood. A client recounted a childhood memory involving his father. Another, the beauty of the Ga language. An experienced father gave advice on raising daughters to a new father. A linguist talked on similarities of pidgin languages.

'It takes a whole village to raise 'is child' is one of the many sayings indicative of the nature of African communities. It points to the deeply socialist structures many were built on before colonisation and capitalism changed them. Of all the cities I'd visited, this philosophy seemed most alive in Accra, such that it had inhabited Christianity and localised it. Aunt Mary was in the church business. On the first day, Ebo, who worked for her, asked if I'd accompany him on his morning errands. It involved visiting a church Aunt Mary was building. I jumped in the taxi and minutes later, we stood before an unpainted concrete structure the size of a small sports stadium. Inside lay high-tech sound systems, pulpits and podiums for preachers, a broad stage with a cascading blue curtain, magnificent natural light through slits cut in the roof and large windows for cross-ventilation. It sat four thousand people comfortably. A primary school was attached to one side of the church, architectural plans for a secondary school had just been completed, and behind lay a small but rapidly expanding shop. Ebo explained about the financial ecosystem built into the church, those it employs, the lives it supports, how vital it'd become to the neighbourhood, how, some Sundays, so many attend that they set up a canopy and cinema screen to relay the service to those standing outside.

#IfAfricaWasABar Ghana would be that guy who gets drunk and starts – for some reason – talking about how much God loves us all.
– @SiyandaWrites

England

One night in Battersea a young actor entered the barbershop and admitted he doubted he'd get the role he'd just auditioned for. We asked what the role was.

He said, 'Black man.'

'Anything else?' I asked.

'Strong black man,' he said and continued that he doubted he fitted the director's concept of 'black' masculinity.

I asked what his concept was, he said he didn't have one. I claimed this was his problem, until he asked if anyone really had a definite grasp on what 'black' was, or 'masculinity', for that matter. We failed to answer him then, and I fail still, but travelling had given me a broader sense of the issue.

The term 'Black' was employed by African Americans as both a political and socially conscious alternative to 'negro' (or the much darker *nigger*). It was as an act of defiance, self-identification, and as a way to distance themselves from the 'African' label, which had abundantly negative connotations at the time. Nowadays, the label is used for darker-skinned people of sub-Saharan descent everywhere: in the Americas, Asia, Europe and on the Africa continent itself. In Europe where whiteness is the default, blackness stands in contrast and any race is 'other'. On the African continent, not only is blackness NOT the default, given North Africans who are generally lighter-skinned, but blackness isn't the default in all sub-Saharan countries; countries like South Africa, Angola, Namibia or Zambia have large British, French or German communities. In the countries I visited that have a greater percentage of 'black' nationals, the concerns, motivations and emotions of the men I met differed, not just from country to country, but within countries, along tribal and socio-economic lines – differences so sharp and clear they had become stereotypes. Dividing them along tribal lines, those six countries alone break down to 558 different types of 'black' men. 'Black' men from all 54 African countries live in England, so even a conservative estimate would put a least 1,000 different types of them in the country.

England is also home to 'black' men from the various

Caribbean Islands, from North and South America, as well as 'black' men born in England, who have never touched African soil ... men of different tribes, temperaments, natures, political and socio-economic backgrounds and beliefs. Despite these obvious nuances, phrases like 'black-on-black crime' or 'black community' are used to suggest a monolith and when there are disagreements within said monolith, it is portrayed as dysfunctional, rebellious, animalistic and mutinous. The African continent is so vast the land can hold Portugal, Spain, Belgium, France, Germany, Switzerland, Italy, Eastern Europe, India, United States, China, Japan and the United Kingdom at the same damn time. As we know the earliest human, 'Lucy', was found in Ethiopia, it's safe to say inhabitants of these countries and all of humanity came from sub-Saharan Africa, that sub-Saharan Africans are genetically coded with all of humanity's assemblage, that they contain all hues, variations and cultures: eye shape, pupil colour, hair texture, hip thickness, bone density, finger width, tongue and skin tone. To put it mildly then, it is insulting, reductive, counter-productive, lazy, disingenuous and deeply, deeply, deeply, problematic to attach a single label – one of Western invention as a shield against racism, one as porous a description of skin pigmentation, as 'black' – to a group of people so vastly varied and numerous. Whenever we beg for nuances, for our differences to be articulated, for more diversity and accuracy in how our communities are described, in the characters written for 'black' actors on stage, on television, or in film, our voices are either silenced or ignored.

#IfAfricaWasABar there would be a load of groupies hanging around outside claiming they know what's going on inside better than the bar staff.
– @fil

WEARING WHERE YOU'RE AT: IMMIGRATION AND UK FASHION

SABRINA MAHFOUZ

I thought you'd be, you know, darker ... You don't look at all how I imagined ... Well, I have to say, I thought you'd look more, ha ha, I suppose, foreign ... You look a bit, English though ... It's quite a relief you're, well, you know ...

These comments were spoken by different people of different backgrounds at different times of my life, but put together they could easily be one continuous musing by a confused person on what it means to have a name that indicates non-whiteness, but a skin tone that indicates a happy harmony with the politically and economically dominant racial group of the previous few centuries. There is so much to delve into from this that it would require another essay with a different focus. What I'd like to particularly point out from it for the purposes of this piece are two things. Firstly, that the way whiteness is defined seems to differ person to person, country to country. Many people from North Africa and the Middle East regard themselves as white, whilst stating that there are also black people of that nationality. In Egypt, for example, those who have a darker skin tone and more of a sub-Saharan African physiognomy may be called 'Black Egyptians' by other Egyptians who, if pressed, would self-classify as 'White Egyptians' – even though they themselves would most certainly be regarded as a non-white ethnic minority in a white majority country such as the UK or USA. It is interesting to note that the classifying seems to be done by those with lighter pigmentation. This is a direct colonial legacy of course, encouraging racial divides and appealing to those with a lighter skin tone to self-classify as white in order to create feelings of superiority and aspirations of assimilation into the politically dominant race, which they are not recognised as being once outside of their locality. The first existing documentation on racial classification was François Bernier's, written in 1684. Bernier divides all of humankind into four racial groups – calling those who live in Europe, North Africa, South Asia as well as the Native Americans to be of the same race, whilst sub-Saharan Africans were another, as were the Lapp race (indigenous people from Lapland area). The Central, South and South East Asians were the final category.[42] This 'typological model' influenced later anthropologists such as Johann Friedrich Blumenbach who created explicitly racist theories, which in turn influenced the eugenics movement and the persistence of the slave trade. Although these theories, and Bernier's simplistic classification system, are thankfully now wholly discredited, we can see from the self-classifications of Egyptians, as mentioned above, that this original theory still permeates the consciousness of people. There are those who would narrow these outdated categories even further. I have had conversations with educated people

42 Siep Stuurman, 'François Bernier and the Invention of Racial Classification', *History Workshop Journal*, Issue 50 (Autumn 2000), 1–21.

of all ethnicities in the UK who truly believe that if someone is not black, then they are white and vice versa. This narrow and negating dual classification tool has been promulgated so that people are unwittingly encouraged to choose 'sides' and discouraged from regarding race as something unfixed and far more complex than many seem ready to admit. I see this as a huge societal issue that can only be dismantled by constant discussion, hence my inclusion of it here, even though it could be argued to sit slightly outside of the remit I have set myself. However, as this is an essay that talks of race throughout, I'd ask the reader to bear in mind the above and to note that despite the imperfection of all classification systems, I will be using the classification of whiteness throughout which relates mainly to Northern and Central European ancestry.

The second aspect of the above I'd like to pluck apart is my own discomfort at feeling as if I don't meet people's expectations of what somebody from 'somewhere else' should look like. This reclassification of my identity by others has often made me feel guilty that I have this background, and even more so that I am connected to and highly interested in it. It is part of our endemic racism that we immediately attribute the experience of otherness to somebody who fulfils what otherness is supposed to aesthetically be. Whilst I appreciate that any negative experiences of otherness are exacerbated if you *do* occupy that aesthetic, it is part of the problem if we do not accept, or expect, diverse heritage experiences from those who don't conform to our inherited and constructed ideas of what 'diversity' looks like.

I am a bit white. I'm part-Danish and part-English via Wales. I'm also as much part-Amerindian and Madeiran Guyanese. But the largest part of my heritage is Egyptian, which is where the Arabic Muslim surname comes from and why some of the (openly pleased) people quoted at the start of this piece thought I would look 'more foreign'.

I have seen these surprised smiles enough to know I am not in a position to complain about my ability to assimilate into the cold embrace of dominance due to my pale skin tone; but on a micro level, I think that whenever anyone questions your identity, you have the right to get a bit pissed off and on a macro level, what this questioning represents is problematic, as I've already talked about. What I've found interesting and worrying in varying degrees is the extent to which my ethnic identities can be validated, dismissed, or even prove offensive to others in the UK, just from me wearing a particular piece of clothing, arguably a luxury others who look 'less white' don't ever get.

I'll share a couple of examples. My Egyptian great-grandmother and my Guyanese great-grandmother both wore headwear in styles reflective of the country and time they were in. My Egyptian great-grandmother wore a thin, silky turban of sorts, with a costume jewel in the middle, fashionable but conservative in the days when not many middle-class women in Egypt covered their heads. She was a practicing Muslim, but in those days this did not mean what it often does today in terms of Egyptian women's attire. She chose it partly because her husband was an active Islamic scholar and both of them felt more comfortable if she covered her head in public, as they were often attending places of worship and religious importance. The other factor was that despite Egypt being credited with the emergence of the turban thousands of years ago, it had unexpectedly become globally fashionable in the 1950s, so she was doubly happy. My Guyanese great-grandmother wore colourful cotton scarves tied up around the front of her head in little knots, a style that those with African heritage had popularised in the country, many of whom she had grown up with in the city orphanage as a mixed-up, light-eyed child, nobody would take in.

Waiting at the bus stop in South London one day, I was wearing a black turban similar to the style my Egyptian great-grandmother wore. I hardly knew her, but I have always been more comfortable with my head covered, albeit not in a traditionally religion-specific style. When living in Cairo for a few years of my life at various times and whilst exploring aspects of my faith, I have worn hijab, but in London I have always worn a wide variety of head coverings. On this particular turban-wearing day, a white English man came up to me just before I stepped onto the bus, pointed at my head-covering and shouted, '*All Muslims should die*', before scurrying away to dissolve in the acid of his hatred (hopefully). I am well aware that this is light conversation compared to what Muslim women wearing hijab or niqab have to face every day in this country. But it astounded me, as it always does, that somebody could be driven to such vociferousness by a piece of cloth and the 'difference' this might represent.

Another day, once again in south London, but this time *on* a bus (all of this is making me think I should probably just save up for a car), I was wearing a headscarf similar to the ones my Guyanese great-grandmother used to wear. Two girls who appeared to be of mixed heritage behind me were loudly complaining about '*white people wearing black people's headscarves like a trend*' and stared at me pointedly when their stop came along and they left the bus. I understand appropriation is a very real, very sinister thing. Cultures who are left devastated by Western power and policies – in some cases almost entirely annihilated by them (such as the Aboriginal and Native American peoples) – are constantly used as sources to 'inspire' fashion trends and art of all kinds.[43] At the same time, in the case of this scenario, I feel strongly that headscarves are not owned by one culture and, even if they were, what the comment made by the young women highlights again is this problematic assumption of an individual's heritage based purely on an aesthetic they appear to fulfil. Maybe I should have said all of this to them through the open window. But I didn't because I was busy playing a game on my phone and let's be honest, confrontation on London transport is always better as a 'shoulda woulda coulda'.

Except for the one time on a night bus to Lewisham around 12 years ago, when I heard two drunk, young, white men abuse two much younger black men at the back of the top deck. There were quite a few passengers, but they all stared ahead. I got up and told them to leave it out. I was wearing a faux snakeskin pink biker jacket from Morgan (don't, I know). Both of the young men left the boys at the back and came swaggering towards me. As one of them started taking his belt off to presumably threaten to hit me with or take down his jeans more efficiently, the other one provided the commentary.

'*You think you're fucking J. Lo, don't you?*', he said, pointing at my jacket.

The upside of this distraction caused by my dubious fashion choice was that the other boys ran off the bus unbothered.

Meanwhile, I was trying to simultaneously figure out why my wanting to be J. Lo in a snakeskin jacket (which I didn't, I really only ever listened to UK Garage) made him so angry he was ready to unleash a belt buckle into my face. I was saved

---

43 See Kristin Knox's *Culture to Catwalk* (London, Bloomsbury, 2011), for numerous contemporary examples of fashion appropriation.

by a tannoy announcement that the driver was recording what was going on and the two racists rushed down the stairs, out of the doors and on their merry way. That story, though loosely related, was a slight detour on what is basically a wondering on my part as to both fashion's impact on the identity of immigrants and the children of immigrants in the UK and the impact of immigration on current British fashions.

I asked the two direct immigrants in my family – my granddad (from Guyana) and my dad (from Egypt) – to tell me what they could recall about their experience with British fashion when entering the country as an outsider.

My granddad arrived in Hartlepool in the 1950s on a merchant navy ship that had set sail from Guyana, shown the young Pedro the metropolis of New York and the arbitrary aggression of the open ocean. It was due to carry on around the globe, but my granddad hired a moped and decided he liked the sights he saw around the north of England.

There were the ladies, in their stilettos, nipped-in waists and flouncy skirts. He had Ray-Bans, Hawaiian shirts and could freestyle on the bongo drums. This made him an instant celebrity in the foggy streets of the North-East. There were just enough Caribbean immigrants in the area for him to have allies and understanding, but not too much competition when it came to novelty.

Flip-flops were the items he remembers as having the biggest shock factor. Now one of the most-worn items of footwear in the warmer months, in the 1950s British people were as likely to be seen in them as they were to move to Germany. My grandma, from the North-east of England with Welsh heritage, could never fully get over his apparent disregard for the looks people gave him if they went to the pub and he had his toes out. He says he did it *for* the looks, his toes were freezing and anyway, he preferred winkle-pickers, a British fad he discovered after a few nights out in Newcastle.

My dad arrived in Britain in the 1980s, having already married my mum in Cairo. He was subjected to months of interrogation and mockery of his marriage to a British woman before he was granted temporary citizenship. He wanted to fit in. But not with the fuddy-duddy pen pushers who made up the majority in the south London suburb where he lived, oh no. He wanted to fit in with the fashion crowd, with the young ones living it up in one of the coolest cities in the world. He might have been married, but he was in his early twenties and his love of the disco life was made of strong stuff (it still is).

It's likely he funded the entire leather jacket industry at the time and he was certainly a fan of the plain white T-shirt. He stocked up on Levi's and loafers; he left the socks in the drawer. One thing he couldn't get on board with though, was the clean-cut coiffed hair look. He had the moustache and slight beard of Cairo movie stars and he removed them for nobody, not even the Home Office.

A country wears where it is at. Most people can visit a place and, after seeing a few dozen passers-by, make a judgement based on the fashions being worn about a number of cultural, social and political aspects of that place, whether they're conscious of doing this or not. They may be wrong – that's the tricky thing with judgements after all, they're no science. For example, standing at Old Street Underground station entrance on a Thursday at 8.30am and the first groups of people that pass by have smart suits on, but they wear backpacks and more casual shoes than brogues and stilettos. They have scarves on. I can make a judgement based on those simple observations that this area is business-orientated but slightly more casual and youthful in approach than Westminster or Mayfair and it's cold outside. These judgements may be partly right, but stand in the same spot at 9pm and the people I observe are wearing party clothes, many of them outside of the mainstream, metallic trousers and neon glasses, multiple piercings and bubble coats. This could lead me to think the area is one full of bars, clubs and somewhere more alternative than, say, the West End. Again, this would be partly true, though not the whole story. Most of us like to imagine our individuality is reflected in our style and reveals nothing about the system we are inextricably linked to, but of course it does.

So is what the UK's wearing today related in any way to immigration?

Yes.

Even in the most mundane high street stores you'll see colours, fabrics and styles that have been taken from every part of the globe. The ones that are popular here are often ones that originate from the very places that have a large diaspora in the UK.

Indian embroidery, East African beaded jewellery, Caribbean colour palettes, North African styles such as the kaftan, West African prints – the list continues. In no way does this mean the people from these diasporas are the ones buying (or making) these things, but it does indicate how these groups have heavily influenced what is perceived as 'British style' today. A quick Google image search shows plenty of the above included in the visual definition of 'British style', alongside a multitude of well-tailored jackets, tartan patterns and twinsets.

Of course, nothing can be called 'British' without including the huge array of cultural influences that make Britain what it is, but sometimes that is not what it feels like. The rhetoric around the term 'British' insidiously attempts to equate it with a pre-multicultural England (whenever that was, seeing as North Africans were guarding Hadrian's Wall nearly 2,000 years ago, but whatever) that owes its celebrated arts, style and 'values' to nothing and nobody except the ancient British families and their rambling estates that get rolled out for every period drama.

Despite this grievance with the whitewashing of British history, I readily admit it's not only elsewhere that has inspired British fashion. It also works the other way around. Many immigrants came to the UK, were inspired by the fashions they found here and integrated these into their existing wardrobe – resulting in London in particular being world-renowned for some of the most exciting and eccentric clothing combinations.

However, by not widely acknowledging the influence immigrant groups and individuals have had on UK fashion, we allow the story of colonial superiority in all realms to perpetuate.

I see fashion as the cultural crystal ball, an immediacy reflecting what will later be seen in other art forms, once the artists have had time to filter the nuance and the nausea into a cohesive piece of work.

Fashion-makers (and in this I include designers, printmakers, sewers, pattern-cutters, and others I don't have the expertise to credit) are driven by a practical need, as well as a creative and financial one; to create things that people can wear. They don't always have time to filter or to muse on the profundity of a moment – they take the moment and sew it onto fabric and we see it walking down the street and don't think twice about it, unless to admire or object to it.

After saying all of this – what, specifically, is the majority of Britain wearing in 2016?

I couldn't find any research that had been done into individual items of clothing purchased in Britain, outside of broad categories such as 'shoes' or 'leather goods'. There was no literature on how immigration, outside of very specific groups, had influenced British fashion and it is easy to see why. The impact of immigration to the UK on contemporary UK clothing is impossible to accurately document. Therefore what follows are simply some of my musings, triggered by my fruitless searching for studies on the subject.

Amazon, despite its dubious morality regarding workers' rights, thankfully came up trumps with a current list of the top 20 bestselling clothing items on the UK site. Not all UK residents use Amazon, or even the internet. I have no illusion that this is the definitive source of purchasing information for the country. However, I do think it reflects at least a part of our national fashion footprint and so I have chosen to expand on some of the items shown there, evaluating how their emergence into a top 20 list could *possibly* be linked with immigration to the UK.

Number nine on the list is a 'Ladies Chiffon Wrap Scarf'. It has flowers printed on it and comes in a multitude of colours.

Chiffon as a fabric was invented in early-twentieth-century India. It can be made from silk, cotton or polyester fibres, but nowadays is most widely available as polyester. This particular wrap scarf is reminiscent of traditional Indian scarves that have been worn for thousands of years, with a European-influenced flower design printed on them.

Indians have been present in the UK for hundreds of years – as have people from many areas of the world – albeit in small numbers to begin with. Global trade has been happening since people were able to travel and this resulted

in traders and workers living temporarily or permanently in
countries outside of their birthplace. India was under various
forms of British colonial rule from 1612, so this migration
of traders and workers would have been even greater. There
is evidence of Indian seamen being buried in London during
the 1600s and one probable theory is that the East India
Company employed Indian seamen for their voyages back
to Britain and their home.[44] The first large migration to the
UK by Indian women, who brought with them versions of
the fantastic chiffon scarves that today sell so prolifically in
the mainstream, seems to have been from Kenya in 1968,
when 100,000 Indians arrived in Britain following Kenyan
independence from Britain – mostly as families invited here
and promised passports and citizenship. The scarves worn by
these women were already reflected in the popular Western
fashions of the time – the loose-flowing hippy garments
and Indian-influenced designs. Much fashion of that era
disappeared along with the feelings of peace and love, but the
chiffon scarf evidently remains a strong staple. This is likely
to be due to its versatility, durability, resistance to wrinkling
and its ability to be stored in very small spaces. All of these
traits became even more important by the advent of mass
access to international travel. The 'twice migrants' of Indian
origin knew this well, having travelled the globe with their
belongings more times than most. Who knows if they would
have had any idea that the scarves that covered them, warmed
them and cooled them would become one of the most worn
fashion items in Britain less than 50 years later.

44 Rozina Visram, *Asians in Britain – 400 Years of History*, (London, Pluto Press,
    2002).

Worryingly, number two in the most popular clothing bought on Amazon.co.uk is the 'FeelinGirl Latex 9 Steel Boned Waist Training Corset Cincher for Women'. Considering the Rational Dress Movement (1881) was a significant player in feminist activism and eventual suffrage for women, campaigning as they did to free women from clothing that 'impeded physical movement or deformed the figure',[45] it is depressing to see this elaborately named item of clothing maintain such a prominent position on the sales list, at a time when many women and men say there's no need for feminism and/or feel a discomfort at describing themselves as a feminist. This discomfort must pale in comparison to the aches imposed by wearing the chart-topping 'Steel Boned Waist Cincher'. French migration to Britain brought along the early obsessions with corset-wearing, although its current popularity may be more directly linked to TOWIE or Kim K. It's generally accepted that the garment first became popular in Italy and was introduced to France by Catherine de Médici in the sixteenth century.[46] It was also during the 1500s that the largest numbers of French migrated to Britain to put down permanent roots, as the Protestant Huguenots fled religious persecution in their homeland. It is from this point onward that corsets become common in Britain and throughout Europe, something which doesn't change (although the style of the corset does) until the 1920s, as women had been asked to stop buying corsets in order to save steel for the war from 1917.[47] They continued to exist as items of fashion worn in Britain for

45 *The Rational Dress Society Gazette*, (1889).

46 Elizabeth Ewing, *Dress and Undress: A History of Women's Underwear*, (London, Batsford, 1978).

47 'Mary Phelps Jacob', Phelps Family History in America. http:// phelpsfamilyhistory.com/bios/mary_phelps_jacob.asp

stage costumes and in sex shops as 'erotic wear'. Perhaps their mainstream popularity resumed in the 1990s with the onset of pseudo-female empowerment branding, such as the mass commercialisation of 'raunchy lingerie' by companies like Ann Summers.

Prior to writing this, I would have imagined that the French presence in Britain had resulted in far more stylish items of popular fashion than the 'cincher', but there you go.

Now, the moment we've all been waiting for – the number one selling item of clothing on the UK site of Amazon … The white T-Shirt. It's been there for 1,887 days. What is it about white T-shirts? I own two, but I just wear them under furry vintage jumpers to stop the scratchiness sending me barmy. I borrow my partner's sometimes for bed. They have long been worn by all sexes, yet there still seems to be something quietly masculine about them. Perhaps this is attributable to their origins. Worn as all-in-one undergarments in early nineteenth-century America, these 'union suits' were hailed as emancipatory fashion for women, allowing them to wear more comfortable and 'masculine' clothing in an effort to rid themselves of the restrictions placed on them by society and manifested for all to see in the fashions of the time. These then became two-piece undergarments worn by both sexes and in the late nineteenth century buttonless versions were issued as standard US Navy undershirts. Around the same time, these easy to slip on garments became popular globally amongst miners and stevedores (a waterfront manual labourer involved in loading and unloading ships). They were convenient for hot environments and comfortable to work in underneath layers in cold environments. This global popularity may have been initiated by the US Navy presence from the 1820s in all

African countries where the British Navy was stationed.[48] I am purely speculating, but it is possible that the dockworkers in these countries used the white T-shirt more than the British Navy did, as all of the British Armed Forces have their own strict uniform codes. Considering that in the early twentieth century, Britain began urgently recruiting people from its vast colonies to work on British ships and dockyards[49] and large numbers of Somali, Sudanese and Yemeni dockworkers took up the offer of employment, perhaps they were the ones who brought the white T-shirt to British docks long before Hollywood did – influencing fashion (and Amazon sales) in a way they would surely be unable to predict, or benefit from. Whatever the truth about its introduction to Britain is, this enduring popularity of the plain white tee is surely down to more than just practicality? I would make some guesses that it speaks to individualism's irony and capitalism's sustenance by allowing the wearer (and the 'viewer') to project any of their multiple identities onto the blank face of the top. It allows the wearer to appear theoretically classless and unclassifiable.

As my dad showed with his very own collection of bright white T-shirts, this rare opportunity for equality is often more valuable to an immigrant than others could ever imagine.

48 Christopher Lloyd, *The Navy and the Slave Trade: The Suppression of the African Slave Trade in the Nineteenth Century*, (Hove, Psychology Press, 1968).
49 David Killingray, *Africans in Britain*, (Hove, Psychology Press, 1994).

AIRPORTS AND AUDITIONS

RIZ AHMED

To begin with, auditions taught me to get through airports. In the end, it was the other way around.

I'm an actor. Since I was a teenager I've had to play different characters, negotiating the cultural expectations of a Pakistani family, Brit-Asian rudeboy culture, and a scholarship to private school. The fluidity of my own personal identity on any given day was further compounded by the changing labels assigned to Asians in general.

As children in the 80s, when my brother and I were stopped near our home by a skinhead and a knife was put to his throat, we were black. A decade later the knife to my throat was held by another 'paki', a label we wore with swagger in the Brit-Asian subculture and gang culture of the 90s. The next time I found myself as helplessly cornered, it was in a windowless room at Luton airport. My arm was in a painful wrist-lock and my collars pinned to the wall by British intelligence officers. It was 'post 9/11', and I was now labelled a Muslim.

As a minority, no sooner do you learn to polish and cherish one chip on your shoulder, it's taken off you and swapped out for another. The jewellery of your struggles is forever on loan, like the Koh-i-Noor. You are intermittently handed this

Necklace of labels to hang around your neck, neither of your choosing nor making, both constricting and decorative.

Part of the reason I became an actor was the promise that I might be able to help stretch these Necklaces, and that the teenage version of myself might breathe a little easier as a result. If the films I re-enacted as a kid could humanise mutants and aliens, maybe there was hope for us.

But portrayals of ethnic minorities worked in stages, I realised, so I'd have to strap in for a long ride.

Stage One is the two-dimensional stereotype – the minicab driver/terrorist/cornershop owner. It tightens the Necklace.

Stage Two is the subversive portrayal, taking place on 'ethnic' terrain but aiming to challenge stereotypes. It loosens the Necklace.

And Stage Three is the Promised Land, where you play a character whose story is not intrinsically linked to his race. In the Promised Land, I'm not a terror suspect, nor a victim of forced marriage. In the Promised Land, my name might even be Dave. In the Promised Land, there is no Necklace.

I started acting professionally during the post 9/11 boom for Stage One stereotypes, but I avoided them at the behest of my 18-year-old self. Luckily there was also a tiny speck of Stage Two stuff taking shape, subverting those stereotypes, and I managed to get in on the act.

My first film was in this mode, Michael Winterbottom's *The Road to Guantanamo*. It told the story of a group of friends from Birmingham who were illegally detained and tortured there. When it won a prestigious award at the Berlin Film Festival, we were euphoric. For those who saw it, the inmates went from orange jumpsuits to human beings.

But airport security hadn't got the memo. Returning to the glamour of Luton Airport after our festival win, ironically-named 'British intelligence officers' frog-marched me to an unmarked room where they insulted, threatened, then attacked me.

'What kinda film you making? Did you become an actor to further the Muslim struggle?' an officer screamed, twisting my arm to the point of snapping.

The question is disturbing not only because it endangers artistic expression, but because it suggests our security services don't quite grasp the nature of the terror threat we all face. A presentation outlining Al-Qaeda's penchant for 'theatrical' attacks may have been taken a little literally. Their suspicion of thespians may also explain why those Guantanamo Bay prisoners are so goddamn photogenic.

It turned out that what those Special Branch officers did was illegal. I was asked by activist lawyers if I wanted to sue, but instead I wrote an account of the incident and sent it to a few journalists. A story about the illegal detention of the actors from a film about illegal detention turned out to be too good to ignore. I was glad to shed some light on this depressing state of affairs.

I went on to write a song inspired by the incident, called 'Post 9/11 Blues', full of sage advice like: 'We're all suspects so watch your back, I farted and got arrested for a chemical attack.' The song got the attention of Chris Morris, who cast me in *Four Lions*.

In the end, having my arm nearly torn off by people whose salary I pay led to me exploring loads of Stage Two work – loosening the Necklace. It felt good, but what about Stage Three, the Promised Land?

It turned out there was no clear pathway for an actor of colour in the UK to go to Stage Three – to play 'just a bloke'. Producers all said they wanted to work with me, but they had nothing I could feasibly act in. The stories that needed to be told in the multicultural mid-2000s were about the all-white mid-1700s, it seemed. I heard rumours that the Promised Land was not in Britain at all, but in Hollywood.

The reason for this is simple. America uses its stories to export a myth of itself, just like the UK. The reality of Britain is vibrant multi-culturalism, but the myth we export is an all-white world of Lords and Ladies. Conversely, American society is pretty segregated, but the myth they export is of a racial melting-pot solving crimes and fighting aliens side by side.

So America is where I was headed. But it would not be an easy journey.

You see, the pitfalls of the audition room and the airport interrogation room are the same. They are places where the threat of rejection is real. They're also places where you're reduced to your marketability or threat-level, where the length of your facial hair can be a deal breaker, where you are seen, and hence see yourself, in reductive labels – never as 'just a bloke called Dave'. The post 9/11 Necklace tightens around your neck.

I had so far managed to avoid this in the audition room, but now I faced the same threat at US airports. It didn't help that *The Road to Guantanamo* had left my passport stamped with an Axis of Evil world tour – shooting in Pakistan, Afghanistan, and Iran within six months. I spent the flight sweating in defiance of air-conditioning, wondering what would await me.

When I landed, the officer assessing me shared my skin colour. I wondered whether this was a good sign or if he was one of the legendarily patriotic Cuban borders officers I had heard about, determined to assess how star-spangled I was with a thumb up the anus.

He looked at my passport, then at me, frowned and drew a big 'P' over my immigration card. I immediately thought it stood for Paki.

'Protocol!'

I was led down a long corridor without explanation before turning in to a side room that felt instantly familiar.

Apart from a Chinese family and a South American pilot battling the indignity with his spotless uniform, the holding pen was filled with 20 slight variations of my own face, now all staring at me. Kinda like a Bollywood remake of *Being John Malkovich*. It's a reminder that you are a type, whose face says things before your mouth opens. You are a signifier before you are a person. You are back at Stage One.

The holding room also had that familiar audition room fear. Everyone is nervous, but the prospect of solidarity is undercut by competition. You're all fighting to graduate out of this reductive purgatory and into some recognition of your unique personhood. In one way or another you are all saying, 'I'm not like the rest of them.'

The fresh-faced desk officer was no older than 23. By the time I was called up to audition for him, my spiel to explain the passport stamps was ready. I'd show a letter from the film's producer, I'd say 'award-winning film', and I'd flash a shiny new DVD. But the kid questioning me seemed more nervous than I was. He'd clearly been to the same 'beware bloodthirsty actors' seminar as the intelligence officers at Luton.

'Step back from the counter!'

I was pinballed up the chain for a proper interrogation with a dangerously fat man and his moustache. I sat and waited, rehearsing my lines. When the interrogation came, it was more of a car crash than my *Slumdog Millionaire* audition.

'Oh yeah? Afghanistan? What kinda movie were you making there?'

The question shot through me with a shudder. It reminded me of the questions I faced at Luton airport, but also of the question I ask myself all the time. Was I adding to the catalogue of Stage One, Two, or Three? Was it a film my 18-year-old self wanted? Would it make the Necklace looser or tighter?

I thought about the right way to answer him. *The Road to Guantanamo* was a documentary-drama, but maybe saying I was in a documentary about Guantanamo Bay wouldn't be wise. Drama should do.

I said, 'Erm, it's an award-winning drama called *The Road to Guantanamo*.'

There was a long silence. He raised an eyebrow. I offered up the DVD; it had a photo of me handcuffed in an orange jumpsuit on its cover. I immediately regretted it. Longer silence. Second eyebrow went up. He leaned in.

'Do you know anyone who wants to do harm to the United States?'

I shook my head and made Hugh Grant noises, venturing a 'gosh!' in there somewhere. He absorbed my performance before holding up a book from my luggage. It was Mohsin Hamid's novel *The Reluctant Fundamentalist*.[50]

'What's this book?'

I explained, but he wasn't really listening. He deployed a state-of-the-art intelligence protocol by Googling me, which returned a news clipping about the Luton Airport incident. Fuck. My heart sank. This was it. No Hollywood for me. I was

---

50 Though I didn't know it at the time, I would go on to act in the film adaptation of *The Reluctant Fundamentalist* – I'm sure in part because its title doubled as a description of my casting perils up until that point.

never gonna be Brad Pitt. I wasn't even gonna be Apu from the fucking *Simpsons*. What was I thinking?

When after an agonising three hours I was waved through, I couldn't believe it. I felt relieved, grateful, lucky – and then suddenly incensed.

On the way out past my look-alikes, I gave a loud 'As-Salaam aliekum'.

No one leapt to return the greeting. Perhaps they lacked the safety net of a convincing 'gosh!'.

I joined a friend in Manhattan for dinner, apologising for being three hours late, and zoned out while they discussed astrology. Someone at the dinner turned to me.

'You're such a terrorist,' she said.

I blinked. What the fuck? My face screwed itself into the expression I wish I'd pulled instead of mewling apologetically at the border officers.

'What the fuck is that supposed to mean?'

My friend put her arm on mine and squeezed.

'Riz, she asked if you're a Sagittarius.'

I swallowed. Baffled faces pinned me with concern.

'Right. Sorry. Yeah. Yes, I am,' I said.

A similar version of the same thing happened again soon after. And again. And again. And again. I grew belligerent.

One officer asked if I had had any military training. My school had a cadet-force programme that I was swiftly ejected from, but I just answered 'yes' without expanding. I was asked if I had travelled to Iran, Iraq, or Afghanistan recently.

'All except Iraq, but if it helps I've also been to Pakistan and Saudi Arabia,' I smiled.

Childish perhaps, but the situation itself is infantilising. Feigning obliviousness to an officer's suspicion and refusing to pander to it was my only defence.

But the farce rolled on.

Twice when applying for a US Work Visa I was subjected to a Section 221G – a lengthy background check against a global database of terrorists – which almost lost me the jobs. I saw the email correspondence between the state department and my attorney:

'Hey Bill, looking at your client Mr Ahmed – pretty British-sounding name, huh? Saw his "Post 9/11 Blues" song, what's with the "I heart Osama" routine?'

Fair enough, you might think. Search him. Look at his racial profile and his passport stamps and his dangerously hilarious rap lyrics. But since I had been let into the US and deemed safe just the previous month, another rigmarole this month was obviously fruitless. The possibility of radicalising me in under thirty days is laughable if you know how entrenched I am in a Satanic Internet Porn addiction (and the CIA and NSA surely do).

In the end, I was always let in, so these airport auditions were technically a success. But they involved the experience of being typecast, and when that happens enough, you internalise the role written for you by others. Now, like an over-eager method actor, I was struggling to break character.

I tried not to ingest all the signs telling me I was a suspect. I tried not to buy into the story world of this 'protocol' or its Stage One stereotype of who I was. But when you have always moulded your identity to your environment and had your Necklace picked out by others, it's not easy. I couldn't see myself as 'just a bloke'. I failed at every single audition I went up for.

Rehearsing a scene beds a role into you. But sometimes if you over-rehearse it without unearthing any new meaning in it, you can suddenly forget your lines. You realise that you are on a stage, not in the real world. The scene's emotional power and your immersion in it disappears.

And so it dawned on me that these searches were a fictional role-play taking place in a bubble, rather than an assessment of my worth.

This was the way to see it.

And it turns out this is also the way to see auditions.

The protocol lost its chokehold on me, and I started getting roles again.

One big job secured me a proper US visa, and soon I was getting waved through without the protocol. I began inching towards the Promised Land.

Now, both at auditions and airports, I find myself on the right side of the same velvet rope with which I was once clotheslined. But this isn't a success story. I see most of my fellow Malkoviches still arched back, spines bent to snapping as they try to limbo under that rope. So although these days it's likely that no one resembles me in the waiting room for an acting audition, the same is also true of everyone being waved through with me at US immigration. In both spaces, my exception proves the rule.

Don't get me wrong: although my US airport experience is smoother, I still get stopped before boarding a plane at Heathrow every time I fly to America. But now I find it hilarious rather than bruising. Easy for me to laugh with my work visa and strategically deployed 'gosh!', perhaps. But it's also easy for me to laugh, because the more I travel, the more ridiculous the procedures become.

Heathrow airport draws its staff from the nearby Asian suburbs of Hounslow and Southall. My 'random selection' flying to LA was so reliable that as I started travelling more, I went through a six-month stretch of being searched by the same middle-aged Sikh guy. I instinctively started calling him Uncle, as is the custom for Asian elders. He started calling me 'beta', or son, as he went through my luggage apologetically. It was heart-warming, but veered dangerously close to incest every time he had to frisk my crotch.

'How are you, son?'

'I'm er, ooh, er, good, Uncle.'

As I've travelled more I've also done more film work, increasing the chances of being recognised by the young Asian staff at Heathrow. I have had my films quoted back at me by someone rifling through my underpants, and been asked for selfies by someone swabbing me for explosives.

The last kid who searched me, a young Muslim boy with an immaculate line-beard and goatee, was particularly apologetic.

'Sorry, bro. If it makes you feel any better, they search me before I fly too.'

We laughed, not because he was joking, but because he was deadly serious. It was the perfect encapsulation of the minority's shifting and divided self, forced to internalise the limitations imposed on us just to get by, on the wrong side of the velvet rope even when (maybe *especially* when) you're on the right side of it. We cracked jokes and bumped fists.

As I left, he called after me with a question.

'Bro, what kinda film you doing next?'

I looked at the ID badge hanging from a string around his neck. I told him I hoped it would be one he liked.

PERPETUATING CASTEISM

SARAH SAHIM

Most people are aware of the discriminatory Indian caste system, but many do not realise that this form of intra-racial segregation has extended beyond South Asia and into the United Kingdom through the diaspora. While the British were not directly responsible for the caste system's creation, their own system of classism and the violence of racism imposed on Indians during colonisation reinforced it.

Caste is an ancient and complex social stratification system, with Dalits (Marathi for 'oppressed') at the very bottom and Brahmins – the spiritual and scholarly class – at the top. Such is the status of Dalits in Indian society that they are excluded from the *varna* (an ancient Hindu form of classifying civilisation) entirely.

Those around today are still paying for – or, for those who are privileged, reaping the benefits of – the results of past generations' mistakes with regards to casteism. Caste continues to affect our lives despite it being supposedly eradicated. There is a colonial 'hangover' of sorts and it isn't just limited to the borders of India. It pervades other countries and the Indian diaspora. It takes place in Britain itself: the colonial source. Yet, the question remains: why do Indians who have migrated to Britain (as well as other Western countries, such as the

United States) and their children continue this discriminatory practice?

'Caste' itself was a British construction, showing up on Indian census forms in 1871.[51] This helped create a hierarchy of castes that worked to give Brahmins more privilege and societal advantages through their misunderstanding of the complex *varna*. This is not to say that the system on its own – prior to British arrival – was without fault. And notwithstanding discrimination based on caste being illegal in India, casteism has permeated factions of Indian society both domestically and internationally. The caste system has supposedly been eradicated from India,[52] and was not necessarily part of the original structural inequality in other countries in the Indian diaspora. However, casteism is just as vehement today, and those who refuse to acknowledge its existence are in abundance.

The relationship between castes is also complex. As a young light-skinned woman with a Gujarati Brahmin mother and Afghan Pashtun father, I have access to a wealth of privilege: something I have taken for granted. My family never concerned themselves with casteism and neither did I: we didn't discriminate or abide by its rules. However, this 'caste-blind' attitude is extremely harmful and you cannot and must not turn a blind eye to injustices that your people are responsible for. I have the freedom to be wilfully ignorant, but others, especially Dalits, cannot afford to do so.

The recent suicide of Rohith Vemula, a Dalit, on

51 'Caste not class is the main British problem, Lords', *The Huffington Post*. http://www.huffingtonpost.co.uk/jasdev-singh-rai/caste-not-class-is-the-ma_b_2989148.html

52 'Why India is still fighting over caste system', *CNN*. http://www.cnn.com/2015/08/28/asia/india-gujarat-caste-protests/

January 17th 2016, reified the horrific realities of caste-based discrimination, especially amongst younger Indians. Vemula was a 25-year-old PhD student at the University of Hyderabad. Just two weeks away from turning 26, Vemula hanged himself after being expelled from his accommodation because the university refused to carry on paying him a grant of 25,000 rupees per month, an apparently clear case of caste-based discrimination by an academic institution.

In his suicide note he wrote, 'I always was rushing. Desperate to start a life. All the while, some people, for them, life itself is curse. My birth is my fatal accident.'

His death subsequently sparked protest and a much-needed discussion about the state of casteism in India.

One of the ways the conversation has evolved is through New York-based journalist Yashica Dutt's *Documents of Dalit Discrimination* blog on Tumblr.[53] The page is intended for Dalits and witnesses of Dalit discrimination to share their stories; a 'safe space for conversation that goes beyond "reservation" and "merit" and voices that echo the hurt so many of us suffer silently'.[54]

As well as charting the history of discrimination, she also seeks to record the toll that the caste system continues to exact on it lower caste victims. The page documents instances of casteism denial – which in itself is casteist – instances of slurs being used against Dalits, job discrimination, assuming

---

53 Documents of Dalit Discrimination (blog). http://dalitdiscrimination.tumblr. com/

54 'Coming out as a Dalit in Rohith's memory: New York journalist's project to document discrimination', *The News Minute*. http://www.thenewsminute. com/article/coming-out-dalit-rohith%E2%80%99s-memory-new-york-journalist%E2%80%99s-project-document-discrimination-38083

that someone of a lower caste was employed due to positive discrimination, unprovoked physical abuse, and how many Dalits have to attempt to pass as Brahmin in order to circumvent all of these experiences. 'Passing' is not only a precarious decision, but the fact that it is possible at all, just goes to prove that delineations between caste are meaningless and harmful. Dutt even used the blog to recount an abhorrently violent incident that happened to her own mother: '[Her neighbour] had … hit her with two different mid-sized boulders from a distance of less than two feet. One he brutally bruised her face with, using its sharp end. The other, he used to strike her forehead.' These were stones that her mother had used to block sewage coming from his drain. Unfortunately the neighbour did not stop there as he 'kick[ed] her twice in the shin and [struck her], using the boulders'. She immediately contacted the police but the neighbour denied attacking her. The police were of no use and she told Dutt this was because 'everyone knows our caste'. This encapsulates the myopia through which perpetuators of the caste system perceive their world and just how tangible its effects are, but is only one of hundreds of thousands of stories about the mistreatment of Dalits.

The South Asian non-binary and trans 'performance art duo' DarkMatter tweeted on May 30th, 2014, 'Hinduism is a huge and complex and contradictory religion but it has been repurposed by upper caste for nationalism #NoHindutva', which was just one of a series of tweets about casteism.[55] It's evident that the issue of casteism and exploring methods to undo the poisonous nature of this obsolete and divisive

55 Twitter user @DarkMatterPoets. https://twitter.com/DarkMatterPoets/status/472505155817316353

structure is one that younger people prioritise. While conversations about casteism by white people and non-South Asian people of colour can easily careen into racist, xenophobic, or culturally insensitive sentiment, that does not mean that the conversation should not be held at all. It should be led by people who bear the brunt of casteism: lower castes, depressed classes, Dalits.

After the supposed end of the caste system in India, a system akin to positive discrimination emerged there, a so-called 'quota system'. This was developed to help disadvantaged castes succeed without regard to their social status. The system created groups of 'Other Backward Classes', 'Scheduled Castes', and 'Scheduled Tribes'. Though it was intended to counter years of oppression of lower castes,[56] systems such as this one are not always successful. Despite attempting to mitigate institutional oppression, putting people in a workplace where they might be assumed to be there only because of this, brings about its own issues. Quite a few instances of everyday casteism mentioned on Dutt's blog discuss problems with the quota system. Some of them expressed worry about accepting scholarships because they had been pretending to be Brahmin.[57]

In Dutt's *Huffington Post* article 'Today, I'm Coming Out As Dalit', she articulates the struggle of passing. 'I was born in a Dalit family in Ajmer, Rajasthan. And I grew up learning to hide it. My convent school education, a non-Dalit-sounding last name, and a skin colour that was "dusky but still not dirty", eased

56 'Why India is still fighting over caste system', *CNN*. http://www.cnn.com/2015/08/28/asia/india-gujarat-caste-protests/

57 Documents of Dalit Discrimination (blog). http://dalitdiscrimination.tumblr.com/post/137820923502/i-never-came-out-of-my-shell-became-introverted

my passing as a non-Dalit,'[58] Dutt writes. She also mentions that early in her career as a journalist she wrote about things associated with upper castes that she thought would help her continue to pass as non-Dalit, such as 'fashion and lifestyle'.[59]

One thing that Vemula's suicide did for Dalits such as Dutt was remind them that their pain was rooted in oppression: not in shame or the notion that they are 'dirty'. This victim-blaming mentality echoes the negatives of colonialism too. Removing the actual source of the blame serves to place it on those who are experiencing the most pain in society; the most marginalised. Vemula's suicide is still a tragedy, but with young trailblazers and activists like Dutt, there is a chance that he might be one of the last. What Dutt, *Documents of Dalit Discrimination*, and other Dalits who are seeking self-empowerment and community empowerment are doing is similar to what Dr Ambedkar argued for.[60] He stressed that he wished for Dalits to gain 'self-pride, self-improvement, and self-confidence so as to have an equal share in society'.[61]

The census imposed on India by the British Empire in 1871 served to solidify the institutionalisation of caste for years to come, many remnants of which have survived into the

---

58 'Today, I'm coming out as Dalit', *The Huffington Post.* http://www.huffingtonpost. in/yashica-dutt/why-im-coming-out-as-dali_b_9035094.html

59 'Coming out as a Dalit in Rohith's memory', *The News Minute.* http://www.thenewsminute.com/article/coming-out-dalit-rohith %E2%80%99s-memory-new-york-journalist%E2%80%99s-project-document-discrimination-38083

60 India's first minister of law and justice and prominent campaigner against the caste system.

61 N.S. Gehlot, 'Dr Ambedkar, Mahatma Gandhi, and Dalit Movement', *The Indian Journal of Political Science,* Vol.54, No.3/4 (July–Dec 1991), 382–387.

modern era. The way the caste system manifests itself today
is the combined product of both the British and privileged
Indians. Another article that followed Vemula's suicide makes
this clear: 'The discussion surrounding the suicide on the
other hand is evidence of the colonial hangover our society
suffers from; of our incapability to elucidate societal divisions
without resorting to the concept of caste, which was born
out of a combined effort on the part of the British and the
Brahmins to maintain governing status in the country'.[62] The
first census in 1871 counted and classified Indian people based
on caste, which contributed to the institutionalisation of the
caste system under British colonial rule.

This step to maintain British and Brahmin Indian power
demonstrates the British involvement in modern casteism, and
they must be held accountable. The British also used other
means of classifying Indians[63] as they had with many other
colonised populations, including skin colour/shade, head
measurements, body measurements, and other objectifying
means, designed to help determine physical traits and their
supposed relation to caste. This embodied archaic distinctions
anthropologists used to separate 'Negroids', 'Mongoloids',
'Iranids', and other offensive racial classifications. Western
colonialism stunted many societies' ability to advance by
enforcing regressive views on race, gender, and sexuality. Though
some may try to argue that colonialism was, on balance, a good

62 'Our obsession with caste is really a colonial hangover', *The Indian Express*.
   http://indianexpress.com/article/blogs/rohith-vemula-dalit-suicide-
   hyderabad-our-obsession-with-caste-is-really-a-colonial-hangover/

63 'Caste not class is the main British problem, Lords', *The Huffington Post*.
   http://www.huffingtonpost.co.uk/jasdev-singh-rai/caste-not-class-is-the-
   ma_b_2989148.html

thing (a sentiment that derives from the British believing they abolished 'uncivilised' cultural practices), the fact of the matter is that the British ruled with an ardent cruelty that stemmed from their inflated sense of racial superiority,[64] and they passed this attitude on to Brahmins (not to mention that the notion of the British 'civilising' other cultures is inherently racist).

While Gandhi was regarded as a bastion of peaceful protest who fought against the evil British Empire, his methods left many unsatisfied, including Dr Ambedkar. Granted, Gandhi's efforts ameliorated the anti-colonialism movement but that does not automatically render him unaccountable for his casteism. Gandhi opposed Dr Ambedkar's demand for separate electorates for the Dalits, dating back to 1931 at the Second Round Table Conference in London.[65] Dalits then protested against Gandhi's stance on this situation upon his return to Mumbai. And when the lower and depressed classes were given separate electorates, Gandhi went on a petulant hunger strike in protest until Dr Ambedkar relented. Dr Ambedkar was concerned that without their own electorate, the Dalits would remain 'at the mercy of the Hindus' and, with hindsight, it looks as though his fears were justified. Gandhi, on the other hand, believed that 'untouchability' would soon be a thing of the past.[66] The reframing and manipulation of history has been in Gandhi's favour. A hunger strike is seen to be a valiant form of political defiance and this further romanticises perceptions of Gandhi. This sentiment is not shared by the lower castes,

64 'Wake up, Britain. Should the empire really be a source of pride?', *The Guardian*. http://www.theguardian.com/commentisfree/2016/jan/23/britain-empire-pride-poll

65 N.S. Gehlot, 'Dr Ambedkar, Mahatma Gandhi, and Dalit Movement'.

66 N.S. Gehlot, 'Dr Ambedkar, Mahatma Gandhi, and Dalit Movement'.

however, as their lack of political power remains unaltered.

Despite the part the British played in helping to reinforce this caste discrimination, the racism practised by white British people extends to all, not just those of a lower caste. Racial discrimination does not distinguish between Dalits and Brahmins; to racists, all Indians are the same. Even when the politics of respectability encourage variation in the way Indians of different castes or socio-economic status are treated in Britain, the end result is still racial discrimination.

Racism in society often works through a divide and conquer strategy, more often than not it is also intertwined with classism as well as other forms of oppression. Structural racism can divide a community that would be stronger together, by keeping individual groups entrenched in their own class – in this case, caste discrimination. This form of racism combined with the inflated white British sense of self-importance means that from the outside it appears that they dismiss casteism without holding themselves accountable. In some ways, one could argue that lingering caste discrimination in the UK is fortified by British classism – a capitalist structure that seeks to segregate people without any chance of social mobility is very reminiscent of the Indian caste system.

British Indians are the largest minority community in Britain[67] and while most young British Indians may not pay much mind to the caste system, they are no doubt still on the receiving end of its negative effects as it manifests in many ways. Although children are independent and formulate their own opinions, watching their elders partake in the caste system

---

67 'British Indians seek legal protection from caste system', *CBC World.* http://www.cbc.ca/news/world/british-indians-seek-legal-protection-from-caste-system-1.2224275

can leave a lasting impression and encourage them to become directly complicit in casteism. Their privilege as upper-caste Indians gives them an arbitrarily higher status over other Indian children who might have to resort to hiding their caste, even in a country where the Indian caste system is not a familiar concept. Those who are conscious of, and engage in, the boundaries that casteism presents, perpetuate discriminatory and odious practices such as forbidding inter-caste marriage so as not to 'spoil' a bloodline. But the divide extends beyond marital relationships as higher castes make efforts to exclude lower castes from partaking in events and functions that are intended to bring communities together for dancing and celebrations. This is particularly rife in the North Indian community as many British Gujaratis host and attend garbas (a form of traditional Gujarati dance with sticks), which are segregated by caste and most are exclusively attended by the higher castes.

Whether an Indian from a higher caste admits it or not, they are always indirectly complicit in perpetuating the caste system, because their existence means that they're more advantaged than Dalits by default. Young children have been known to taunt other children from lower castes with casteist slurs[68] and British-born Hindu Indians are still at risk of being shunned for their caste, no matter what generation.[69] They experience caste discrimination at work, '… in public services, music, social media as well as at religious and community

68 'No escape from caste prejudice even in UK', *The Times of India*. http://timesofindia.indiatimes.com/nri/No-escape-from-caste-prejudice-even-in-UK/articleshow/18998712.cms

69 'British Indians seek legal protection from caste system', *CBC World*. http://www.cbc.ca/news/world/british-indians-seek-legal-protection-from-caste-system-1.2224275

spaces',[70] and when casteist slurs like 'Jat'[71] are being used in lieu of 'dirty' it evokes a cause for concern.

In 2013, British Indians protested to the British government about casteism, demanding government protection. While these protests were successful, with the British government eventually agreeing to explicitly prohibit caste discrimination within the 2010 Equalities Act, changing the law does not simply end discrimination right there and then. When systems of oppression are so deeply ingrained in the Indian – and human – psyche, it's impossible for people to do a complete *volte face* with regards to their bigotry, even if it is illegal. All British Indians are still subject to white supremacy,[72] despite Britain's claims that race is less important in this than class. Additionally, it's hard to ignore that Britain was the perpetrator of modern casteism and thus the hierarchical social order in India. Usually those claims that racism is no longer an issue are paired with assertions that the United States is the sole culprit of institutional racism. While it is true that the United States has a huge history of and problem with racism, that does not erase the history of racism and white supremacy in Britain. It was Britain who formed the second point on the transatlantic slave trade triangle (the path African slaves would travel in order to reach America) and most recently, the death of Sarah Reed – a London black woman who died in 2012 after a brutal beating while in police custody – bears

---

70 'Long range of prejudice', *Outlook Magazine*. http://www.outlookindia.com/article/long-range-of-prejudice/293121

71 The Jat people are an Indo-Aryan people based in Northern India and Pakistan, most of whom still live in farming communities.

72 The notion of 'white supremacy' in this instance is to be taken as a global concept rather than in the context of America's relationship with black and Native American citizens.

many similarities to the fate of Sandra Bland, who died under mysterious circumstances in a Texas prison cell in 2015.

In order for anti-racism to become a reality – at least in the context of Indians – it's important for Indians higher than Dalit on the *varna* to be fully aware of the arbitrary privileges bestowed upon them and those who possess major social and financial power to make the environment safer for Dalits. This is not something that can happen overnight. Acknowledging the pain that Dalits experience is the first step. The conversation of caste cannot start and end with Vemula's suicide. The work of today's existing generations fighting against caste discrimination cannot go unnoticed either. Yashica Dutt's *Documents of Dalit Discrimination* and the work of other activists like DarkMatter is vital in moving forward into a future that betters the lives of the lower castes and in turn enhances the lives of all castes.

The British must be held accountable for their reinforcing of the caste system and their continuing indirect support of discriminatory practices. It's clear that the caste system, taken to the extreme it has been, is not an inherently Indian convention. If the British are partially responsible for classifying Indians during colonialism, why is there a need to continue this practice – why not abolish caste discrimination and work as a better-formed community, embracing the diversity of the castes, to challenge British authority? Indulging casteism is not going to earn upper castes the privilege that white Brits have by design. It is clear that the continuation of caste is not beneficial for anyone in the Indian community and especially within white institutions. Looking down on lower castes or classes and using them to navigate your way to the top does not guarantee you will achieve a white person's status in this white supremacist world. Uniting against white oppressors can only be achieved by eradicating these quasi-sectarian oppressions.

SHADE

SALENA GODDEN

*Shade: Comparative darkness and coolness caused by shelter from
direct sunlight.*
  The darker part of a picture.
  A position of relative inferiority or obscurity.
  *To publicly criticise or express contempt for someone, to act in a
casual or disrespectful manner towards someone, throwing shade,
acting kinda shady.*

Sometimes I think I am about the same shade as Beyoncé. But
it is hard to tell because it depends how much light they give
her. Some days I think I'm about the same shade as Rihanna
but that's also difficult to say as she switches shade too. Your
shade is not skin deep. Your shade is not just about your heart
and soul; your religion and spirituality, your elders and your
history, your connection to a country, to geography and to a
time and place. Your shade is an industry, your shade is a token,
shade is a passport, shade is a cage and shade is a status.
  You tick: Other.

I am in Bangkok. The billboards on the streets and sides of
buses are dominated by adverts for a skin-lightening product
called 'Snail White'. Glossy pictures of westernised Thai

girls with cheerleader smiles and faces of palest ivory. In the markets and restaurants I observe Thai residents with bleached skin and powder-white faces; in the streets some wear gloves protecting their brown hands and thick white tights to conceal brown legs in 40-degree heat. I never noticed this so much before. I think I missed a memo, but the internet informs me that skin bleaching has been trending for years – from India to Africa, the Caribbean, all over the world, skin bleaching is big business and the shade of your skin is your freedom or your prison. The colour of the outside of you dictates existence and acceptance. Your shade is the symbol of your wealth, your beauty, your worth and your success.

Here we are then, this is Britain, where white people dye themselves as brown as tea stains. The desire to tan continues to thrive, people toasting themselves to sunbed death. The first sign of a UK heatwave and our beaches and parks are awash with salmon pink bodies and barbecued lobster faces. Celebrities on the covers of gossip magazines are crab orange; reality television stars are streaky antique teak.

Wherever you live, wherever you are from, it seems it is all about shade. Universally we are divided and whatever shade you are born it is not right or good enough. We are in a giant brainwash, we are being organised by colour and tone, the natural shade of your skin must be improved, altered and filtered. Your skin is a living organ. Your skin is the casing for your sausage-meat soul. And the armour for your muscles, bones and flesh. Skin is the protective layer of the interior of you with the exterior world, but it is always wrong. You are too white or too black. Too light is bad? Too dark is bad? I get confused. I am in the middle here. Hang on a minute, what shade am I to you?

My mother is the same shade as Oprah or Maya. Some

summers I have seen my big brother almost as brown as Idris but closer to Obama in the winter. Bob Marley was mixed, Jamaican and Celtic, same as me, his shade looks pale in some photos, sometimes much darker. You see, it all depends on the filter and the time of year, it all depends on the light, it all depends on the shade. It depends on what point people are trying to make, to advertise things, to sell you things, to make money. That is the point, to get the shade right, to make shade the issue. To give shade, to put someone in the shade, to put someone in their place, to let someone know they are less, more or less, because of their shade. Advertising companies, big corporations, banks and politicians need to maintain this, to control the division of people through racism and shade, throwing shade of difference and indifference, good immigrant and bad immigrant, refugee and benefit scrounger. This keeps us in our place, humans bickering, focusing on their differences, distracted, and at each other's throats, competing and separating –

Divide and rule.

I now imagine a giant separating people like he is recycling glass at the bottle bank: brown skin glass there, yellow skin glass here, white skin glass over there. But most people aren't simply one or the other, either black or white. What about me? Where are you putting the two-tone people?

I wish the giant would pick the glass people up and hold us all up to the light. Then he'd see that together and united as a people we are a beautiful picture, a multicoloured mosaic, a glorious stained-glass window. But the giant just scratches his head and continues flinging people in separate buckets. Referencing his colour chart guide for shades of human – Paddy Field Brown is Poverty. Greasy Chip White is Skint.

Black Panther Beret Black is Super Bowl Uproar. Shot Teenager is Chalk On Bloody Concrete. Crack White is Baby Momma's Bitch. Geisha is Pink Cherry Blossom. Ping Pong is Ladyboy White. LA Orange is Porn Slut. Tangerine Queen is Essex Teak. Cardboard Grey is Benefit Scrounger. Rat Tail Beige is Food Bank. Cheerleader Pink is Under-Age Pop Tart. Fox Hunt is Tory. War Crime is Blood Diamond Red. Arab Oil is Gold Dust. Drowned Brown is Refugee. Immigrant Brown is Better Media Coverage. The giant shrugs. He throws some people in the *other* bucket and some in the sea to die. His supervisor reminds him it is vital to tell the difference between Immigrant Brown and Refugee Brown. Let's be diligent about that. Let's make sure we pay attention.

News just in …

What is the shade?

Boko Harem Black. Entire village. Over 80 people burnt to death in their homes.

No. Not newsworthy. Not important.

Bring Back Our Girls.

No. Not Today.

Black Lives Matter.

No. Not Today.

Say Her Name.

Not newsworthy.

Terrorist bomb, blood on European soil.

Headline. Front page.

The indifference is clear. The difference is as clear as oil and gold. We must know the divide. Know your shade. Whose shade are you on? Whose side are you on? None of us can ever un-see the violent images of immigrant children washed up on beaches and plastered over the front page of newspapers. Or the ashy broken babies trapped beneath rubble and bomb debris. How safe are the children? How safe is it for immigrant children in transit? All over the world, wherever they end up, whatever the shade of their skin, refugee brown or immigrant brown, who is protecting the kids from the predators, traffickers, from rape and murder?

Do you mind me asking you a question: where do you come from?

You tick: Other.

I pull up a chair and wait to be processed. I wait here while you print off your labels, and consider me for your boxes marked black as in black-black or black as in brown-black, or brown as in half-black or brown as in half-caste. But hang on a minute. Surely if I am from two colours, two races, I am two shades, and therefore not half-caste, not half anything, but whole, I am double-caste. But half sounds shadier. Half is best because half means less. You lose. You are half a person. We don't want you getting all empowered, now do we.

Half-caste.

Half-breed.

Mulatto.

Ah, now there's a shady word we don't hear too often, but a word used liberally throughout my teenage years. And most recently a word revived in the US press in a piece about Halle Berry, a shitty article that debated what we should call her mixed children. How rude and how old money is the word mulatto? That word is pure shade with its connotations and meanings. The word mulatto comes from the Spanish and Portuguese – it is derived from *mula*, meaning mule, the hybrid offspring of a horse and a donkey. But I am not a mule and I am not made from two species.

My parents are Jamaican and Irish-English. My passport is British and I have lived in England all my life. My fire and spirit is pure Maroon rebel. They didn't teach us about the significance of the Maroons at school, but growing up Jamaican it was always *Black History Month* back home. My grandparents wanted me to know where we all came from, how the Maroons rebelled to rise and fight against slavery. Through storytelling in the kitchen my grandparents gave me history lessons, a map and a time machine.

Welcome aboard my Good Ship. Let us sail to the colourful island of mixed identity. You are free to use your own rules and savvy because they haven't invented a filter for our shade yet. You are a pirate and you're itinerant. You eat from the cooking pot of mixed culture and bathe in the cool shade of being mixed-race. You disembark and hesitate, your pen hovers over your boarding pass.

You tick: Other.

'I don't think of you as black, not really black-black …'

Not black enough. But not white enough either. You are in the playground and you keep your mouth shut as your classmates argue. 'She's not black, she's brown, but she's not black-black, not like really black …' Your plaits are too frizzy and messed up for the Strawberry Shortcake girls, you are too loud and bright and boisterous for them. Maybe they are too girly and pink for you, anyway. They smell of Parma violets and baby powder. You smell of cocoa butter. You stay in the shade they provide, you find your own light inside, you find strength and you are taught that you are outside.

You tick: Other.

There's a rising fashion for golden-brown skin and curly hair. Mothers at the school gates coo and nudge each other.

'She's so lucky, she has a sun tan all year around, mine comes out of a bottle!' They laugh as someone's mum pats your head, her hand bounces a bit.

'I wish I had your curly hair, can I touch it?'

You tick: Other.

After school, spotty white teenagers in Tacchini tracksuits writhe and jolt, body-popping and breakdancing, competing at caterpillars and windmills on a piece of lino in the street to hip-hop on their ghetto blaster – they call it a Ghetto Blaster. Breakdance has exploded and suddenly everyone wants to be a rapper, everyone wants to be *other*. These same white boys who might have teased you and called you *golliwog* a year or two ago, now suddenly call you 'sister' in a fake Yardie accent.

You tick: Other.

You go to live in the city. You and your friends have been studying drama and you go for castings, auditions for extra work and modelling jobs. Most of the time you are turned away for being too exotic. Casting agents look at you with a puzzled expression and shrug and say:

'We don't book your look … we don't really specialise in exotic girls.'

Someone suggests you join an agency for *exotic people* and scribbles down an address. You are penniless and desperate for work so you go. When you get there, there are film stills of aliens, photographs of dwarfs on the walls. Ah, penny drops! Of course, brown people belong in the circus, with the aliens and the dwarves, not in beauty campaigns, but with the elephant man, with the outsiders and the other others. You give them your CV and hope to get offered extra work, non-speaking parts the prostitute, drug dealer or dead girl. You get a part as an extra in a prison riot scene, it pays the rent that month.

You tick: Other.

My mother is a black immigrant. She was born in Port Antonio, Jamaica. She lived in the Robinson family home on Colonels Ridge, Bulls Head Mountain. There are more shades of green there, and more shades of sky, than anywhere else in the world, it is so beautiful. My mother's tropical childhood days were idyllic. She was barefoot and carefree, picking mango fresh from the tree and swimming in clear, warm turquoise oceans. My mother had no idea what England was, or who King George was. She knew nothing of the war, there was no shortage of sugar, cocoa or coffee. Jamaica was the centre of the world. Her father was in the RAF and posted to Dover and so just before my mother's seventh birthday, December 1951, my grandmother and my mother left that warm paradise and stepped onto a banana boat to set sail for England to join my grandfather.

The passage took several weeks. My mum vaguely remembers the ocean crossing, my grandmother making friends with the other passengers. Most of all she remembers how they switched boats off the coast of Ireland and she was terrified as she was winched across from the shipping boat onto a passenger ship, as though she were just like a box of bananas. My mother had been born in the colourful paint box of Barrington Watson and suddenly she found herself in the coal grey industrial frame of a Lowry. England was one long bitter winter's day; my seven-year-old mother shivered at the docks in a short-sleeved cotton dress. Her feet, so used to being bare, were now shoved into these hard shoes she hated. And the flags were all at half mast, King George had just died, February, 1952.

She remembers all of this as a traumatic time.

Back in Jamaica they had told her how wonderful England was, that the streets were paved with gold. But she recalls arriving to find an atmosphere of lost hope, of people's dreams being dashed, a collective depression and disappointment. Newcomers to England found it hard and cold, cold with animosity, cold in the shade cast on them.

She has an early memory of a white child, just opposite, across the street, pointing at her:

'Mummy, Mummy, look at the blackie.'

The mother yanks her child's hand,

'Now, now, dear, don't stare.'

At her new English school, my mum remembers the teachers, how they always put the immigrant children to work together in groups. The brown faces, teeth chattering, shivering on the field, stuck in pairs for sports. Keeping the outsiders outside, keeping the others, other. The newcomers were united as outsiders and lived in a community. One of my grandmother's first friends when she arrived in England was a neighbour, a Polish woman who showed her some practical things, like the way to the shops and how to keep the house warm and keep out the draughts. That Polish immigrant neighbour knitted my mum her first wool cardigan, a kindness my mother remembers even now.

Meanwhile my father was white, his mother was an Irish immigrant. We don't know much about this side of my story because he was adopted and his birth mother disappeared without trace. My paternal grandmother was an Irish 15-year-old scullery maid, working below stairs in a big house. When she fell pregnant with my dad, the case went to Juvenile Court, she said she'd been *taken advantage of* by the lord of the manor, the big boss of the house had got her in the family way. It is all very *Downton Abbey* in my mind, but not much of a happy ending, this 15-year-old girl disappeared as the ink dried on the adoption papers and we now know nothing of my Irish roots. And the fact remains that my paternal grandfather must have been a wealthy and reprehensible brute as he kept his name well out of it and off the record. It was his word against hers in the 1940s, that of a poor 15-year-old Irish immigrant maid against a white man of means and wealth, she didn't stand a chance did she? And nor do immigrant teenagers in this century. Wherever they end up, wash up, whatever the shade, refugee or immigrant, torn away from their parents and homes, I repeat my question: who is protecting the kids from traffickers, from rape and murder?

My parents fell in love and married in the swinging 1960s. They were part of a circle of open-minded, cosmopolitan groovers, musicians and bohemians. My father was a brilliant jazz musician and my mother was a go-go dancer. That was how they met, my father down in the pit, looking up at the legs.

Every time I tell people my father was a jazz musician they picture him as a black man and my mother as the white, funny, isn't it?

But away from their mix of bohemian jazz friends and swinging sixties hippy circle, the prejudice showed its ugly self, primarily as an ignorant curiosity about their sexual relationship. People sniggered and said the most filthy things, the racist connotation being that my mum was untameable and wild from the jungle. Men would nudge each other dirtily and make crass jokes that my father was a lucky man, the common joke going along the lines of:

'… I bet he has his work cut out in the bedroom.'

The fetishisation of the sexuality of black people comes from centuries of dirty dark shade. It starts with sleazy old jokes that black men have huge cocks, or that black women are hyper-sexual, and it festers to become something toxic and sinister. This continues now, mostly unquestioned, with the sexual objectification of women, rounded fat bottoms and full lips all across the media industry. But once the canned laughter dies down or the fashion shoot is done and dusted, and you stop and take a cold hard look at the root history of these jokes and stereotypes, it all comes from a shade so bleak and so ignorant, that it has a sub-human subtext to it – brown people for sale in a human pet shop window.

When my mother had her babies she remembers that the immigrants, the black and Asian mothers, were all put together at one end of one ward. She recalls some nurses were unkind, a bit snotty, making sure they knew they were in the shade, that they were being cast aside, treated differently and were somehow inferior. And afterwards, in the street, as a new mum were proudly pushing her pram, people would stop to look, peering in, curious to see her offspring. Staring down at me, a chubby pale blonde bundle in the pram.

'Are you sure that's your baby?' they'd ask rudely, without a flicker of thought for the hurt that comment might cause.

James Robertson, my great-great-great grandfather, is known in my family as the Colonel. By the time he died he was in fact a General, General James Robertson. A Scottish man, who we recently discovered is buried at Edinburgh University. The Robertson mausoleum is in Greyfriars Cemetery. His oil painting hangs in the National Army Museum, it is a portrait of a white man in a white wig, red jacket, medals and epaulettes. I believe that he was rewarded for his excellence in capturing

Maroons with hunting dogs. I feel uncomfortable when I see his portrait, and visiting his grave I can visualise it all–

Gnarling dogs snapping in the moonlight, Maroon warriors waiting in ambush, camouflaged in the rain forest undergrowth, a human fox hunt, the masts of distant ships, hidden treasure, piracy and subterfuge. We weren't taught about the Maroons at school. They were renown for inventive guerrilla warfare and fierce courage, living by the Maroon mantra that called for them to fear no death:

'To never bow head or knee, to hear only their own voice, to stand in the shadow of none and to be masters of their own destiny.'

Robertson was given land in Jamaica, and this whole area of Clarendon is still called Colonel's Ridge to this day. Robertson married a Maroon - she was in fact a Zulu princess - and through miseducation and misdirection his name changed from Robertson to Robinson, he didn't correct anyone's spelling because he faired better in Jamaica. He abandoned his wife and children in Scotland for a life living as a wealthy plantation owner in the blue mountains of Jamaica.

So now what shade are we? I am a child of immigrants, the first being this Scots man, Robertson or Robinson, an immigrant from Scotland to Jamaica. We are all connected. We live in the shade and shadow of secrets and lies, this shared dirty history of colonialism, rape, land theft and slavery. Slavery was abolished, at a cost, with promises of land and wealth and freedom. Jamaica may have gained independence from Britain in 1962 but today we still chase those broken promises and fight for truth, justice and reparations.

Now, these are just a handful of the things that I hardly ever talk about, these are memories that give me uneasy feelings of doubt and things that remind me that to some I am nothing but a shade. And these are also the moments that inspire me to keep writing and to keep fighting to speak and to be heard and to be read. This shade I wear, this outer skin, this isn't a lovely natural perm or a lucky all-year tan, this is my past, present and future, this shade is my identity. As a kid I was the curly-haired, brown girl with bright green eyes. I was an alien and I stood out in the school group photographs, you can spot us right away, me and my brother; the two grinning brown faces in a sea of white. But you pass any playground now and there are millions of us. I occasionally work in schools, teaching poetry workshops and giving talks, and I'm delighted to walk into a classroom to see a sea of countless colours and mixes, beautiful mixed-up, double-dipped, curly-tops. Most of us are mixed something or other, the world is majorly populated with minorities.

We tick: Other.

There is a dream, a grand idealism, that mixed-race people are the hope for change, the peacekeepers, we are the people with an *other* understanding, with an invested interest in everyone being treated equally as we have a foot and a loyalty in many camps, with all shades. We are like love bombs planted in the minefield of black and white. It is as if our parents intended to make us, with courage, and on purpose, as vessels of empathy, bridges for the cultural divide and diplomats for diversity and equality.

As you grow older, as a mixed-race person, you become a chameleon, you are born with natural camouflage. When you travel everyone assumes you are some version of Latino or Spanish. In the first minutes of meeting you, people have to figure out what shade you are and this is your superpower, it buys you valuable time. People will show their hand and ask, 'Where do you come from?'

And if you reply, 'I just jumped on the tube at Tottenham Court Road,' they'll tut and shake their head.

'No,' they say, 'where do you come from, as in …'

Pause '… *come from*, come from?'

You earn time to chameleon, to camouflage, to make your shade darker or lighter. To morph into what is required or expected. Whatever it takes to survive, whatever it takes to be heard, whatever it takes to get the job. Whatever armour you must wear that day. It's all positive discrimination. Right? No. Wrong. Very. Wrong.

You hesitate, your pen hovers over your boarding pass.

You tick: Other.

Being other, another shade, hasn't ever been a free pass: at the time of writing this I have been reading articles about the aggressive backlash aimed at actress Zoe Saldana for not being *black enough* to play Nina Simone in a new biopic of Simone's later years. As far as Saldana is concerned she is black enough, and woman enough and good enough. When confronted like this, are they asking her to pass up the opportunity to play Nina? Should she know her shade and therefore her place? Decent lead parts for strong female actors are so few and far between, I am keen to see how she plays it. In spite of the shade thrown her way, I suspect Saldana will have worked ten times harder to prove she is good enough, a skilled actor, to portray the legend that is Nina.

For me, being another shade has not been a guarantee of being published by a BAME publisher, to be included in black literary magazines, or that my work will be supported by the black press or BAME media. I haven't relied on tokenism or any positive discrimination. I have, however, always felt that I have to work ten times as hard and that my voice is mine, but that it is different. I keep my head down, I keep on keeping on and I show up to work to write every day. I like to believe that I am booked for festivals and events and published for my merit and talent, and not for the tokenism of my shade or even my gender. I have hope and feel strongly that diversity and equality is improving in the UK, it's a long and slow simmer, but I have seen improvement since I started out in 1994. I perform regularly, and share the stage with a comparatively even mix of boys and girls, black, mixed and white. But we still have such a long way to go; the headline acts are still mostly white and male. I continue to survive and thrive due to my own tenacity and the generous support of others, people who identify as being other: the warriors and outcasts, rebels and renegades, the revolutionaries, the circus, the outsiders and underdogs, the working-class heroes, the punks and the poets and the LGBTQ+ community too. We have learned to belong in the un-belonging. Spirited and colourful souls, of all shades.

We tick: Other.

Some people seem to think that BAME writers, *coloured folk*, are all in some clique, saluting our saviour Zadie Smith sipping coconut water and sharing jerk chicken sauce recipes. That is not true. And neither is it true that BAME writers write with BAME readerships in mind. It also isn't true that all our books solely contain stories for each other, about each other, and about our roots, like travel diaries, tales that will only interest other homesick BAME people. I call bullshit on all of that. The shade of your skin is not the whole content of you and your work. The shade of your skin should not be the measure of your worth. The shade of your skin is not your only audience nor should it be a limitation.

The universal job of being a writer is to write, to write with empathy, to be brave and honest, to find joy conveying a journey and in sharing your passion. Your ink is replenished by your life experiences, by taking off the mask and using your limitless imagination, by stepping out of the shade and into the light. As a woman may write in the voice of a man, I don't see why a writer cannot imagine the voice of another shade and culture, that is what imagination is all about. Whatever shade you are, as a writer, you have just one task each day, one battle, and that is you against the blank page. Every writer should have just that in mind, nothing else matters, just that one fight is more than enough to contend with, each and every morning.

You and your pen against the empty page.

Britain is an island surrounded by salt seawater and inhabited by people of every shade. On a whole I do not think of people as flocks of sheep but more as shoals of fish, swimming to find food and heat and migrating to survive. We could protect each other better if we swam together in unison, we could protect each other from great white sharks dominating everything. We could, but we are like fish, as fickle as fish.

I finish writing this piece at Arvon. I'm working at the writing residency, The Hurst in rural Shropshire. This week I'm tutoring an all-BAME and all-female group of writers, poets and playwrights. I just discovered that this is the first time that Arvon have programmed an all-BAME and all-women course since Arvon began in 1968. I feel honoured to be chosen to be here this week. I observe the women sharing stories, the challenges of being women writers, the struggles to be funded and to publish work. I am stunned by the openness of the dialogue, moreover the shocking lack of confidence which

...an eat from the cooking pot of mixed culture ...e in the cool shade of being mixed-race. There is no ...d for a passport. There are no borders. We are all citizens of the world. Whatever shade you are, bring your light, bring your colour, bring your music and your books, your stories and your histories, and climb aboard. United as a people we are a million majestic colours, together we are a glorious stained-glass window. We are building a cathedral of otherness, brick by brick and book by book. Raise your glass of rum, let's toast to the minorities who are the majority. There is no stopping time, nor the blurring of lines or the blending of shades. With a spirit of hope I leave you now. I drink to our sameness and to our unique differences. This is the twenty-first century and we share this, we live here, in the future. It is a beautiful morning, it is first light on the time of being other, so get out from that shade and feel the warmth of being outside.

You tick: Other.

Librarian.

A villain with a good heart.

Hairdresser.

One by one, accepting smiles spread around the room, our fates were tantalisingly dished out. The person next to me is bequeathed 'Nurse'. She's happy. She tells me later that she'd been fearing 'Student'. We are all pleased for her.

It's my turn next. I'm in a drama studio, sitting in a circle with the 33 other people that I've spent the last three years with. Three years spent desperately clinging to the hope that we will leave this place and won't spend the rest of our days working in a call centre instead of setting the BBC alight with our acting majesty.

Today is an infamous day in drama school folklore. This is the day that we are all going to discover how to best market ourselves. After three years of trying to make ourselves as versatile as possible, we are now going to be told how the world would be seeing us. Our training is almost at an end. Just a few weeks to go until we're kicked out into the world, comes from having to lower your expectations, shrinking your dream because of a stream of constant rejection and the lack of opportunities here in the UK, especially if you are a BAME woman and aged over 30. Above all, this week is evidence to me of things improving, new platforms being provided and good people helping to change things. Things are slowly getting better, I can see an improvement since the 1990s, but it is just taking way too long.

All I can do is keep on keeping on, keep sailing my Good Ship. Human colour is the colour I'm truly interested in, the colour of your humanity. May the size of your heart and the depth of your soul be your currency. Welcome aboard my Good Ship. Let us sail to the colourful island of seized identity. You can eat ⟨...⟩ and bath ⟨...⟩ nee ⟨...⟩

THE WIFE OF A TERRORIST

MISS L

Doctor.
Lawyer.
Farmer.
Librarian

comes from having to lower your expectations, shrinking your dream because of a stream of constant rejection and the lack of opportunities here in the UK, especially if you are a BAME woman and aged over 30. Above all, this week is evidence to me of things improving, new platforms being provided and good people helping to change things. Things are slowly getting better, I can see an improvement since the 1990s, but it is just taking way too long.

All I can do is keep on keeping on, keep sailing my Good Ship.
    Human colour is the colour I'm truly interested in, the colour of your humanity. May the size of your heart and the depth of your soul be your currency. Welcome aboard my Good Ship. Let us sail to the colourful island of mixed identity. You can eat from the cooking pot of mixed culture and bathe in the cool shade of being mixed-race. There is no need for a passport. There are no borders. We are all citizens of the world. Whatever shade you are, bring your light, bring your colour, bring your music and your books, your stories and your histories, and climb aboard. United as a people we are a million majestic colours, together we are a glorious stained-glass window. We are building a cathedral of otherness, brick by brick and book by book. Raise your glass of rum, let's toast to the minorities who are the majority. There is no stopping time, nor the blurring of lines or the blending of shades. With a spirit of hope I leave you now. I drink to our sameness and to our unique differences. This is the twenty-first century and we share this, we live here, in the future. It is a beautiful morning, it is first light on the time of being other, so get out from that shade and feel the warmth of being outside.
    You tick: Other.

THE WIFE OF A TERRORIST

MISS L

Doctor.

Lawyer.

Farmer.

Librarian.

A villain with a good heart.

Hairdresser.

One by one, accepting smiles spread around the room as our fates were tantalisingly dished out. The person next to me is bequeathed 'Nurse'. She's happy. She tells me later that she'd been fearing 'Student'. We are all pleased for her.

It's my turn next. I'm in a drama studio, sitting in a circle with the 33 other people that I've spent the last three years with. Three years spent desperately clinging to the hope that we will leave this place and won't spend the rest of our days working in a call centre instead of setting the BBC alight with our acting majesty.

Today is an infamous day in drama school folklore. This is the day that we are all going to discover how to best market ourselves. After three years of trying to make ourselves as versatile as possible, we are now going to be told how the world would be seeing us. Our training is almost at an end. Just a few weeks to go until we're kicked out into the world, desperately waving our *Complete Works of Shakespeare* like it's a ticket for the *Titanic*. Sat before us is the head of the acting school, a woman who has been getting to know us for three years and is now telling us what it's worth.

She turns to me and there's a pause. Wow, I think. A dramatic pause. Clearly this is going to be good. My versatility over the last three years must mean my tutor can't possibly pick just one role for me. I can practically hear every film studio sweeping their doorsteps in preparation for my arrival. She takes a deep breath and I suddenly realise what she's going to say.

'Terrorist.'

People laugh. I even think I laugh. I'd honestly been expecting 'pharmacist'.

'Actually, no,' she says, changing her mind. Well of course, she'd realised what a narrow-minded thing that was to say. That's okay, we've all been there, we've all put our recycling in the regular rubbish without thinking of our great, great, great-grandchildren and the awful world we're creating for them.

She looks at me again and says, 'The wife of a terrorist'.

Now I'm definitely laughing. Three years of getting up at 7am, three years of movement classes that made my feet bleed, three years of singing that made me cry at my atrocious voice, three years of phonetics that made me want to rip my own soul out, three years of time, money, effort, hope, love, hate, hangovers and it was all to play the wife of a terrorist, the most silent, unseen role you can possibly think of.

I wish I'd had the courage to shout back. I wish I'd found my voice before she moved on to tell me that the man sat next to me would be best suited to play a politician. I'm reeling harder than the time Dad was doing Ramadan so it meant we had to wait until the evening for our Christmas dinner ... I know, our household was nothing if not multicultural.

Until now, acting was being everything that I wasn't. I, the brown girl at school with a funny name, had played everything. I'd been a villager from Oz, I'd been Jack Frost, I'd even played Gordie from *Stand By Me* when, aged 10, my friend and I inexplicably decided to turn it into a full-length play for our class. Yes, I, a 10-year-old girl with frizzy hair and a better moustache than all the boys in my class, had pretended, in 1993 in front of our Year Five class and painfully patient teacher Mr East, to have a leech on my penis. It's this kind of tolerance of my foolish endeavours that almost definitely lead me to believe I could prance about for a living. When you've spent most of your life wanting to make a living out of pretending to be someone else, suddenly being told you can only play one role because of how you look is quite the rap across the jazz hands. One of the first steps to becoming an actor, after the realisation that people will always ask if you've been in anything they might've seen, is telling yourself it's okay to want to be other people. It's not that you don't want to be you, it's that you also enjoy not being you, and that's fine. You took the Halloween fancy dress invite, and instead of just buying a cheap wig like most people, you decided to make a career out of it.

The whole point of acting is versatility. Of course, there are some actors who make a glorious living out of playing the same role for ever more, but the reason why we become actors is because we never know which role will come in next. Look at Meryl Streep, you need to set aside a whole day if you want to spend some time with her CV. I kept telling myself there would be other roles on offer to me. If Renée Zellweger could play Bridget Jones then I was allowed to dream of being more than sad set dressing. I'd played Jack Frost, goddammit. Really though, that wasn't the problem on that warm spring afternoon in April. The problem was that I'd finally been told how the industry would see me, and it was only on my walk home that I had the withering realisation that I was being judged by both my skin colour and my gender.

The first question I had to deal with was why I was being seen as the wife of a terrorist. I'm going to go out on a pretty strong limb here and say that, despite the fact I once drunkenly broke a locker, this wasn't due to any particularly disruptive tendencies I'd shown at drama school. In fact, I was so keen to not disrupt things that I even rather foolishly once came in for a dance showing with chronic food poisoning. I often wonder how many people in the world have attempted a grand *jeté* to Kanye West and contemplated which orifice is going to give way first. So no, that can't be it. Therefore, I'm going to have to make a pretty bold assumption, much like she did, that my terrorist casting is down to the colour of my skin and my slightly unpronounceable name. Apparently, because of this, I was much less likely to be a doctor and far more likely to be something that has sadly become synonymous with the Middle East.

Now don't get me wrong, I was under no illusions that I was going to be the next Lizzie Bennet. I'd already come to terms with the fact that I was probably never going to appear in a Sunday teatime adaptation. Those quaint period dramas were never going to be for me, girls with my complexion don't get to wear a corset as their father worries about the upper field drainage. I mean, it's supposedly fine to cast white actors in ethnic minority roles (Angelina Jolie, Emma Stone, Mickey Rooney, I could go on …) but the other way round? There's more chance of seeing Benedict Cumberbatch in the dole queue. This would be fine if ringlets and riding crops didn't reign supreme on our TV screens, but you currently can't look at a screen without seeing a white person worrying about a dowry. It's no wonder ethnic actors are heading to America instead, somewhere they have a chance of not being elbowed out by corsets and fancy hats.

As a kid who grew up being mildly obsessed with *Brief Encounter*, the realisation that I'd never get to be in any of these of course made me sad, but I consoled myself with the fact that this was the twenty-first century. This was the era of diversity and I, a woman once called 'funny-coloured' by one of her drama school peers when wondering how she'd be best described, should surely thrive. I hate to go on about it but, come on, I'D PLAYED JACK FROST. The sallow-skinned girl with a big nose had played the whitest male character the world has ever seen. So why was I being pigeonholed before I'd even begun?

I should be used to assumptions being made about me since it has been happening pretty much my whole life. From kids at school incorrectly calling me 'paki' to teachers constantly presuming that I and the other Middle Eastern girl at school must be sisters, despite us having different surnames. And then there is, of course, this conversation:

'So where are you from?'

'Oxford.'

'No, where are you really from?'

'It's a little village in the sticks. You really won't have heard of it.'

'No, like where are you originally from?'

'Do you want my address?'

'No, what's your heritage?'

Your heritage, like you're an antique vase or a listed building. The other lesson I quickly learned was that being unwhite also seems to mean that people make assumptions about what you can do. I remember once going to an audition for another familiar scenario, 'Middle Eastern woman in a relationship with a white man and they have to fight everyone's prejudices'. The audition was so far away that I nearly had to pack my stuff up in 100ml bottles, and I got there to find it was being held in the director's attic. Already this didn't bode well. We did the scene and he frowned at me. 'Can you do the scene in Hindi for me?'

'Nope.'

'I think it would be a good idea.'

'But I can't speak Hindi.'

'Why not?'

'Because I'm not from India.'

He grabs my printed out CV. 'Well, what do you speak?'

'English.'

'And you don't speak any other languages? You should be ashamed of yourself.'

Should I? Would they be saying this to a white actor who hadn't bothered to learn German? At no point had I claimed to speak Hindi, and nor should I, but people can presume I can, just because I look a little bit like I might come from somewhere near there. It's also been presumed I can speak the following (deep breath) Italian, Spanish, Portuguese, Hebrew, Farsi, Arabic, Urdu and Turkish.

The wife of a terrorist.

Suddenly being released into the world as a newly trained actor is tough enough but I also had to contend with being both Middle Eastern and a woman. This is something I've battled against since day one and is the reason why I set up my *Casting Call Woe* blog. Born out of frustration and horror, it's a look at the very worst casting calls I've seen on my desperate hunt for work. From female roles described as 'her cleavage is her best feature' to actors being asked to do an 'immigrant accent', it's a terrifying insight into the stereotypes still being maintained despite it supposedly being the twenty-first century.

I'd love to say that once I stepped out into the big, bad world I actually got to play a whole host of interesting roles. I mean I did, sort of. Over the last 10 years I played an eight-year-old boy, a nine-year-old girl and even a stag, but a good 75 per cent of the roles I went up for very much fell under the heading of Middle Eastern Women. If I wasn't auditioning for the wife of a terrorist (yes, she was right), then I was up for the role she hadn't warned me of, that of a woman in an arranged marriage. It was nice that there were some surprises still in store for me but, really, a BAFTA nomination would've been nicer.

In fact, it was the arranged marriage situation that I found myself in most. Pretty much every role I went for was either being set up for an arranged marriage or was suffering terribly during one. One particular role I went up for was of a woman desperate to escape her marriage. I turned up to the audition to find a note tacked to the door saying the room was no longer available and instead to go and wait outside the McDonald's. Odd, but whatever. I wandered around to find that the audition was actually being held inside the McDonald's. Great. Because there's nothing that aids getting into the character of someone who's just set themselves on fire than seeing someone tucking into their cheeseburger. I checked a few months later and saw that the very white director had decided to cast herself instead. I consoled myself that night with a KFC.

When I complain about the lack of female representation in film and TV, I can guarantee someone will helpfully shout some suggestions in my face. Granted, these suggestions will probably be from a few years ago (yes, *Girls*, *Bridesmaids*, *Mean Girls* … funny how they all have something female in the title …) but they tend to shy away when I bemoan the lack of Middle Eastern females. They might flounder for a bit and then quietly – just in case they're wrong and they can then claim I misheard it, like someone pretending not to hear a question in the pub quiz because they know they really should know the answer – they'll mutter, 'Princess Jasmine?' 200,000 years of humans and all we get is a Disney princess to represent us. To be fair to them, Middle Eastern women are few and far between when it comes to the roles we see on our screens and stages. There's a reason why you can't think of any famous wives of terrorists, because who would remember a woman in a hijab who features in the corner of one shot? Once you've exhausted P-Jaz and Cleopatra, you're already starting to run out of ideas. More recent additions include Ms Marvel, *Persepolis* and *A Girl Walks Home Alone at Night*; there's progress, but it's slow and can just as easily take a step backwards rather than forwards.

Much of this came from the fact that I was graduating during the Noughties, a time when our perception of the Middle East was particularly primed to be one based around fear and misunderstanding. Maybe if I'd been graduating a bit earlier then I might've been able to play the wife of a taxi driver or a kebab shop owner, maybe the wife of a rug maker if I was really lucky.

There are such connotations linked with being Middle Eastern that you generally can't play a role unless it has something to do with your race. Sure, I can play a doctor or a lawyer or a street cleaner, but only if I'm being forced into an arranged marriage in the background or providing a cover-up for my terrorist husband. If there's some really daring casting then I might get to play a character that defies my father's wishes, if that happens then maybe I get to wear a nice dress and not wear a hijab. But very rarely do I get to play a role that isn't defined by the preconceptions made about the colour of my skin.

What really gets me is that all the roles are so helpless, and this is something that's often true of a lot of female roles. Every role I go up for that is specifically Middle Eastern is a woman that is basically having her life controlled, and her story is that she's either suffering through it or trying to escape it. In fact, I'm reading a casting call for such a role right now, 'a rebellious Pakistani Muslim girl who lives with her traditional father and brother. She decides to run away with her boyfriend.' Now, don't get me wrong, these are stories that should be told but we're mistaken to think that Middle Eastern women are limited to being in unhappy relationships. Also, not only are they hugely limiting for Middle Eastern actresses but they're massively insulting to Middle Eastern men.

Looking back over all the Middle Eastern Wife roles I've been up for, not one of them has been in a happy marriage. She's either there because she's been forced to or she's dealing with a terrorist husband through gritted teeth. And of all the Middle Eastern Non-Wife roles I've been for, not one of them has had a father or brother who isn't trying to get them to marry someone. How boringly limiting is that? There are no roles for Middle Eastern girls to aspire to, no roles to show the world that we're capable of more than being a prop in a hijab.

All this is what lead me to, shamefully, deciding to change my name when I first graduated. I've never been ashamed of how I look or the fact that cold callers take a deep breath before attempting the concoction of letters that I call my name, but I couldn't cope with the fact that I was pigeonholing myself before I'd even started. I'd spent so long having assumptions made about me and now, suddenly, I was being handed this little ticket that might allow my acting abilities a second thought. Of course, it was a hideous idea. The name never really scanned properly. I'd suddenly made myself that random person from school on Facebook who gets married and changes their name. Every time they pop up on your feed, you totally forget who they are and only vaguely remember when you squint at their terrible picture. I lived with that feeling as my name for two years until, thankfully, a director I was working with was the first person to be honest with me and sat me down to tell me I'd made a huge mistake. That afternoon, I changed it back and, since then, I've embraced everything that being a part-Iraqi, part-Iranian, part-British actress is.

Yes, I will play the role of a wife or wife-to-be. Yes, I know that I sometimes get work purely because I'm a good diversity box-ticker. Yes, I'll never be cast in *Pride and Prejudice*. But none of that really matters because I get to represent a bunch of incredible women who are so vastly unrepresented. And that's what acting is. It's about telling people's stories as honestly and faithfully as we possibly can. It's being entrusted with a person and showing them to the world. It's not just about us as actors being represented, it's about the people we represent and making sure their tales are told.

Excitingly, as I write this, I've just been asked to audition for the lead in a short film. It's the role of a high-powered Syrian lawyer. She's also married to a controlling husband. Roll on Princess bloody Jasmine.

WHAT WE TALK ABOUT WHEN WE TALK ABOUT TOKENISM

BIM ADEWUNMI

The comments section is different for every story on the internet. For stories about diversity – whether that be across gender, disability, sexual orientation or race – though, there are a few that crop up with a regularity that would be reassuring if it weren't so depressingly samey.

A quick perusal across the breadth of the internet throws up the one that gets me the most heated: the 'but do you want tokenism?' defence. I mean, practically every gathering of internet-opinions has its version of this question; well-meaning people asking – with baffled internet-expressions – if what we as people of colour want is 'tokenism' in popular (and not-so-popular) culture. This is how 'reasonable' people – the people who work alongside you, and manage to have nuanced conversations about so many things in daily life – respond to a call to have more than one type of person in the cultural representations of human life that we absorb every day. I feel sure I have seen every variant of this comment and I am compelled to ask: why is it that the only options ever offered are 'tokenism' (this internet-person's objective, overwhelming concern) or total, yawning absence? How is it, that in 2016, there are only these two stark choices? To paraphrase Eddie Izzard's classic sketch: why do we have to be so 'cake or death' about this?

Sometimes, there are addenda, gracious add-ons, like: 'I'm happy to see people of colour as characters in this TV show *if* the plot calls for it' or 'why put a black dude in the cast "just because"?' (Again, there are many variations of these.) It is important to understand precisely what is being said there: the story that everyone can relate to, the character that we as an audience are supposed to be able to project ourselves onto with the most ease, the 'universal', is white. The default is *always* white. There are no vacancies in that spot – ever – for people of colour. No Nigerian-British everyman. No unexceptional Bangladeshi-British Joe Bloggs/Jaleel Begum. Characters of colour only make it into the mix specifically 'when the role calls for it'.

Let that sink in for a moment.

Whiteness – or, you know, white people – exists as the basic template. And that template covers all human experience, by the way: the ability to be special or ordinary, handsome or ugly, tall or short, interesting or dull as ditchwater. On the other hand, *our* presence in popular culture (as well as in non-stereotypical 'issue' roles) must always be justified. Our place at the table has to be *earned*. We must somehow show we are worthy of inclusion in representations of the culture that we live and breathe in. Does that black woman deserve to be on that show? Give the exact reason that Chinese-British man is in this scene. Explain the series of decisions that led us to having this mixed-race boy in this film. Please show your working for maximum marks.

We live in an age where fandom is less on the fringes: regular people make their own homemade costumes and go to comic conventions now, not just the geeks of yore. So we know the patter of the showrunner who is getting some audience heat – they were 'hesitant' to include POC POVs in their shows because they were 'worried' about issues of 'authenticity'. For about five seconds after hearing these responses, I nod and understand. That quickly passes, though; what I want to do is call up their offices to set up a meeting to discuss *exactly* what they imagine people of colour (usually in the city, town or village the writer is her/himself from) do so damn differently. *Then* I want to offer my services (for a substantial fee, obviously – I'm no martyr) to help them 'bridge the gap'. Here's what black people do: we breathe air, we drink water and we fart noxious gases, just like other people. Our hopes and dreams are similar, and alongside the various hardships we may suffer because of the way we look or where we come from, we largely do the same things – and that includes all the frivolous things too. Things like eating cupcakes, or wanting the chance to write a self-involved collection of essays (let's not even get started on the publishing industry), having sex with unsuitable boys and being monstrously self-obsessed. There, I'm a consultant. NOW, WHERE'S MY CHEQUE?

As an enthusiastic fan of popular culture – and a human being in possession of the full complement of human desires and emotions, narcissism high among them – I like to see myself in the surrounding culture. I want to see a girl with natural hair, or a weave, or relaxed hair and I want to see her doing everything: I want her to go to the movies, I want her to find a cure for a rare disease, I want her to work as a shop girl, I want her to save the world when the apocalypse comes, I want her to fall in love, I want her to fight aliens, and I want her to laugh a lot. As things stand, she simply doesn't exist. This sad state of affairs means I thrilled quietly when I saw Storm in the X-Men movies (even though she has a frankly insulting and vague 'African' accent in the first one – WHO ACTUALLY SPEAKS LIKE THAT, HALLE?), and I squealed and called my sister when I saw Nicole Beharie in the trailer for Steve McQueen's *Shame*. It means I got excited when I read in a 2012 report from the Directors Guild of America that Shonda Rhimes used 67 per cent female or minority ethnic directors in the making of her show *Scandal*.[73]

I'm a big telly fan. It's one of my favourite things in the world – I can quote most of *Friends* (my favourite sitcom of all time, despite its monochrome core cast and myriad flaws) from memory, just give me the prompt – but I am not involved directly in making telly. I don't wish to downplay the importance and necessity of having a diverse writers' room system – clearly there are too few people of colour in these rooms, and that's before we even get into the class issue. But it seems obvious to me, a naïve layman with beautiful dreams, that there are three steps to writing a good character of colour:

1. Write a stonkingly good, well-rounded character
2. Make the 'effort' to cast a person of colour
3. That's it!

I've seen real life applications of this groundbreaking technique in *The Good Wife*, *Master of None*, *Chewing Gum*, and *Community*, among others. But maybe I'm wrong. Maybe there are huge hurdles to clear in order to make television that looks like the world, hurdles that the layman just can't see or comprehend. If you're reading this and do make entertainment television, please correct me if I've somehow misunderstood the complexities.

---

73 'DGA says diversity among TV directors stalled: report', Deadline Hollywood. http://deadline.com/2012/09/directors-guild-diversity-study-tv-directors-veep-dallas-344300/

It appears clear to me that there is a gap in what people mean when they say things like 'we're all one race – the human race' and how they actually see the world. The thing that means a person cannot imagine seeing a Asian man as a superhero (you know, that set of fictional beings with special powers) is pretty much the same thing that makes a person cringe away from feeling empathy for a fictional dying black girl (Rue, played by Amandla Stenberg in *The Hunger Games*). It leaks into the everyday, too – if you cannot bring yourself to imagine us as real, rounded individuals with feelings equal to your own on screen, how does that affect your ability to do so when you encounter us on the street, at your workplace, in your bed, in your life?

It doesn't have to be this way. Consider these words from Mindy Kaling back in September 2012:

When you are the only Indian-American female lead in a television show, you seem to be making sweeping statements about that person simply because you are that person and the only one, whereas, for instance, Steve Carell – he's not making sweeping generalisations about white American men on his show because there's so many different white American men on different shows. So I get worried by doing this character that people think that I'm saying that about all those people. And I just have the weight of that on my shoulders, which is something that I do envy other performers for not having.

This is just the everyday shit of being a pop culture fan living in black skin. And it's so tiring.

DEATH IS A MANY-HEADED MONSTER

VINAY PATEL

My father's father, my dada, is staring at me, trying to wrap his head around what I've just told him.

'Crocodiles?'

I nod.

'Yes, Dada.'

By the staircase in my house there is a framed photo of a woman that I've passed every day of my six years. I've always known, looking at that photo, that this woman died when I was very little, littler than I am now. I've always known that this woman is my mother, a mother being someone a bit like my grandma, my Ba, but younger and with better English. I know that when someone dies, it means they're not around anymore. I even know how it can happen.

'Too many angry white shells,' is how Dad, sitting on the edge of my bed late one night, explained lupus to me. Despite mishearing 'cells' as 'shells' and imagining my insides as a tiny beach, I'm already more *au fait* with death than your average kid.

But the possibilities of what death might be like for the person dying have only recently snuck up on me and they are more horrifying than any movie monster. At bedtime, before I switch off the light, I picture death. I see myself floating in a void for a finite but excruciatingly long amount of time before being allowed into heaven. Like fifty thousand years. Long enough for you to lose all sense of self, all points of reference. Maybe Mum, trembling and alone, is a few years into that long haul. Then the idea of time vanishes and I grapple with the darkest thought to enter my young mind so far: when you die, you are dead for ever. No feeling. No thinking. Just nothing. Forever. I started to leave the light on. However, the stillness of a lit room in an otherwise dark street had its own sense of a timeless void so I would throw myself into different worlds in order to escape. I would read – *Star Wars* novels, a copy of *Great Expectations* someone had bought me without irony, *Improving Your Golf Swing*, whatever I could find – until a drowsy adult would stumble past (I come from a family of light sleepers) and check in. I'd pretend to have dropped off mid-sentence, they would turn the light off and I would hope I had tired myself out enough not to think.

Thankfully, this exhausting state of affairs could now come to an end since, on my way to confront my bed, I've poked my head in to watch a BBC nature documentary someone's left running on the living room telly and I've heard something wonderful, something that's going to change my life for ever and I've run upstairs to tell my dada. I repeat myself to him to dispel the confusion on his face:

'Yeah, crocodiles! They said on the TV that crocodiles reincarnate and if crocodiles can reincarnate, I can too.'

The idea of death being final might have been new to me but this reincarnation lark was not. Nobody had explicitly talked to me about it yet, but it featured very strongly in the children's storybooks I'd been given depicting the two central

Hindu myths, the *Mahabharata* and the *Ramayana*. These were epics about Gods-incarnate and 10-headed demons and arrows that could destroy seas. They were tales where at the start a woman could be spurned by a suitor and kill herself from the shame, only to turn up near the end, born into the body of a young warrior prince, ready to revenge herself on her former lover. What a twist! However, twists are devices for stories and whilst I thought they were awesome stories, it was clear to me that there was no connection between those mythic worlds and my reality.

That had all changed now. Already at the age of six there was a deep part of me that recognised David Attenborough's calm voice as one that spoke with a weight of knowledge. I could trust what this man from the documentary told me about the world because this wasn't a story, this was *science*.

It takes Dada a while, but he eventually figures out that this is yet another mishearing on my part and what Mr Attenborough actually said was 'crocodiles reproduce', not 'crocodiles reincarnate'. My dada is a proud, self-taught businessman who likes to pamper his grandkids, using the gains from a lifetime of hard work to create a cushion from the harshness of the world that he never had. So to crush the hopes of a child and then round it off with a much-needed chat about the birds and bees must've been quite tricky. But he bloody well managed it.

My thoughts about The End spread from bedtime to every spare moment. Showers are particularly bad. They start off well enough; I enjoy being naked, our boiler is the absolute business and our showerhead provides several options to keep things fresh. And then, as the ballast of everyday cares drop away, my mind inevitably drifts to the moment of my death and I consider how one minute I'll exist and the next I won't, that the line was that fine, that it was absolutely, definitely going to happen to me one day. One day I won't touch or smell or see or even care that I couldn't and …

Screaming.

Eventually, always, I ended up screaming in terror for a good minute or so until the small worries of life crept back in.

'You might be dead one day, buddy,' they'd say. 'But you've still got us to deal with.' I was never more grateful for Monday morning homework hand-in than in those moments.

My poor concerned Ba asked me every time what was wrong, and I always sulked the question off. How could she empathise or understand? She was full of the comforting conviction of faith, so much so that she dedicated half of every morning to the shrine in her bedroom – bringing a flame from downstairs in a tiny golden cup and placing it before her equally tiny idols of the Gods, of which there a multitude. I only recognised the bronze Hanuman that I had picked up myself from a ramshackle market stall in Ahmedabad. I was told that I could choose the God I wanted to be the one who would look after me and I went for Hanuman, the mercurial monkey king from my *Ramayana* story book. He spends his time wrestling, arguing with mountains and burning down cities with his tail for japes. That's the guy I want watching my back. When I pointed him out, the merchant nodded, applied some badly-painted plastic eyes to the metal, and handed him over. I found it really funny to see this boss-eyed monkey man sitting on my ba's immaculate shrine but it was clear to me from this practised routine, during which you *must not* disturb her, that it all meant a lot to her. Any solutions to my screaming were going to come from this faith, this dedication and I didn't trust them.

None of this anxiety was helped by the family events I was now trusted to come to. Typical of immigrants from poor countries, my extended family was huge on both sides, which meant an endless stream of weddings and funerals, at which I knew no one and cared very little. The weddings were traditionally Indian: flowers, saris, bad dancing, carefully portioned food served into specially made plastic trays with dividers that helpfully kept your khichdi and puri dry and separate from the dhey. The funerals, on the other hand, had a stronger English infusion. Black suits, churches and solemnity. The weddings were boring but at least you could run around and have fun with the other kids. No such luck at the funerals. All there was to do was absorb the sadness and hope that if you fell over, someone might take you home early.

I eventually tamed my existential dread by doing what I continue to do with all deadlines to this day: I pushed it back. I can't remember what triggered it but one day I just told myself 'It's OK, I'll find religion when I'm twenty-one', and with that I was satisfied that All Would Be Well One Day. It was a Pascalian pragmatism that held for a couple of years until, ever so gradually, the obvious issue reared its head.

Exactly **which** religion would I be finding?

Being raised in a Hindu family but going to an explicitly Christian school (where I played Joseph in the nativity play, yet somehow lost out on Mowgli in *The Jungle Book* to a ginger kid called Charlie) in a nominally Christian country meant a strong dissonance not just in tolerance of spices and film lengths but also in end-of-life theories. With Hinduism there wasn't even an Abrahamic link like there was between Judaism, Islam and Christianity that would allow you to do a reasoned 'well, when you think about it, it's all from the same place, the same people, what do the differences really matter?' number on it.

People I loved, people I trusted, people I thought were cool, all backed wildly different beliefs about what happened after death and how to live the life that came before it. My grandmothers had a fervent Hindu faith, but adding together everyone else around me it was clear there were so many others available to offer a contradiction: my Sikh friends with their little swords and turbans; the proud owners of the Punjabi kebab house I'd visit with my dad on Commercial Street with Islamic art on their walls; my Chinese teacher at primary school who taught me all about which numbers were lucky and which weren't in her culture; even a Jehovah's Witness who turned up at our door once and made a good go of explaining how she was one of the chosen few. There seemed to be as many ways to live as there were to be dead. They couldn't all be right, even if I wanted them to be, which led me to what felt like the only logical conclusion: they're all wrong. Dread had morphed into pragmatism, which now gave way to a wary, sometimes sneering atheism shared by my sister and dad – the cynical school run trio – that carried me through secondary education and informed my choice of friends.

It wasn't until university and my encounters with the Christian Union there that I found anything matching my grandmothers for intensity of belief. These weren't the half-hearted C of E types I knew from home, or traditional old ladies for whom religion went a long way to standing in for the education denied to them. These CU types were confident, smart and *nice* – so bloody nice. It's hard to be snarky about people who hand out free cheese toasties with a smile and no expectations. I became good friends with a few of them and started to see how their faith helped guide their lives. It gave them patience, hope, a mission, all things I was desperately lacking in. I was still cynical about religion but I could see the appeal; when compared to a first-year student body loaded with horny drunks, it was hard not to think that the world would actually be better off with more people like them – community-minded and doing regular Good Deeds – than people like me.

To show my appreciation, I made posters about how their hall rep was 'a really fucking great guy!', which wasn't appreciated. Eventually I started going to their meet-up groups, along with my Belgian Goth flatmate, Michael. He was there to give them a hard time, I was there to listen.

As it happens, God did finally find me during second year, two years before my self-imposed deadline, but it wasn't the Christian Union that got me in the end, despite their best efforts. I was lucky enough to have all four grandparents around for my childhood; however, the counterweight of that luck was knowing you were going to see them all die one day and you wondered which would go first. It wasn't the one I was expecting. It turned out to be one of my grandmothers, my mother's mother, my biji ba (a name, along with biji dada, that I think of with much affection, but which basically means 'other grandma' and 'other grandad' – useful in distinguishing between them but somewhat suggestive of a bit of a hierarchy). She was both the youngest and the most devout. One of the last things she said from her hospital bed was, 'I'm coming back as a bird.'

Hearing this, I wanted to reply, 'That's stupid, you're here, be here, don't be talking about being somewhere else, something else.'

I didn't, of course. I couldn't crush her like my grandfather had done to me. She wasn't six like I was but sixty-six which, to my mind, was still far too young for this to happen. She was the first person that I really knew to go and I found that first death is the evil mirror universe version of first love – life-changing, raw, an experience that will superficially come again but will never be felt in the same way.

My childhood was spent between the homes of both sides of my family, and if the photo of Mum in my dad's house was a subtle memento mori, the funeral home opposite my mum's parents' estate was an altogether more overt one, somewhere they were probably going to end up if the place stayed in business long enough, and so it proved. They had Biji Ba in the back room of that funeral home (isn't it strange they're called homes?), her concrete-grey, stern face – an expression she'd never worn in life – contrasted with the bright sari she'd been draped in. The colour amongst the grey felt a fitting tribute to her time in this country. Before I left, I decided I really, really needed to knock on her forehead. Was she in there? In the void? A bird? There was, of course, no reply.

The funeral and the events around it I went into with a detached clarity. Living within two religious traditions had robbed me of any belief in the holy or spiritual but it allowed me a greater appreciation for why those traditions are important. They hold us when we need it. Traditions are just nonsense that binds, and whilst the nonsense might take on a different hue, the binding is universal.

My grief lingered and, in the time it was with me, it felt possible to believe that maybe, just maybe, my grandma *was* a bird. I tortured my sceptical brain around the science of it – we're all just atoms to be rearranged, right? – and it felt that there must be something to this world that I was missing. I wanted to believe that the sacrifices my family had made to create a life for me, that took them so far from their home, would be validated somehow by a merciful god. It had to be. Had to. So I asked my newly widowed biji dada for a copy of the *Bhagavad Gita*, which he gladly provided. In doing so, he told me of his own journey from non-belief to belief over his years moving through the last outposts of Empire and ending up in his ex-council house in Battersea. Is it harder to have faith when you're in another land, I wondered? Or, in a search for meaning and purity in a place that can often resent you, does your faith harden in reaction?

For my part, I started to push against my evangelical friends who I had previously got on so well with. What did *they* think had happened to Biji Ba? To my mum? What did they think would happen to me, this heathen in their midst?

During a night I'm not particularly proud of, I pushed one of them so hard that she confessed that, yes, they thought my mum and grandma were in hell and that I was going to end up there too ... but she prayed that I wouldn't. I was being a prick. She was my friend. She was in tears. She clearly found it agony to say it. But she did say it, and I told her to go fuck herself. It was ugly, and proved an uglier time still for Exeter evangelicals in general as their group found themselves in disputes with other Christian societies as well as the secularism of the uni itself. An increasingly rancorous chain of events that culminated in them attempting to sue the student union[74].

Meanwhile, I dived into the *Bhagavad Gita* and was thrilled to find more poetic, adult versions of the storybooks I had as a kid. I spoke to priests. Read forums. Did I know Hinduism isn't a religion but more a pagan-style collection of beliefs? No, I did not. Did I realise you could worship Jesus and still be a Hindu? No way. This was great. It all tied up! Hinduism was older than everything else, it was flexible, if there was one that

---

74 'Christian group to take university to court', *The Guardian*. http://www.theguardian.com/education/2007/jul/27/highereducation.uk2

was going to be *right* across the millennia it had to be this one – the faith I needed had been staring me in the face ever since birth. I was brown Luke Skywalker. I was a Hindu, like my mother before me. Of course. Of course! Peace and purpose were around the corner.

This religious ecstasy lasted, all in all, about a couple of months before withering away.

Nowadays, having for the most part accepted I'm just a chimp with airs, with no mighty sky chimp looking out for me, I think less about what happens to the souls of me and my loved ones after and more about what will be done with our actual bodies, which we at least have some control over.

At the time of writing this essay, I still have three grandparents left. Fingers crossed this figure doesn't shift too significantly before publication, but it will one day and how they choose to be mourned says as much about their journey as their actions in life. Three generations of my family have been born on three different continents: most of my grandparents in India, both parents in Kenya, me in England along with my sister and cousins. Asia. Africa. Europe. Every continent we've been through has left a mark on us. I'm half-amused, half-annoyed that the little Gujarati I speak is infused with Swahili words and dialect, a coded language fully available only to those who have made that particular journey. Broadly useless to me, but in itself a wonderful reminder of how far they've come in every sense. We are happy to change and adapt even something so fundamentally important to us as language in order to start sinking into our new homes. In death, though, so far they've all returned to the 'motherland' and had their ashes spread over the Ganges. There's a religious element to that of course but, in choosing this way to be laid to rest, it suggests to me that this diaspora, these brave wanderers, always yearned for home no matter how successful they were at integrating abroad.

What about me then? After all, I'm racking up the days myself and when I dwell on the numbers they warp into curious, morbid trivia. This year, for example, I turn thirty and so soon my mum – that picture on the wall – will become, in a way, the youngest member of our family. If my sister and I live until we're eighty, it will have been a whole hundred years from my family arriving in the UK to someone born here dying here. And, I imagine, we'll also wind up getting our ashes spread here or somewhere nearby. We aren't religious. There's no spiritual connection to some 'homeland' for us. Will that be the final moment of integration? When we've not just been born, lived and died in this country, but are interred somewhere in its soil as well? When there's, to rephrase an old poem, some corner of an English field that is forever foreign.

For my part, I hope in death I create another branch to my family's story. If I die where I am now, I don't believe I'll reincarnate, I don't think I'm going to heaven or hell or the void, but at least I will already be home.

THE UNGRATEFUL COUNTRY

MUSA OKWONGA

So here's my experience of growing up in Britain; it was always a case of making sure that I was grateful. Maybe that wasn't such a bad attitude to have; after all, my parents were brought to the UK as refugees, fleeing the hyper-violent regime of Idi Amin, and so there was no question that they had been given a second chance at life. At the time of their departure, Amin was busily wiping out anyone who might represent a future threat to his rule, and my parents – then attendees of two of the best schools in Uganda – were firmly within his target demographic. And so they came to West Drayton, and a few years later I turned up: the eldest son of two doctors, with an eagerness to please their adopted country.

I didn't notice that eagerness until I was 11, when I was given a bursary to attend Sunningdale, a boys' prep school. Until that point, I hadn't given much thought to my skin colour, since everywhere I'd studied before had been racially diverse: now, though, I was one of two black pupils out of 130. What's more, my new peers and their families weren't like the white people I had met before, whose lives were reassuringly everyday, and who generally only owned the one home. My new classmates seemed to have the most glamorous of existences. Many of them lived abroad. Their holidays were spent skiing and shooting. One had a butler. The richest ones were always the most shabbily dressed: if a boy had holes in his sweater, he was more likely than not to be descended from some emperor.

Following the overthrow of Idi Amin in 1981, my father returned to Uganda to help build what he believed would be a better country. He became the military physician for Major General Oyite-Ojok, the commander who defeated Amin, and he died with him. On December 3rd, 1983, their helicopter crashed – or, most likely, was shot down – in a moment that was seen as the turning-point in the struggle for control of the country. My mother, widowed, was left to raise four young children alone; and with her attention divided between us and endless shifts as a local GP, I learned that the last thing she needed was additional problems from me. No: what she needed was for me to be smart, dutiful and responsible. So I turned up at Sunningdale School, black and from a miraculously solvent single-parent home, amongst the sons of white millionaires.

I became an unofficial ambassador for black people. There were so few of us in the boarding-school world that I felt driven every week to prove that we could be just as good as our white counterparts. Returning home for my holidays, I saw the implications of a world where people were judged by their skin alone. My cousins and I were starting to be stop-searched by police, on one occasion merely for waiting by a bus stop. 'Loitering' became a code word for 'being dark-skinned in broad daylight'. And here I was, at school with boys whose parents had the potential to change things for people who looked like me; with boys who, one day, might be running the country themselves. I approached my studies with a furious sense of mission: believing that, if I made a good impression here, I could help to erode some of our society's firmest prejudices.

Maybe, in attending Sunningdale, I felt as much of an immigrant as my parents had in their schooldays. My mother had gone to Gayaza High School, in Kampala. As one of its few pupils from the northern part of the country, she had been mocked by her classmates, who said that members of her tribe were rumoured to have monkey tails. Perhaps, like my parents landing in the UK, I was in an alien landscape, grateful for the opportunity I had been given. It didn't help that, never having been taught Latin, Greek, French or Tudor history, I was immediately bottom of almost every single class. I only remain thankful for being good at English, which allowed me to reassure those around me that I wasn't academically useless, and for being decent at football, which among most boys that age was a pretty immediate path to social acceptance.

After two years at Sunningdale, I found myself at Eton College. This, I told myself quietly, was The Big Time. I had watched a documentary about it on Channel 4, *Class of 91*, and was captivated. Here, I thought, was a place an outsider had to go to prove himself. Some of the world's greatest leaders had been here, and now their sons were presumably going there too. If I was to achieve anything in life, I had to acquit myself against them, and excel. As Frank Sinatra once sang of New York, if I could make it there, I could make it anywhere.

I took to my studies with such a spectacular seriousness that, for a couple of years, I carried my work around school in a briefcase. That must have looked excessively formal, even by the standards of a school where we wore wedding clothes to class. Desperate to make the best of an education that so few people, let alone black ones, would ever experience, I got involved in every school activity I could. If there was an arts magazine anywhere in sight, I wanted to edit it; if there was a school society I liked the look of, I wanted to run it. I enjoyed my work, but I didn't much enjoy my social life. Whenever I went back home, I discovered that I was considered too posh to hang out with most of the locals there; and during the school holidays I rarely saw my classmates, since most of them seemed to have prohibitively expensive tastes. Moreover, there had been the warning that an Old Etonian, one of my mother's patients, had asked her to pass on to me when I was just about to start my first term there. 'Tell him he will never be one of them,' he said. I scoffed at that advice then, but with each passing term I was less and less sure.

I remained grateful to the UK. Then the murder of Stephen Lawrence in 1993, horrifying in itself, exposed a police force so addled with discrimination and alleged corruption that it could not even complete what, at first, seemed to be a reasonably routine investigation. Lawrence's death annihilated the lies we told ourselves – that if we were just good little black boys and girls, that if we just stayed away from the bad crowds, no harm would come to us. Lawrence was a budding architect who spent most of his final hours playing video games with his best friend; it didn't get anymore innocuous than that. Yet that didn't stop him from encountering a gang of white youths who found his mere presence so offensive that they spontaneously set upon him and stabbed him to death.

In the five years between Lawrence's murder and the end of my time at boarding-school, I was grateful for the sanctuary of Eton. West Drayton, for that period, endured a surge of racism apparently at odds with the normal torpor of this suburb. The British National Party, oblivious to the fact that black people lived in our particular cul-de-sac, posted campaign fliers through our door. Studying at the local library, I found National Front logos carved into one of the desks. Heading towards the train station, I found stickers bearing considerate advice for foreigners. 'West London pakis beware,' they read. 'Combat 18 in the area.'

And there, next to Yiewsley Methodist Church and along a wall 30 metres across by 10 metres high, you could find graffitied every form of white power insignia you could imagine. The one I remember best was a burgundy Ku Klux Klan logo, lovingly stencilled inside a star: it looked like the kind of thing a sponsor might emblazon across a football shirt. Once, a man waited for my sister and me to emerge from the local opticians, and then, seeing that we had crossed the street to avoid him, opened his leather jacket to reveal a patchwork of swastikas of various different shades and sizes. Multiracial racism, if you will.

Eton taught me some vital things about people and their judgments. One was that I could not change some of my peers' perceptions of black people merely by being as hardworking and as agreeable as possible; I became the exception that proved their rule. I realised this when having a pub meal with a friend. Out of nowhere, he launched into an astonishing rant against migrants, and, when I pointed out that my parents and I were no different from those he was denigrating, he told me that 'I don't see you as a migrant, Musa. I see you as a friend'.

Even the calling-card of being an Etonian was not enough to shield me from prejudice in the upper-class world. I will never forget the time when, just after my A levels, I went to stay at a friend's flat in West London. His stepfather had not been at home when I had dropped off my bag earlier that afternoon. When I returned that evening, though, the stepfather took one look at me and asked me to leave, not even allowing me to enter the house. It was a quarter-to-midnight as my friend shamefacedly handed me my bag on his doorstep, and stepped back into his home.

I only really started being myself when I was 22, a year after I left university. During my three years at Oxford, where there were fewer than 100 black students of African or Caribbean descent out of a total 15,000, I still felt I had ambassadorial responsibility. I was used to being part of an ethnic minority by now.

I started being myself at 22, because that's when I had my first drop of alcohol. I don't mean to say that drink liberated me, in some profoundly spiritual way: I simply mean that I felt comfortable enough to get drunk. Because, until my friend passed me that first fateful shot of tequila, I had tried my very best to keep control. As ridiculous as it might seem, I believed that since my white peers had grown up seeing so many negative stereotypes of black people their entire lives, I had a duty to counteract as many of them as possible. That meant never getting drunk, never getting that Afro I had long wanted, never taking the joint when it was offered. And, in truth, I was a little scared about what my intoxication might reveal. I was afraid that, beneath my straight-laced veneer of the Good Immigrant, there seethed a boorish, brutal womaniser. And, of course, no such monster emerged. I was merely a slightly louder, slightly merrier version of my sober self. And I saw then, after several years, that I had absorbed many of the racial stereotypes that I had feared others would see in me. Raised without a father, lacking many black male role models – most of whom were probably quietly struggling away just like me – I was left only with media portrayals of what black men were, and most of those were overwhelmingly negative. What's more, 22 was also the age when I realised that I was attracted to men as well as women: an experience that was traumatic at the time, but for which I am now thankful. It was so life-altering an event that it forced me no longer to see myself as some sort of diplomat for my people, but instead to live for myself. London was a place where identity did not matter nearly so much as it had until that point in my life. Surrounded by Turks, Kiwis, Poles, Nigerians and many more, there was no need to worry further about who I was, but simply to get on with the business of being.

I thought I would never again see anti-immigration feeling as strong as I did in my teens, and so when UKIP's votes started to rise rapidly I was taken by surprise. By the 2015 general election, they found themselves walking away with 6,346 votes, over a quarter of those claimed by the winner of the seat for Uxbridge and South Ruislip, one Boris Johnson. In hindsight, though, UKIP's progress makes total sense. A sprinkling of foreign-looking people here and there was all very well, but the arrival of many of us at once bewildered locals who were not accustomed to such swift cultural change. That was to say nothing of white working-class people who found themselves undercut by labourers from the EU and beyond, who were prepared to work for far less. To some of them, it must have felt like looting.

And here's the problem. There's only so much you can do to convince your fellow citizens that a multiracial society is A Good Thing, especially when they perceive that it's hitting them too hard in their pockets. It's remarkable how so many of the country's economic problems were blamed, not on the misfiring calculations of the financial sector, but instead on the ills of mass immigration. The momentum was probably building from around 2005, when Michael Howard's Conservative Party put out a billboard campaign I saw each day on my way into work. 'Are you thinking what we're thinking?' it said. And just in case you weren't sure, it gave you the punchline: 'It's not racist to impose limits on immigration'. That second sentence always made me pause. It wasn't inherently racist to impose limits on admission – after all, if a nightclub is full, it's not racist to say that no-one else can come in. What is racist is when you begin denying admission to people purely on the basis of their race and culture – which, incidentally, is something that has been happening in London nightclubs for years.

There's nothing new about a country wanting to cherry-pick the best of all the foreigners who want to come over. Some might even argue that there's nothing wrong with it. But as I got older, I began to notice more and more that the very moment immigrants were seen as contributing anything less than wholesomely to the national effort, they were viewed with contempt. It was as if, even though we had been born here, we were still seen as guests, our social acceptance only conditional upon our very best behaviour. I began to have less tolerance for this infantilising outlook, particularly when I looked at how much of the capital's, and indeed the country's, lowest-paid work was being done by immigrants with very little complaint. If there was anyone ungrateful about their presence in the country, it wasn't them, it was Britain.

And this, I think, is what I hoped to see the media coverage of the immigration discourse – a recognition of what people like my parents brought to the country, both economically and culturally. But that nuance was often absent, and took a *Daily Mail*-esque tone.

I remember, during the 2012 Olympic Games, the *Mail*, having taken offence at a scene from the opening ceremony, which featured a happily married mixed-race couple, wrote the next day that '[the ceremony] was supposed to be a representation of modern life in England but it is likely to be a challenge for the organisers to find an educated white middle-aged mother and black father living together with a happy family in such a set-up'.[75] And to my surprise, because I am normally a fairly temperate soul, I lost it.

I think I lost it because the *Mail*, presumably read with approval by millions, had finally exploded the lie that had been comforting so many of us for so long – that even if you lived a decent, law-abiding life, there were countless communities in this country that might never accept you, merely because of how you looked. The thought that a black man somewhere in the UK might somehow have infiltrated the affections of a white woman apparently filled the *Mail* with disgust. Perhaps this story affected me so much because the *Mail* said what I feared so many white middle- and upper-class parents silently believed: that someone like me would never be good enough.

By now I was in my mid-thirties, and travelling abroad with work. During these short trips, I would occasionally check back in with the British press, and the anti-immigrant anger in its pages struck me time and again. These days, though, I was increasingly greeting that fury not with fury but exhaustion. I was tired, as one of the few black journalists writing with reasonable frequency for some of the country's main publications, of being summoned by the media to defend the basic dignity of black people; of being called upon every single time a public figure said something flagrantly bigoted, or, as they or many of their softly cackling fans might put it, 'provocative'. It felt more like bear-baiting than how the news ought to work. I was better than this: black people were better than this. Since my schooldays I hoped that the quality of

75 The *Daily Mail* pulled the article after all the backlash, but thanks to the wonders of the internet, you can find it here: http://www.freezepage. com/1343493744VDGIBPHPUW

my writing might one day speak for itself; now, though, I was becoming The Race Commentator. It was all that some news editors would come to me for. For a period of several months, I turned down every single media invitation to debate or write about race, even as they increased in frequency. *Let others discuss it among themselves*, I thought. *Let others sit and reflect on just how low the discourse has fallen.*

Here's the truth of the matter. I find racism boring – really dull. I wish it didn't exist, and have spent most of my life trying to help to counteract many of its worst effects in society. Contrary to the belief of some of the digital pitchforkers who jab away at the bottom of each of my blogs, I genuinely wish that I never had to write about it again. Unfortunately, however, that is a luxury that I do not have. Because even though we're well into the second decade of the twenty-first century, young black people are still being shot on sight in the USA because they are regarded as inherently criminal due to their skin colour; black people are dying unexplained at police hands; black people are having disproportionate trouble renting apartments in the world's most cosmopolitan cities or even getting job interviews because of the foreign-looking names on their CVs.

I had just grown tired of all of this. More pertinently, on a personal level, I had grown tired of spending my time fighting those battles in the country of my birth. Naïvely wishful as it seems, I had thought that there would by now have been a better public understanding of why so many immigrants seek to come to the United Kingdom. I had thought that there would be a greater level of awareness about the British Empire and its historical role in shaping the world as we see it today. But I was wrong, and to that extent I had to admit some form of defeat.

I decided to leave the United Kingdom. The decision was heartbreaking. I never thought it was something I could do. I had long since realised that if there was greatness in Britain, then it lay in its everyday citizens, and not in its institutions. Britain was not great because of its papers and politicians who relentlessly denigrated us, it was great in spite of them. Britain was great because of the spontaneous community spirit you saw as soon as a small town was flooded, because of the volunteers who turned out in their tens of thousands to act as stewards for the Olympic Games. But that wasn't a spirit that I felt my country was doing nearly enough to nurture.

I quietly shuffled off to Germany. It wasn't lost on me that the very advice that racists in the UK had long spat at foreigners – 'if you don't like it, then go ahead and leave' – was that which I took. I suppose; in that sense, they won. I had my new home of Berlin to look forward to – one which, though not without racial issues of its own, had shown a great willingness to embrace newcomers from all quarters. A year or so after my arrival, this city of misfits greeted thousands of Syrians, fleeing war in their homeland. A cluster of supremely grateful immigrants, they were looking, just as my parents had done, to make a new life, to form part of a greater and hopefully more glorious whole: and, in their welcome, I saw confirmation that a town this generous was the perfect place to start again.

ACKNOWLEDGEMENTS

Thanks so much to:

The Secret Cabal.

Nikesh: Thank you to everyone at Unbound, especially Rachael and John, for supporting and championing this project; all the contributors, Katie, Niven Govinden, Julia Kingsford and Charlie Campbell, Sarah Shaffi, Melissa Cox, Candice Carty-Williams, Harpreet Purewal, Elaine Wong, everyone at *Watershed/Rife Magazine*, Sam Asumadu and Henna Butt from Media Diversified (especially for publishing an earlier version of Darren Chetty's essay), Sunny Singh, James Smythe and Will Wiles, Nerm and Sangna Chauhan, Anita Rani, Josh Idehen, Nimer Rashed, Sam Binnie, Sharan Dhaliwal, Josie Long and Neil Griffiths and everyone at Arts Emergency.

Extra special thanks to Chimene Suleyman, Rosie Knight, Inua Ellams and Musa Okwonga for level heads and emotional support.

Vera: Thank you to Haruka Abe, Julie Cheung-Inhin, Shera Chok, Kathryn Golding, Catriona James, Jennifer Lim, Diana Ly, Anna Sulan Masing, Rani Moorthy, and Caroline Teo for talking to me as I mulled over the intersection between East Asianness and gender. Thank you Daniel York for being a champion, and James for the support. Love to GS, CAG, SLF, JT, LS and TWH.

Inua: Thanks to Siyanda Moutsiwa.

Ming: Thanks to Katy Lee, Jackie Tang and Viki Cheung, Katy's friend Vera, Jiaqi Hou, Jun Kit Man and Cohan Chew from The BC Project, Paul Courtenay-Hyu, Nina Crisp, Kim Liu Leach, Rebecca Yip, Professor Yaojun Li, Louie Stowell, Jeremy Curtis, Katherine Webber, Kevin Tsang, Alice Sutherland-Hawes, Manisha Matharu, Kwaku Osei-Afrifa, Joelyn Rolston-Esdelle, and Jasnam Channe. Final thanks to my family and to Liz Wawrykow.

Kieran: Thanks to Bally Yates.

Riz: Thank you to Bilal Qureshi, Farrah Jarral and Anya Raza.

Daniel: Thank you to Jennifer Lim and Elaine Wong.

Sarah: Thank you to Haleem, Rabia, Ishwarlal, Tarla, Hanif, Meena, Amina, Samie, and Roxanne for standing by my side and believing in me. I'd also like to thank my friends and masala chai for keeping me going.

Musa: For my parents, the two immigrants who gave me everything they had.

Bim: For Ade, who is the reason I am a writer.

Darren: Thanks to Samantha Asumadu and Media Diversified. Thanks to Judith Suissa, Sam Berkson and Bréanainn Lambkin for helpful comments on my writing. Thanks to Steve Cockett, Geoff Fox and Steve Williams for encouraging me to share my stories. Thanks to the primary school children who have shared their stories with me. Special thanks to Rageshri Chetty, for her love, support and inspiration.

Miss L: Thanks to T, my mum, dad and nan.

Chimene: Always, Mum and Dad. And the Turkish Cypriot community who have more strength than they are ever recognised for.

Nish: Amy Annette, Jack Barry, Tez Ilyas, Sara Pascoe and whoever made the 'Confused Muslim' meme.

Himesh: Thank you to the friends I've made since the beginning of my career for feeding my soul and showing me a world beyond my front door – I'd still be naïve and clueless without you. Thank you to my sister for setting the stage, to my dad for his silent wisdom, to my mum for putting love above all else and to all three of them for opening the window and giving me the faith to leap through.

Coco: Thank you to Beena for making me, and Stephen for rating me (enough to get me writing).

Salena: Thanks and love to my Mum, to my elders and cousins, and my mixed up immigrant family. Thanks to my Dickie. Thank you to Nikesh and all the crowd funding Unbound comrades for making this extraordinary book happen.

Vinay: Thanks for my grandparents for putting my hardships into context and loving me before I was even born.

Varaidzo: For my siblings.

Thank you to immigrants, the children of immigrants, relatives of immigrants, friends of immigrants, employers of immigrants, and anyone who made a journey from there to here and opened the world up in the process. This is for you.

SUPPORTERS

Unbound is a new kind of publishing house. Our books are funded directly by readers. This was a very popular idea during the late eighteenth and early nineteenth centuries. Now we have revived it for the internet age. It allows authors to write the books they really want to write and readers to support the writing they would most like to see published.

The names listed below are of readers who have pledged their support and made this book happen. If you'd like to join them, visit: www.unbound.co.uk.

With special thanks to
Harriet Tyce, Super Friend of *The Good Immigrant*.

@BooksandJohn
Tom Abba
Lauren Ace
Claire Adam
Gemma Addy
Morenike Adebayo
Crud Man Adz
Kate Agar
Ore Agbaje-Williams
Afua Agyeman-Mensah
Ailah Ahmed
Mediah Ahmed
Jon Aitken

Furquan Akhtar
Karen Al-Jeboury
Aria Alagha
Carolina Albuerne
Georgie Aldridge
Emma Alexander
Max Alexander
Firdos Ali
Becca Allen
David Alsmeyer
Amy Alward
Tanuja Amarasuriya
Annissa Amrani

J. Ander
Stuart Anderson
Josephine Andrews
Christina Angeloudes
Susan Angoy
Catherine Annabel
Mark Appleton
Clare Archibald
Marian Armour
Jesse Armstrong
Stuart Armstrong
Jason Arthur
Will Ashon
A. J. Ashworth
Jenn Ashworth
Claire Askew
Cicely Aspinall
Tim Atack
Tanya Atapattu
Jacqueline Auma
Suzanne Azzopardi
Bolu Babalola
Hannah Bacon
Suki Badesha
Dinesh Kumar Badhan
Zara Bain
Ali Baker
Amanda Baker
Upekha Bandaranayake
Adam Banks
Catherine Banner
Fozia Bano
Tutku TUTS Barbaros
Kate Barker

Paul Barley
Sarah Barnard
Chris Barnes
Amanda Barokh
Nick Barreto
Georgia Barrington
Cara Barry
Stuart Bartholomew
Cath Barton
Neda Barzegar-Befroei
Avneet Basra
Jessica Bateman
Bath Novel Award
Georgina Bawden
Rachael Beale
Cole Beauchamp
Charles Beckett
Mark Beechill
Farhana Begum
Jo Bell
Carolyn Belson
Julianne Benford
Jendella Benson
Trine M Bergestuen
Claire Berliner
Gillian Best
Sanjeev Bhaskar
Nirpal Bhogal
Nikki Bi
Karn Bianco
Elizabeth Billinger
Georgie Billings
Sam Binnie
William Binns

Bugs Binny
Matthew Birnbaum
Indira Birnie
Joshua Bishop
Sophia Blackwell
Joanna Blake
Ellie and James
    Blatchley-Asfa
Hana Blumenfeld
Pascal Blunk
Rich Boakes
Amna Boheim
Steph Boland
Thomas Bonnick
Shane Boothby
Ruth Boreham
Euan Borland
Mair Bosworth
Emily Boulter
Andy Bower
Gavin Bower
Deborah Bowman
Jo Bradshaw
Serena Braida
Eishar Brar
Joti Brar
John Brassey
Carys Bray
Corrie Bray
Richard W H Bray
Bread Matters Cultural
    Foundation
Miriam Brent
Andy Brereton

Madeleine Brettingham
Laura Brewis
Sam Brhaspati
Laura Brooke
Chris Brosnahan
Jack Brougham
Ellie Broughton
Helen Brown
Kat Brown
Lauren Brown
Pendrick Brown
Nick Bryan
Josh Bryson
Gary Budden
Clare Bullock
Cheresse Burke
Ed Burness
Peter Burns
Cai Burton
Jessie Burton
Rachael Burton
Anna Burtt
Virginie Busette
Aisha Bushby
Sam Byers
Tanya Byrne
Helen Cadbury
Lucy Caldwell
Kit Caless
Eleni Calligas
Neill Cameron
Sophie Cameron
Alia, Luke & Zara
    Campbell-Crawford

Kirby Costa Campos
Rosie Canning
Anna Carey
Perdita Cargill-Thompson
Clare Carlin
Caroline Carpenter
Daniel Carpenter
Victoria Carr
Tobias Carroll
Eva Carson
Joel Casey
David Castle
Stephanie Catala
Lucy Catchpole
Nao Cathcart
Karan Chadda
Yann Chalmers
Niki Chang
Priya Changela
Zelda Chappel
Sarah Chappell
Elisabeth Charis
Ava Charles
KJ Charles
Tom Chatfield
Hinesh Chauhan
Navreet Chawla
Andy Checker
Darren Chetty
Dushy Chetty
Rageshri Chetty
Viki Cheung
Lumiere Chieh
Alex Chisholm
Zen Cho
Vera Chok

Sarah Chong
Ekwy Chukwuji-Nnene
Matt Clacher
Nick Clark
Caro and Cat Clarke
Evelyn Clegg
Laura Clements
Roxanne Coady
Dave Coates
Richard Coatsworth
Matteo Cocco
Alex Cochran
Jacob Cockcroft
Jonathan Coe
Joe Coghlan
Oliver Colegrave
Julian Coleman
Fen Coles
David Collier
Andrew Collins
Simon Collinson
Jane Commane
Louise Conlin
Sinéad Conneely
Philip Connor
Rosie Cooke
Josephine Corcoran
Isabel Costello
Charlie Coulthard
M. Cox
Dan Coxon
Ellie Craven
John Crawford
Maria Crawford
Kate Crowther
Thom Cuell

Shannon Cullen
Fiona Cummins
James Cuningham
Rachel Cutts
Poetcurious DaGriot
Ciarán Ua Dálaigh
Wasi Daniju
Ishita DasGupta
A M Dassu
Rishi Dastidar
Sheila David
Beth Davies
Hannah Davies
Harriet Fear Davies
Maxine Davies
Sara Davies
Dan Davis
Daniel M Davis
Hayley Davis
Joshua Davis
Susie Day
Becca Day-Preston
Rachael de Moravia
Peter de Silva
Jim Dean
Will Dean
Will Dean
Elelta Demissie
Grace Denton
JF Derry
Ellie Devereux
Sandi Dheensa
Roseanna Dias
Marija Maher Diffenthal
Lanré Diko
Ben Dilley

Tom Dissonance
Isobel Dixon
Sareeta Domingo
Kirsty Doole
Louise Doughty
Nina Douglas
Corin Douieb
Tiernan Douieb
Angela Drayton
Sam Dub
Jane Duffus
Hannah Duncan
Rachael Dunlop
Edmund Dunsdon
Joe Dunthorne
Sam Eades
Kathryn Eastman
Cariad Eccleston
Jean Hannah Edelstein
Steven Edwards
Aniefiok Ekpoudom
elaine.wong elaine.wong
Lauren Elkin
Matthew Elliott
Joanna Ellis
Camilla Elworthy
Luke Emery
Mine Ertanin
Fergus Evans
Tanis Eve
Stuart Evers
Charlotte Eyre
Katherine Fabian
Megan Farr
Claire Farrow
Jumoke Fashola

Rahnuma Feist-Hassan
Emma Felber
Gillian Fenner
Abigail Fenton
Manisha Ferdinand
Rebecca Ferdinand
Hannah Ferguson
Maria Fernandes
Jamie Fewery
William Fiennes
Nathan Filer
Becky Fincham
Ailsa Fineron
Natalya Fineron
Arlene Finnigan
David Fisher
Anna-Marie Fitzgerald
Kim Fitzpatrick
Jean Flack
Catherine Fleming
Chrissy Fleps
Catherine Fletcher
Chelsey Flood
Sarah Flynn
Christina Fontaine
Louise Forbes
Susan Ford
Charlotte Forfieh
Charles Forsdick
Lauren Fortune
Nicola Foxfield
Dan Franklin
Sarah Franklin
Sarah-Jane Franklin
Laura Fraser

Maureen Freely
Tim Freeman
Naomi Frisby
Hilary Gallo
Cathy Galvin
Dian Garrett
Duncan Gates
Vanessa Gebbie
Amro Gebreel
Emma Geen
Jonathan Gibbs
Daniele Gibney
Jo Gibson
Aly Gillani
Salena Godden
Richard Godwin
Caroline Goldsmith
Sophie Goldsworthy
Maya Goodfellow
Sophie Goodfellow
Charlotte Goodhart
Serine Goodmond
Kim Curran Goodson
Sakura Gooneratne
Sam Gordon
Chris 'Chairs' Gough
Miles Gould
Santhie Lau Goundar
Niven Govinden
Roshni Goyate
Samuel Gray
Martin Greaves
Mrinalini Greedharry
Michelle Green
Bedene Greenspan

Ami Greko
Siobhán Grennan
Chris Gribble
Helen Griffiths
John Griffiths
Guy Gunaratne
Rohan Gunatillake
Julia H
Daniel Hahn
Francesca Haig
Matt Haig
Steve Haines
Sue Haldemann
Emylia Hall
Mary Halton
Thomas Hamid
Chris Hamilton-Emery
Kirsten Han
Ellen Harber
Jessica Harby
Donna Hardcastle
Louise Hare
Jonathan Harper
Mary-Anne Harrington
Claire R E Harris
Jane Harris
Richard Harris
Shelley Harris
Kate Harrison
Ruth Harrison
A.F. Harrold
Damian Harte
Madeleine Hartley
Françoise Harvey
Ramsey Hassan

Louise Hawkins
Paula Hawkins
Molly Ker Hawn
Lucy Hay
David Hayden
Rob Haynes
Abbie Headon
Nick Hearne
Eric Heath
Rachel Heath
David Hebblethwaite
Alexandra Heminsley
Michael Henry
Emma Herdman
Johanna Herman
Marta Bausells Hernanz
Tania Hershman
Imali Hettiarachchi
Philip Hewitt
Clare Hey
Tim Higginbotham
Colin Hill
Matt Hill
Sabina Hinchliffe
Juliet Hirst
Tom Hodges
Ed Hogan
Rachel Holdsworth
J.A. Holten
Sarah Honey
Antonia Honeywell
Seth Honnor
Jennifer Hunt
David Hunter
Kirsty Hunter

Rebecca Hunter
Emteaz Hussain
Rabiah Hussain
Sairish Hussain
Vicaas Hussain
Louise Hussey
Emma Hutson
Lizzie Huxley-Jones
Ben Immanuel
Suzey Ingold
Tanya J.
Nico Jabin
Sinead Jack
Jade Jackman
Diane Jackson
Rob Jackson
Lisa Jacobs
Lorna Jaggard
Anna James
Rebecca James
Emma Jamison
Jay Jay
Anna Jean
Diana Jeater
Hamza Jeetooa
Lisa Jenkins
Elizabeth Jenner
Natalie Jester-Carter
Jan Jewkes
Tara John
Amber Yeshpaul Johnson
Catherine Johnson
Holly Johnson
Kate Johnson
Mitchell Jones

Nicholas Jones
Sammy Jones
Susan Liu Jones
Zainab Juma
Kamal Kainth
Karthik Kakarala
Savita Kalhan
Wei Ming Kam
Prithi Kanakamedala
Nikita Kanani
Hannah Kaner
Dino Karapittis
Isha Karki
Julia Karmo
Shaheen Kasmani
Sandy Kaur
Robert Kazandjian
Seamus Keaveny
Anna Kelly
Stephen Kelman
Al Kennedy
Ross Kennedy
Laura Kenwright
Rachael Kerr
Amy Key
Simon Key
Hammad Khan
Katie Khan
Mariam Khan
Mobeena Khan
Shahjehan Khan
Henna Khan-Hussain
Saida Khanom
Alison Kidd
Dan Kieran

Peter King

Julia Kingsford

Daniel Kitson

Hannah Knowles

Joseph Knowles

Ian Korner

Maris Kreizman

Jessica Krstičević

Joanna Kurlbaum

Pierre L'Allier

Mit Lahiri

Zoe Lambert

Breanainn Lambkin

Stefanie Lamprinidi

Line Langebek

Sara Langham

Patrick Langley

Jo Lansdowne

Becky Lavender

Patrice Lawrence

Tom Leach

Diane Leedham

Helen Legg

Elizabeth Lehtola

Ilona Leighton-Goodall

Chloe Leila

Paula D Lennon

George Lester

Tala Levin

Philip Levine

Sydney Levinson

Liza Levy

Fredrik Lindroth

Rob Lingo

Colm Linnane

Dan Lipscombe

Cath Little

Olivia Little

Natasha Ying Liu

Marilyn Livingstone

Frances Lynch Llewellyn

Josie Long

Éireann Lorsung

Laurie Louise

Catherine Love

Jo Lovesdancing

Charlie Lowe

Juliet Lubega

Rachael Lucas

DeAndra Lupu

Frances Lynn

Amelia MacDonald

Karen MacKelvie

Michael MacKian

Lorna Mackinnon

Seonaid Macleod

Lucy Macnab

Jon Macqueen

Anand Madhvani

Ravi Madhvani

Anthony Madigan

Erin Maguire

Hannah Maguire

Mellini Mahadevan

Crystal Mahey-Morgan

Francesca Main

Marianthi Makra

Claire Malcolm

Gita Malhotra

Ayisha Malik

Preeya Malkan

Gautam Malkani

Jane Maltby

Halimah Manan

Philippa Manasseh

Kat Mandu

Rachel Mann

Sophie Manners

Sarah Manvel

Rebecca Marcus

Eben Marks

Ellen Marsh

Ella Marshall

Lucy Marshall

Philippa Martin

Kate Mascarenhas

Sapphire Mason-Brown

Janina Matthewson

Ada Mau

Chloe Mavrommatis

Paul May

Sarah May

Stephen May

Kevin Maynard

Jazza MC

Rachel McCormack

Chris McCrudden

Lexie McD

Heather McDaid

Eleanor McDowall

Amanda McGrath

Jon McGregor

John Patrick McHugh

Sarah McIntyre

Belinda McKeon

Anna McKerrow

Kate McNaughton

Kiera McNeice

Martin McNulty

Marie-Anne McQuay

Tessa McWatt

Elizabeth Meade

Glen Mehn

Chloe Meineck

Mina Meiß

Joe Melia

Zak Mensah

Erinna Mettler

Jess Meyer

Sophia Miah

Carly Miller

James Miller

Duncan Mills

Bridget Minamore

Priya Minhas

Saima Mir

Sam Missingham

Anupa Mistry

Malissa Mistry

Josie Mitchell

Pete Mitchell

John Mitchinson

Lucy Moffatt

Virginia Moffatt

Stefan Mohamed

Sarah Monk

Penny Montague

James Montgomery

Mimi-Beth Montgomery

Maxine Monu

Safia Moore
Simon Moreton
Lou Morgan
Charlotte Morris
Cas Morrison
Kate Morrison
Emma Morsi
Juliette Motamed
Durre Mughal
Nafisa Muhtadi
Tanya Mukherjee
Diane Mulholland
Holly Muller
Helen Murphy
Mike Murphy
Rebekah Murrell
Holly Muse
Benjamin Myers
Keshini Naidoo
Fergal Nally
Eric Nash
Stu Nathan
Carlo Navato
Kate Neilan
Graeme Neill
Rachel Nelken
Nerm Nerm
Lorraine Newman
Lydia Nicholas
David Nicholls
Gary Nicol
Jenni Nock
Poppy North
Alexandra Notay
Gosia Nowicka

Khush Nubian
Kevin O'Connor
Meghan O'Dea
Tania O'Donnell
Catherine O'Flynn
Jenny O'Gorman
Dan O'Hara
Emma O'Mahony
Sadhbh O'Sullivan
Therese O'Sullivan
Marsha Gosho Oakes
Rachel Oakes
Georgia Odd
Kam Odedra
Antonia Odunlami
Pey Pey Oh
Natalie Ohlson
Irenosen Okojie
Musa Okwonga
Aimee Oliver
Karen Onojaife
Tasha Onwuemezi
Emily Oram
Elizabeth Orayinka
Katharine Orton
Adam Osborne
Gabrielle Osrin
Susannah Otter
Meg Otto
Marsha Oza
Samuel Palin
Anthony Thomas Palma
Amit V Pansuria
Muna Parajuli
Leonie Parish

Helen Parker
John Parker
Julia Parker
Siena Parker
Claire Parry
Nik Partridge
Damyanti Patel
Jayesh Patel
Maatin Patel
Nikesh Patel
Radha M Patel
Vibhuti Patel
Vinay Patel
Claire Patel-Campbell
Tash Payne
Richard Peabody
Poppy Peacock
Jo Pearson
Genevieve Pegg
Bianca Pellet
Penny Pepper
Tom Percival
Steve Perfect
Sarah Perry
Pamela Peter-Agbia
Bohdan Piasecki
Joe Pickering
Juliet Pickering
Magda Pieta
Candice Pires
Kevin Pocock
Fabia Pollard
Justin Pollard
Lauren Pope
David Porter

Max Porter
positiveimageproject
Nina Pottell
Jackie Potter
Anna Poulton
Lizzie Poulton
Chris Power
Smriti Prasadam-Halls
Alex Preston
Elizabeth Preston
Sharron Preston
Tina Price-Johnson
Simon Prosser
James Pulford
Harpreet Purewal
Emma Pusill
Alice Quigley
Kate Quine
Hazel Quinlan
Sanaa Qureshi
Mandy Rabin
Faisel Rahman
Zara Rahman
Matthew Railton
Kavya Rajagopalan
Polly Randall
Simran Randhawa
Tejal Rao
Nimer Rashed
Leila Rasheed
Kate Raworth
Stephanie Reynolds
Reardon
Clare Reddington
Matt Reid

Nina Renshaw
Cathy Rentzenbrink
Emma Reynolds
Francesca Riccardi
Rahul Ricky
Lorna Riley
Amber Rithalia
Lee.Robb@sky.com Robb
Charmion Roberts
Fay Roberts
Sean Roberts
Imogen Robertson
Neil Robertson
Miriam Robinson
Rachael Robinson
Katie Roden
Anna Roderick
Cynthia Rodríguez
Robyn Roscoe
Annah Ross
Rebecca Rouillard
RowanHisayoBuchanan
Emilie Joy Rowell
C.N. Rowen
Joanne Rowling
Tinni Guha Roy
Harold Rubin
Georgina Ruffhead
Reshma Ruia
Helen Rule
Katherine Rundell
Jalpa Ruparelia
Jonathan Ruppin
Bernadette Russell
Tom Ryan

William Rycroft
Helen Rye
Sid Sagar
Amrit Saggu
Sarah Sahim
SF Said
David Salariya
Melinda Salisbury
Charly Salvesen-Ford
Daisy Samuel
Ana Sánchez-Arce
Christoph Sander
Siân Sanders
Rajpreet Sandhu
Sarah Sandow
Rachel Sanger
Harvinder Sangha
Sathnam Sanghera
Luiza Sauma
Isabel Saunders
Tim Saxton
Samuel Schafer
Erich Schottstaedt
Matthew David Scott
James Scudamore
Cherokee Seebalack
Katharine Segal
Gemma Seltzer
Adeep Sethi
Sarah Shaffi
Amit Shah
Nikhil Shah
Alom Shaha
Farhana Shaikh
Wendy Shakespeare

ShamPhat Sham
Maria Shamin
Samantha Shannon
Dale Shaw
Lucy Shaw
Richard Sheehan
Alexandra Sheppard
Emily Shipp
Leo Shire
Nadia Shireen
Jai Shukla
Neena Shukla
Nikesh Shukla
Grace Ibidolapo Shutti
Amardeep Sian
Kay Sidebottom
Jess Siggers
Joanna Silber
Julia Silk
Ranbir Singh
Sid Singh
Sunny Singh
Leilah Skelton
Jon Slack
Anna Slater
Stephen Slocombe
Iesha Small
Claire Smith
Wendy Smithers
Richard Smyth
James Smythe
Mahsuda Snaith
Amy Zamarripa Solis
Leela Soma
Natasha Soobramanien

Chitra Soundar
Kitty Spence
Josh Spero
Vanessa Bellaar Spruijt
Truda Spruyt
Shefali Srivastava
Emma Stanford
Helen Stanton
Zoe Stavri
Ian Steadman
Cathryn Steele
Daneet Steffens
Katherine Stephen
Robin Stevens
Claire Stewart
Lucy Stewart
Roz Stobart
Peter Stojanovic
Katie Stone
Louie Stowell
Kay Stratton
Emma Strong
Chris Styles
Sarah Such
    and Tony White
Zerrin Suleyman
Recep Süleyman
JC Sutcliffe
Tom Sutcliffe
Alice Sutherland-Hawes
Karolina Sutton
Pete Sutton
SWight SWight
Susie Symes
Laura Taflinger

Paul Talbot
Zeba Talkhani
Preti Taneja
Abeeha Tariq
Shema Tariq
Daniel Tatarsky
Amy Taylor
C M Taylor
Jennifer Taylor
Justine Taylor
Marjorie Taylor
David Taylor-Matthews
Hannah Fort Teller
Matthew Teller
Ally Temple
James Thomas
Joanna Thomas
Caroline Thompson
Fiona Thompson
Selina Thompson
Mike Scott Thomson
Tim Thornton
Rhys Timson
Clare Titley
Charles Tocock
Alice Tomlinson
Francine Toon
Bethan Townsend
Emma Townshend
Angelique Tran Van Sang
Anthony Trevelyan
Claire Trévien
Daniel Trilling
Thomas Truong
Catt Turney

Eleanor Turney
Rik Ubhi
Nilopar Uddin
Asad Ullah
Jack Underwood
Emma Unsworth
Jo Unwin
Bahul Upadhyaya
Mayur Upadhyaya
Reshma Upadhyaya
Shaun Usher
Sabrina Uswak
Francois van Zyl
Liz Vater
Mark Vent
Sophie Verass
Rahul Verma
Iana Vidal
Kelly Vien
Eduard von Fischer
Johanna von Fischer
Erica Wagner
Julia Wainwright
Christopher Wakling
Eloise Wales
Lindsay Waller-Wilkinson
Joanna Walsh
Judi Walsh
Jemma Walton
Miranda Ward
Celeste Ward-Best
Ellie Warren
Emma Warren
Sarah Watkins
Liz Wawrykow

Katherine Webber
Matthew Welton
James Westby
Janet Weston
Emily Wheeler
Hannah Whelan
Jayne White
Simon White
Katy Whitehead
David Whitehouse
Zoe Whitfield
Alison Whittaker-Stewart
Charlotte Wicks
Kishani Widyaratna
Will Wiles
Rebecca Wilkie
Leah Wilkins
Sara Willard
Andrew Wille
Andrew Williams
Eley Williams
James Wills
Fiona Wilson
Johanna Wilson
Terri & Howard
    Windling-Gayton
Gretchen Woelfle
T.M. Wolf
Amy Wong
Joe Wong
Liza Wonga
Jess Woo
Benjamin Wood
Katherine Woodfine
Michelle Woolfenden

Marie Wright
Evie Wyld
Llinos Wynn-Jones
Jane Yates
Pete Yelding
Farrah Yusuf
Helen Zaltzman
Justin Zaman
Eva Zienau